THE TRIATHLETE'S GUIDE TO

Run
Training

THE ULTRAFIT
MULTISPORT
TRAINING SERIES
VELOpress

Recently Published:

Going Long: Training for Ironman-Distance Triathlons, Joe Friel
    and Gordon Byrn

The Triathlete's Guide to Bike Training, Lynda Wallenfels

The Triathlete's Guide to Off-Season Training, Karen Buxton

The Triathlete's Guide to Run Training, Ken Mierke

The Triathlete's Guide to Swim Training, Stephen Tarpinian

Available Fall 2005:

The Triathlete's Guide to Half-Ironman Training, Tom Rogers

The Triathlete's Guide to Mental Training, Jim Taylor, Ph.D.

Available Spring 2006:

The Duathlete's Guide to Training and Racing, Eric Schwartz

The Triathlete's Guide to Sprint-Distance Training, Gary Bredehoft

THE TRIATHLETE'S GUIDE TO

Run Training

Ken Mierke

VELO press®

Boulder, Colorado

The Triathlete's Guide to Run Training
© 2005 Ken Mierke
Foreword © 2005 Dr. Kathy Coutinho

Before embarking on any strenuous exercise program, including the training described in this book, everyone, particularly anyone with a known heart or blood pressure problem, should be examined by a physician.

Printed in the United States of America.
10 9 8 7 6 5 4 3

Distributed in the United States and Canada by Publishers Group West.

Library of Congress Cataloging-in-Publication Data
Mierke, Ken.
   The triathlete's guide to run training / Ken Mierke.
         p. cm. — (Ultrafit multisport training series)
   Includes bibliographical references and index.
   ISBN 1-931382-60-3 (paperback : alk. paper)
         1. Triathlon—Training. 2. Running-Training. I. Title. II. Series.
   GV1060.73.M54 2004
   796.42'57—dc22
                                                              2004023299

VeloPress®
1830 North 55th Street
Boulder, Colorado 80301–2700 USA
303/440-0601 • Fax 303/444-6788 • E-mail velopress@insideinc.com

To purchase additional copies of this book or other VeloPress® books, call 800/234-8356 or visit us on the Web at velopress.com.

Cover design by Erin Johnson.
Composition by Kate Keady Hoffhine.
Interior illustrations by Ed Jenne, E. R. Jenne Illustration.
Cover photo by Tim De Frisco.

Contents

Appendixes

Foreword

Running is one of the most pure sports on this planet, even when combined with swimming and cycling in a triathlon. It is a sport almost anybody at almost any age can enjoy. We can run for recreation and for stress relief, or we can compete—running in the most extreme conditions and distances of racing. But no matter how far or fast we run, we all run for the same underlying reason: deep down we love it and cherish what it can do for our minds and bodies.

However, if performed incorrectly, this glorious outlet and passion can be brought to a quick and emotionally terrifying end. So many runners suffer from injuries. When Ken Mierke began researching running techniques and developed Evolution Running, which was different from everything I'd ever heard about running technique, I was quite skeptical. However, I did have tremendous confidence in Ken, and his explanations did make sense, so I tried it. Since I began using these techniques, while training at a world-class amateur level, the most serious running injury I have suffered was severe poison ivy.

I am a chiropractor, certified in sports injury care and prevention, and, yes, I run with the same addicted behavior that you do. I especially love to run when competing in XTERRA triathlons. However, four years ago I found myself overtraining and running my knees and feet "into the ground." I finally crossed paths with Coach Mierke of Fitness Concepts, and within nine months of being patiently coached through the proper steps I had to take to run safely and with healthy efficiency, I was running faster and longer than I ever dreamed possible—*with no injuries!* I achieved a lifelong dream of qualifying for the Boston Marathon and then ventured into triathlon. In just my second year of triathlon I was fortunate enough to finish third in the female 30–34 division at the XTERRA World Championship.

Despite its apparent simplicity, I have come to learn that developing a runner to her potential is a relatively complicated matter, especially when she has to run far and fast after swimming and cycling. Regardless of how pure running is, human physiology is pretty complex. Some techniques are more efficient than others, some training methods work better for some athletes than others, and what we should do differs at different points in the season.

As my own professional career focuses on injury prevention, I was very motivated to learn the important running skills and training guidelines that are outlined in the following pages. This book will teach you the techniques that will enhance your performance, but they will also enhance your passion and joy with running by enabling you to combine it effectively with your own careers, commitments, and friendships, as it did for me.

Ken Mierke's *The Triathlete's Guide to Run Training* contains all the information any triathlete needs to start taking steps safely in the right direction and to keep moving forward efficiently. This book will help you prepare to run faster and further than you ever thought possible. Ken's great depth of knowledge and experience as a coach for triathletes (as well as for a long list of other sports) and his knowledge as an exercise physiologist gives him profound insight into how to train properly for running, while combining this efficiently with the time-consuming, body-demanding sports of cycling and swimming.

Run free with no limitations.

DR. KATHY COUTINHO
SPORTS CHIROPRACTOR AND COMPETITIVE TRIATHLETE

Preface

This book was written for serious athletes who are intent on making the most of every experience in triathlon. When I say serious, I don't mean elite, fast, or even experienced, but those who are willing to sacrifice to improve in the sport they love and who want to learn how to do it right.

As a less-than-gifted athlete (I have muscular dystrophy), I have always tried to use my brain to find little ways to give myself small advantages in sports. As a football player, I learned to get low and maximize leverage. As a tennis player, I learned to figure out during the warm-up what grips the opponent used so that I knew what kind of spin would give him trouble. I also learned how to angle my shots to minimize how far I would have to run. Gifted endurance athletes overlook so many little things that could give them small, but significant advantages.

When I began coaching, I was working with an elite road cyclist named Skip Foley. He was monstrously strong. This rider time trialed at over 29 miles per hour and could ride away from almost anyone in the region. When in my office for a VO_2max test, I noticed that he had cut the handlebars on his bike to about a four-inch width and put mountain bike bar ends on. The bar was just wide enough to be used for the time trial start, but useless for anything else. Foley had gone to extremes; nothing that could make his bike more aerodynamic was left undone. This was still an athlete that intimidated me terribly, so I timidly joked with him about it. He looked me straight in the eye and said, "Kenny, I'm not strong enough to give anything away." It struck me that this rider, who could sustain far greater wattage than any amateur in the country (and most pros), paid such attention to the most minute of details. That has shaped my paradigm of coaching to this day. If there were something we could do to make you a minute faster, you would do it, but so would your competition. I'll find ten things that will each help you go six seconds faster.

Through the years I have coached hundreds of athletes at all ability levels, from beginner to professional, and I have always thought it was my responsibility to keep track of the little things so that the athlete could concentrate on the big things—workouts and races. I have learned something different from every one of them.

The training system in this book is scientifically based on research in the laboratory and proven by experience on the track, roads, and trails. While there is definitely more than one right way to do something, there are also definitely wrong ways. Many of the training methods used by most athletes are inefficient. While there is clearly an art to applying the science of training to the individual—we definitely coach people, not biological organisms—programs that adhere to sound scientific principles work better than those based on tradition or intuition.

Many athletes believe that a methodical, scientifically based system of training detracts from the joy of the sport. I have found just the opposite. I gain joy from improving and overcoming challenges, and I have found the same thing in every athlete I have coached. Winning races is fun, even if it is yourself you race against. The joy of swimming, cycling, and running is not tied up in spontaneity. Developing efficient technique, planning effective workouts, and going easy when you're supposed to go easy and hard when you're supposed to go hard doesn't detract from the fun. Is it wasting time and energy that makes triathlon fun?

I sign off on e-mails to the athletes I coach: "Train with purpose, Ken," and that is what I propose in this book. Every workout should have a specific purpose, with a specific goal determined before the workout begins.

The Triathlete's Guide to Run Training is divided into four sections. Part One, Technique, covers a topic runners have ignored for years. Please read this section and take it to heart. You have far more to gain by learning to run efficiently than by hard training. Part Two covers training and helps you develop efficient workout programs to make you stronger. Part Three discusses a number of small things you can do to help you to train better and allow you to be more thorough in race preparation. Finally, Part Four talks about racing and how to get the most out of whatever you bring with you to the starting line.

While this book is directed at the self-coached athlete, I highly recommend finding a qualified professional coach to provide additional guidance. Multisport training is more complicated than one might think, and a fully trained coach spends all day learning about effective training. The most serious athlete doesn't know nearly as much as a good coach, who spends much of every day reading lactate assays, nutrition research, or wind tunnel tests. Also, even the most knowledgeable athletes can't be objective about their own training. That is why some coaches say "self-coached" is an oxymoron.

I hope the information in this book helps you to run a little bit faster in your next important race, but even more I hope that it helps you enjoy the wonderful sport of triathlon (or duathlon) a little bit more. Have fun, be smart, and train with purpose.

KEN MIERKE
FAIRFAX, VIRGINIA

Acknowledgments

So many people have contributed to my efforts to produce this book. First, I would like to thank my parents, Ed and Jolien Mierke, for their continued support of me and my business. I am indebted to my wife, Melissa, for always believing in me and for all of her support, hard work, and dedication in helping me chase my dreams.

Thanks to Kathy for your friendship, for keeping me healthy for running, and for all the "business" meetings at Starbucks. Thanks to Melissa, Alan, and Eric for serving as my early guinea pigs. Thanks to Steven Duplinski and Justin Thomas. Your hard work, dedication, and talent showed the world that my methods work. Thanks to David Alleva, my college roommate, who first made me believe that I could actually do a triathlon. Thanks to my two favorite professors, Dr. Thea and Dr. Walberg-Rankin for making me love working my tail off and for making exercise physiology and nutrition fun. Thanks to Skip Foley, the first elite who believed in me, when I had not yet done anything, and gave me a chance.

I sincerely appreciate all of my clients at Fitness Concepts, who continue to inspire me with their dedication, passion, and hard work. Most of what I know about triathlon training I learned through you. Thanks to my coaches Melissa, Margie, Jason, Adam, Brian, Nancy, Geoff, Paul, and Mary for holding down the fort at work while I was writing. Thanks to Bo Duplinsky and Laura Bruch for their help editing.

I would like to thank Joe Friel for the support, trust, and opportunities he has provided me through Ultrafit. Being mentored by Joe Friel, the famous coach (I'm not worthy), has meant the world to me and my business, but having Joe the man as a role model means even more. I hope I can grow up to be just like you.

Introduction

Running is often the most challenging and the most decisive leg of triathlon competition. Triathletes expend significantly more energy per minute on the run than either the bike or the swim. More muscle mass is used for running, and the run is the only triathlon segment in which athletes support their own weight. In addition to fatigue from the high levels of energy expenditure, the high impact of running will beat up athletes far more than swimming or cycling.

The placement of the run segment at the end of the race also adds to the challenge. At the outset of the run, fatigue has already begun to set in. The athlete has already swum and biked between one and 10 hours. On beginning the run, an athlete's muscles may be burning from lactic acid accumulation, fuel reserves may be running low, and dehydration may already be setting in.

With the finish line at the completion of the run, the race ultimately is won or lost on the run. Even a triathlete who is a very strong swimmer and cyclist and heads into the run with a big lead ultimately wins the race running.

Part of the challenge of triathlon running is being able to run effectively after cycling hard for a relatively long period of time. This is both a physiological and a psychological challenge that must be specifically prepared for. The fastest runner in open races (that do not include swim and bike segments) is not always the fastest runner after swimming and cycling.

The physiological challenge involves implementing techniques that enable effective running with fatigued cycling muscles and training those muscles to make the transition from hard cycling to hard running. Specifically, the quadriceps muscles will be extremely fatigued after 40 kilometers to 112 miles of intense cycling. Efficient triathlon runners minimize the use of their quadriceps in their stride through ideal foot-strike mechanics. Brick workouts, as described in Chapter 6, enable the muscles to make the neurological and metabolic transfer from cycling to running more quickly and more completely.

The goals of improving triathlon running are twofold: training the body to run faster for race duration and training the body to perform closer to its potential after hard swimming and cycling. An international-distance triathlete needs to train to run a faster open 10K and to close the gap between his triathlon 10K and his open 10K. Ironman athletes need to become faster marathoners and make their ironman marathon as close to their open marathon as possible.

The psychological challenge involves pushing a high intensity for an extended duration when already fatigued from swimming and cycling hard. Additionally, triathletes will not run nearly as fast in a triathlon as an open race, even when the perceived exertion feels higher. Especially for triathletes with a running background, this can be frustrating. Struggling to run at 6:30 pace, while really suffering, is mentally tough for an athlete who runs an open 10K at a six-minute pace.

This book provides information about running technique, training, and how to integrate running workouts into a triathlon training schedule, as well as a large number of ideas that will allow you to train more efficiently.

THE IMPORTANCE OF SMALL DIFFERENCES

> Sometimes when I consider what tremendous conse-
> quences come from little things . . . I am tempted to
> think there are no little things.
> —Bruce Barton

When an athlete first begins training, improvements come fast. Each workout is faster and easier than the last. As he or she becomes more advanced, progress slows. Even as the athlete continues to improve, the gains come slower and cutting just a few seconds off a run—which used to happen every week—now is a long process that may require many months of hard training. After several years of relatively consistent hard training, athletes are likely to be pretty high on their diminishing-returns curve. Getting stronger and faster will happen gradually. See Figure I.1 for a visual explanation of diminishing returns.

An experienced athlete has trained consistently and trained hard. Increasing volume and intensity may bring slight improvements or no

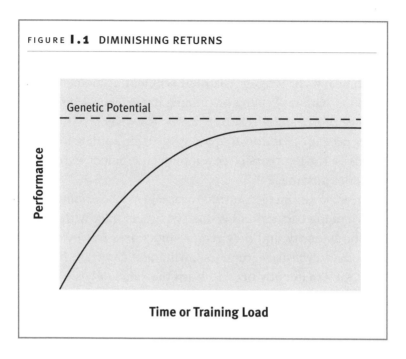

FIGURE **1.1** DIMINISHING RETURNS

improvement at all. At this point, it is time to get more serious about planning an effective training program. An intermediate to advanced athlete has probably done the big things right; now it is time to focus on the little things that, collectively, will make a big difference on race day.

One percent of an hour is 36 seconds. For a hard-training athlete, 36 seconds an hour is an enormous amount of time to be saved in a race. Usually, races are won and lost by less than 36 seconds per hour. One percent is very important. I frequently tell my athletes, "If we could find something to make you 5 percent faster, we would do it for sure, but so would your competition. Everyone uses a wet suit when it is allowed, and everyone uses race wheels and an aerobar. What we can do, though, is find 10 little things that your competition doesn't know about that will each help you go one-half of 1 percent faster." For a serious, hard-training athlete, there are no little things.

Based on his or her athletic experiences before coming to the sport of triathlon, each athlete will bring certain strengths, weaknesses, and predispositions to triathlon. Take these to heart. These tendencies are pretty consistent.

Swimming Background

Even though the swim is the shortest-duration segment of a triathlon, and in many ways the least physically challenging, swimming is the most technically challenging triathlon segment. Athletes who come into triathlon with no cycling or running experience seem to technically master those sports relatively easily. However, cyclists and runners who take up triathlon frequently struggle to develop efficient swim strokes. Having years of developing an efficient swim stroke is a tremendous advantage.

The greatest advantage and disadvantage of beginning triathlon with a swimming background is that swimmers train with enormous volume and intensity, and they require much less rest between hard workouts than cyclists or runners. Swimmers can train hard relentlessly, but they frequently need to learn the value of basic endurance training at an easy pace and the importance of rest days. Especially when running, triathletes who are former swimmers tend to suffer frequent injuries and overtraining.

Cycling Background

Triathletes with a cycling background have the advantage of endurance and efficiency on triathlon's longest segment. The greatest amount of time—and energy—can potentially be gained or lost on the bike. Also, strong cyclists generally come off the bike fresher and are able to run closer to their full capabilities.

The greatest disadvantage for triathletes with cycling backgrounds is that many hours of hard training on the bike have developed muscular and cardiovascular fitness that enables them to run too far, too fast, and too soon. Running stresses the tissues differently than cycling. Similar to triathletes with swimming backgrounds, those with cycling backgrounds will tend to suffer from injuries and overtraining unless they learn to approach running much more conservatively than they approached cycling.

Running Background

With the run such an important aspect of triathlon, we would expect runners to do well quickly, but it does not necessarily happen that way. Runners need to learn to emphasize technique in all three segments and be patient as those skills develop. The cardiovascular fitness developed through years of running is definitely an advantage, but the muscular development that will enable them to swim and bike effectively may take years to develop to the level of their running.

Triathletes with a running background should prioritize the workouts and techniques that will enable them to run effectively even when fatigued from hard cycling.

No Previous Background

Many new triathletes have no experience in swimming, cycling, or running. These athletes generally find swimming the most technically challenging of the triathlon segments and the run the most physically fatiguing. These athletes need to work hard to develop efficient technique in all three triathlon modes and keep their training volume higher on the bike than the swim or the run.

HOW TO GET THE MOST FROM THIS BOOK

Reading and understanding a book like this doesn't pose the same challenge as implementing the information into an effective training program that will fit your life. Following are some suggestions on how the information contained in this book can help you most.

First, I would encourage you to make every effort to improve your running technique. A clinic or private instruction with a certified Evolution Running instructor will help tremendously. Follow the instructions in the chapters on technique, spend just a few minutes on the drills every time you run, and use a metronome to monitor turnover. At every level, runners (especially triathlon runners) have more to gain by improving efficiency than by training to become stronger. Take this part of race preparation seriously.

Altering running technique is an extremely difficult undertaking. Most runners have established incorrect motor patterns through millions of stride-cycles with incorrect technique. The staff of Fitness Concepts has worked with thousands of runners, made all the mistakes you would make if you didn't follow our instructions, and learned from them. I realize that great athletes tend to be impatient. They want results yesterday and are willing to do almost anything to achieve them. These results are worth waiting for and worth being patient with. You are developing the technique you will be using for the rest of your running career. Over the long haul, it will improve your running tremendously. *It is worth doing right!* Take the time to master each aspect of running technique one at a time. Don't rush through to the next aspect, thinking you'll go back and polish up the last technique later—true mastery will only take longer that way.

Second, take the time to plan your season. A skeletal training plan that plots important races, training priorities, and key workouts month by month is vital. Even an advanced athlete or a professional coach needs to include this step in planning training. No amount of experience can prepare an athlete or coach to "shoot from the hip" effectively. Without a plan, time slips up on you and some important steps may be missed. We all tend to overemphasize our strengths, because workouts that emphasize strengths are always an athlete's favorites. Organizing training at the beginning of the year enables an athlete to consistently build upon last month's training and bring it all together on the days of the most important races.

Third, take the little things seriously. This book is loaded with tips to help you train just a little bit more efficiently. Science and experience have proven that they work. Individually, they are little things; collectively, they make a huge difference in race preparation. Hard-training triathletes invest an enormous amount in their sport. So many make the big investments, but ignore the little things: Refuel properly, get enough sleep, take care of your muscles, and go easy when you need to go easy—you will maximize each key workout.

Enlisting the guidance of a qualified coach can be another great investment. The coach takes care of the planning so that all of your energy can be funneled directly into training and racing. Make sure to find a qualified coach and not just a gifted athlete. Kareem Abdul-Jabbar can't teach you to be 7'2".

When planning your season, each month, week, and workout is critical to performing your best—but always use a pencil. The plans are important, and you will train better having made them, but be flexible. We develop long-term plans with the best information that is available at the time, but new information is constantly becoming available during the season. Listen to that new information and make small adjustments to your big picture plan. Always remember that training plans are there for you, not vice versa.

PART ONE

Technique

1

Evolve Your Running Technique

TO IMPROVE "MILES PER GALLON"

Most runners think that performance will improve by running longer and running harder. They assume that faster runners are more gifted, run more miles, and/or run those miles harder than they do. Few give any attention to technique or efficiency. Fitness Concepts research has shown that improving technique will affect performance more than any other factor. Runners have ignored the one thing that will enable the greatest improvement.

ECONOMY

Running economy is defined as the amount of energy required to run at a certain pace. Most triathletes would be shocked at the differences in economy among athletes. The assumption is that faster runners are stronger than those they outperform. Efficiency is not considered a major factor. However, the winner of a race usually expends *less* energy than the third-place finisher. She is able to run faster because she runs more economically. The winner gets more speed out of less energy.

One great thing about technology is that machines do not have opinions, they do not lie, and they are not afraid to break with tradition. I have personally performed over 6,000 VO$_2$max tests, which mechanically measure both an athlete's fitness and efficiency. I have been surprised that performance differences among runners are consistently due to economy more than fitness.

An elite may run 8 percent faster than an advanced runner but only consume 3 percent more oxygen. The elite is 3 percent stronger but runs 8 percent faster. The additional 5 percent in running speed is due to economy. Among the runners I have tested, efficiency played a greater role in running speed at lactate threshold than energy output did 84 percent of the time.

An economical runner uses less energy to run a certain speed due to better technique, stronger muscles, and more elastic tissues. Economy is not an inherent talent, such as high-level aerobic capacity, and it can be significantly improved. Runners who want to improve should make the effort to learn correct biomechanics and implement them into their strides.

Athletes in every sport except running devote enormous attention to perfecting even minute details of the movements required in competition. Most running coaches just tell their athletes to run longer and harder. More miles and more intensity are considered the answer. Technique has been basically ignored for years, as coaches assume a runner's "natural stride" will provide efficiency and injury resistance. That simply is not the case.

As triathletes, we have fallen into this very same trap. How many of your training partners have worked on their swim stroke mechanics? Probably every single one has given at least some thought to how he or she moves through the water. How many have put some effort into bike position or pedal-stroke mechanics? Maybe not everyone, but most serious triathletes have put some effort into improving the efficiency of their pedal stroke and aero position. Even those that haven't worked hard on swimming and cycling skills at least have some vague awareness that they should. How many have given running technique the slightest thought? Far fewer.

The Great African Champions

For several decades, African runners have dominated distance running at its highest levels. Research into what makes these runners faster consistently demonstrates that they have normal VO_2max and lactate threshold levels for elite runners. Their height, weight, limb-length ratios, muscle fiber types, and every physiological variable that we can measure all fall into the normal range for professional runners. No doubt, these athletes are extraordinarily gifted and extraordinarily fit, but so are the other professional runners they beat so easily. Clearly and consistently, what sets the great African runners apart is that they are more efficient than their competitors. They run faster without expending more energy.

Many experts in running economy agree that running barefoot through childhood contributes significantly to the extraordinary success of these athletes. When they put shoes on their feet, they continue to run the way they always have. While I don't suggest that you run barefoot, I will suggest that you take the time and effort to learn the techniques that make these runners so astoundingly efficient and implement them into your technique for running with shoes. Our research with Evolution Running has found that these techniques *can* be taught and that implementing them into almost any athlete's running stride will improve performance and minimize injury risk.

IMPROVING PERFORMANCE

Genetics plays a significant role in triathlon performance. The first thing you must do to win a triathlon is choose your parents well. As we improve our fitness, we all move up a diminishing-returns curve. However, some of our curves have an overall higher peak.

When we first start training for a triathlon, we get stronger and faster every week. We knock minutes off a training run using a consistent amount of effort. By the second year, the improvements have slowed down, but they keep coming. Several weeks of hard, consistent training will still knock a second or two off that run. After several years of training, the gains come harder. Months of hard training are needed to make us just a few seconds faster. As we approach the limits of our genetic ceiling, fitness gains are extremely hard to come by—and this phenomenon is not only for the elite. Yes, gaining even a couple seconds on a climb is hard for Lance Armstrong, but a mid-pack age-group triathlete who has trained seriously for a couple of years faces the same obstacles to improving.

This point in your training is a time when gains in efficiency will enable you to smash through barriers that may have seemed insurmountable. How would you like to knock 36 seconds off your time in a one-hour race? That would be an enormous improvement, right? Thirty-six seconds is huge, but this is only 1 percent of an hour. Many hard-training athletes are at a point where a 1-percent increase in fitness would require extensive training commitments and might even be genetically impossible. Those finishing near the front are probably already within 1 percent of their potential and will never increase their fitness by another 36 seconds per hour. However, almost every athlete could improve his or her economy by 36 seconds per hour and run faster without any increases in training.

Joe Friel, top triathlon coach and author of *The Triathlete's Training Bible*, frequently tells a story about the great American runner Steve Scott. Scott's fitness was tested at a number of different points in his career, and he found a 7-percent difference in economy between times when he was fit and ready to race well and other times when he was "out of shape" (by his standards). For an athlete of that caliber, 7 percent is an incredible improvement in economy. Seven percent is the difference between a four-minute mile and 3:43. If economy made that much difference for Steve Scott, imagine how much difference it could make for you.

Evolution Running

One triathlete I coached, Alan, began working with me to implement more economical techniques into his stride. I already had metabolic test data for Alan, and on our first day at the track, I had him run 400 meters "all out"—as fast as he could possibly run that distance. We met at the track once a week for an hour over a five-month period, and I prescribed drills and workouts for him to follow throughout the week. I had him begin training with a metronome to control his turnover rate (how quickly he moved from one foot to the next).

Alan was not an easy target for quick improvement. He was a high-level athlete and was ranked among the top 10 in the country in his age group. He has run competitively for more than 40 years and has completed 17 marathons plus two Ironman Hawaii® races. He had already worked with another professional coach for years. After all the hard training over such a long period of time, Alan's fitness wasn't going to improve significantly, no matter how hard he trained. In fact, at age 62, his aerobic capacity was likely declining simply due to age. After years of high-volume running, he had established neuromuscular pathways that would be difficult to relearn. That made him a perfect guinea pig. Improvements in Alan's running would almost certainly come from changes we made to his technique, not from increases in fitness. Fortunately, I had access to technology that would enable me to test his running efficiency—directly and objectively.

Each session during those 22 weeks began with drills and a review of what we had worked on the last week. Then we added a new technique. Alan was the perfect student, and he often asked questions to help him understand what we were trying to accomplish and why. He implemented every instruction to the best of his ability. He was incredibly patient and resilient through the frustration of unlearning incorrect motor skills that had been grooved into habit through thousands of hours of running. Alan always began with a set of drills and carried a metronome on every run during those 22 weeks.

The final tests came in week 23: one at the track and one in the laboratory. Alan ran four 1-mile repeats (with 800-meter jog recoveries between) at the same pace he had run just one-quarter mile "all out" 22 weeks earlier. A VO$_2$max test performed later that week revealed an astonishing increase in economy. Alan ran at an eight-minute per mile pace with the same level of oxygen consumption that had yielded an 8:39 pace five months earlier. That represents an 8.4 percent improvement in economy, an amazing change for an advanced athlete. How would running 8.4-percent faster with the same energy expenditure affect your racing?

After Alan's success, another triathlete I coached at the time began implementing these techniques. He had run at a very high level for almost 20 years, was ranked in the top three in the United States in the men's 30–34 age group, and the run was his strength. After working to implement more efficient techniques into his stride, this athlete cut 1:48 from his previous 10K run time on the same course at USAT Nationals. Follow-up metabolic testing showed he had increased his economy at race pace by 4.2 percent, which explained more than 90 percent of the improvement. An athlete at that level would not be able to improve fitness enough to run 1:48 faster with any amount of hard training.

With continued research and experience in teaching hundreds of runners to run faster with fewer injuries, I developed a system for teaching these economy techniques called Evolution Running. My staff and I have worked with hundreds of athletes and found that everyone, from beginner to elite, benefits from developing efficient techniques. Take running technique seriously. This is an area that will improve your performance tremendously.

ELEMENTS OF ENERGY COST

Any discussion of efficient sports movement should begin with an analysis of the sources of energy cost. Where do runners expend energy?

Propulsion

Propulsion should be the greatest area of energy expenditure for an efficient runner. The greater the energy available for propulsion, the greater an athlete's running speed. Efficient running techniques, therefore, seek to maximize propulsion while minimizing all other forms of energy cost. Our discussion here will define propulsion as the energy required to maintain a constant running speed. Note that for flat-ground running, propulsive forces are purely horizontal.

Vertical Displacement

Vertical displacement is the greatest source of wasted energy in most runners' strides. Moving a body against gravity requires a lot of energy. Learning to minimize upward movement of the body's center of mass reduces the energy cost of vertical displacement.

Support

Even with no vertical movement, gravity exerts a constant force upon a runner that energy must be expended to overcome. The energy cost of support is the energy required to hold your body up against the pull of gravity. The energy cost of support is affected significantly by vertical displacement. What goes up must come down. The more a runner's body moves up during each stride, the longer gravity has to accelerate that mass downward before foot-strike. Runners with greater vertical displacement will land harder, requiring more powerful contractions to catch their bodyweight and yielding increased energy cost of support.

Acceleration

Every runner's speed changes somewhat during each stride-cycle, but efficient runners change speed only very slightly. At foot-strike, many runners "brake" and slow themselves dramatically. After "braking," runners must expend a significant amount of propulsive energy to accelerate their bodyweight back to running speed. Our discussion will consider propulsion for acceleration an energy cost separate from the propulsion required to maintain constant speed.

Balance

Some energy expenditure is required just to remain upright. Even the most economical runners constantly make slight adjustments to remain balanced, but efficient running techniques minimize the energy required.

Limb Movement

Moving the arms and legs in space requires energy. Techniques that minimize this energy cost enable greater energy for propulsion and reduce fatigue in the muscles that propel.

ECONOMIC RUNNING TECHNIQUES

As we searched for ways to improve running technique, we used a number of different models to provide insight into how runners might boost their economy.

The Wheel Model

The wheel is an extremely efficient machine. The energy cost of rolling along on a wheel is considerably less than running. Runners can incorporate principles from the wheel into their running technique to run more efficiently.

Machines that use wheels minimize wasted energy in the areas of vertical displacement, support, acceleration, and balance—leaving more energy available for propulsion.

On a flat road, the wheel provides perfectly horizontal movement and, therefore, wastes no energy on vertical displacement and has zero impact stress. The key to the wheel's ability to deliver this strictly horizontal motion is that its center of mass is always directly over its center of support. In addition to eliminating the energy cost of vertical displacement, this minimizes the energy cost of support, balance, and acceleration. Although runners will never have perfectly horizontal movement or zero impact stress, employing techniques that approximate these ideals in the wheel will enable them to move more efficiently.

The African Runner Model

As alluded to previously, African runners, Kenyans in particular, have long dominated the sport of distance running, even though laboratory testing consistently demonstrates that these great champions have fitness comparable to that of other elite runners. What sets the African runners apart is their incredible running economy. Many of the techniques of Evolution Running come directly from analyses of African distance runners' techniques.

THE BASICS OF ECONOMICAL RUNNING

Elastic Recoil

What happens when you stretch out a rubber band and let it go? It snaps back forcefully. What happens when you stretch and release human tissue? The same thing, it snaps back forcefully. This is a tremendous source of propulsion for an efficient runner. Many of your tissues are elastic and capable of storing energy upon landing and returning it at push-off. Correct technique will enable you to harness this source of speed.

When you stretch a rubber band and let it go, it snaps back powerfully. What happens when you stretch and hold a rubber band and then let it go? It snaps back just as powerfully. Unfortunately, human tissue doesn't work that way. When you stretch and hold human tissue, it stretches. The energy stored from the prestretch is lost.

Efficient runners minimize contact time between their feet and the ground to maximize the energy return from elastic recoil. If their feet stay on the ground too long, this source of speed dissipates.

Foot-Strike Placement Used by Most Runners

The most devastating error most runners make in their technique is reaching forward with the foot before foot-strike (see Figure 1.1). Most runners swing their foot forward at the completion of leg recovery in an effort to extend stride length. However, this leads to enormous wasted energy and increases the risk of injuries in a number of ways.

FIGURE **1.1** INCORRECT FOOT-STRIKE PLACEMENT

When the foot hits the ground in front of the body, the runner's leg is not in position to provide propulsion. You have no leverage to pull yourself forward and must wait until your body coasts into position over the foot. Only when your body is directly over your foot can you push off.

Notice in Figure 1.1 that the runner's center of mass moves upward as it moves forward. This runner's mass does not move purely horizontally, but rotates on an upward arc around the position of the foot-strike. This upward movement of the center of mass causes a number of problems. First, lifting mass requires energy. This energy does not contribute to forward propulsion and is therefore wasted.

This foot-strike location also contributes to braking—the slowing of a runner's speed at the moment of foot-strike. From the time the foot first hits the ground to the moment of push-off, the runner's center of mass is rising without significant input from the muscles. The source of this energy is the runner's momentum. Unfortunately, the energy used to do this must be paid back. Using momentum to raise a runner's mass comes at the cost of slowed forward speed. Additional energy must then be used to accelerate back to running speed. This energy is wasted on acceleration instead of contributing to propulsion for fast, steady-speed running.

The upward coast time (waiting for the body to come into alignment with the foot) also increases the energy cost of support. What goes up must come down. The farther the center of mass is raised off the ground, the more time gravity has to act on it before landing and the harder the foot will hit the ground. The muscles that support bodyweight at foot-strike, the quadriceps, must contract much more forcefully to "catch" the runner's bodyweight. This unnecessarily increases the energy cost of support. Fatigue in the quadriceps, especially after long runs at an easy pace, is a sure sign of a forward foot-strike location.

Reaching forward with the foot also increases the energy cost of balance. Balance is best achieved with the center of support directly beneath the center of mass. A runner who reaches forward must contract stabilizing muscles more forcefully. The energy needed to accomplish this would be better used to increase propulsion and run faster.

An out-in-front foot-strike placement also significantly increases the risk for injuries. Obviously the increased vertical displacement causes the runner's bodyweight to come down harder at foot-strike, which maximizes impact stress.

Additionally, this technique places the leg almost in line with the direction of the runner's mass, which also increases impact stress. At the moment the foot hits the ground, a runner's mass is moving forward and down. As shown in Figure 1.2, an out-in-front foot-strike minimizes the angle of deflection (left figure). With this small angle of displacement, the impact of landing provides the foot and leg with a relatively direct blow. Moving the foot-strike back underneath the hips provides a much greater angle of displacement (right figure), which means the impact of landing is a glancing blow, with less impact delivered to the foot and leg of the runner and more energy directed forward to maintain momentum and running speed.

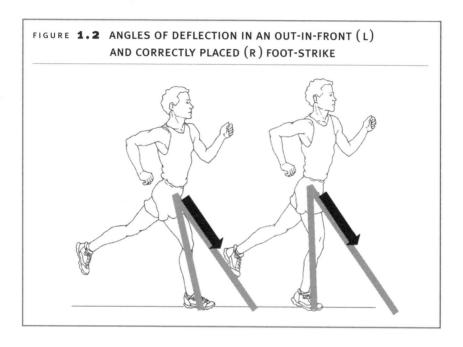

FIGURE **1.2** ANGLES OF DEFLECTION IN AN OUT-IN-FRONT (L)
AND CORRECTLY PLACED (R) FOOT-STRIKE

Finally, an out-in-front foot-strike placement slows turnover and increases the time of contact between the foot and the ground. The upward "coast time" required while the runner waits for bodyweight to move up over the foot before push-off is wasted time. Efficient runners use high turnover and minimize contact time between their feet and the ground to enable maximal use of elastic recoil. The forward foot-strike location makes achieving those goals of efficient running impossible.

Correct Foot-Strike Location

The most critical aspect of running technique is the location of the foot-strike. Placing the foot in the proper position relative to the body minimizes vertical displacement, enables effective use of elastic recoil, prevents braking at impact, optimizes body balance, increases

FIGURE **1.3** CORRECT FOOT-STRIKE PLACEMENT

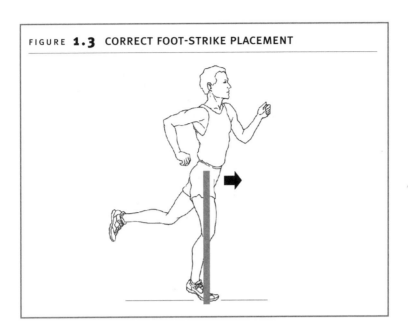

turnover, and decreases the force required at push-off for fast running (see Figure 1.3).

Most of the components of Evolution Running build on this critical technique. Placing the foot-strike in the proper location is necessary before other aspects of good technique can be accomplished. Although this technique is not at all complicated, it may be more difficult to correct than you would imagine. Correct foot-strike placement is natural for very few adult runners. Almost every runner automatically reaches forward with the foot in an attempt to artificially lengthen the stride. When learning to run in shoes with a one-inch slab of rubber under the heel and alongside runners who all reach forward with the foot, this incorrect technique seems natural, automatic, and relaxed.

Correcting the placement of your foot-strike will change your body position, balance, and the basic rhythm of your running. These changes are improvements that will eventually help you run farther, faster, and more injury free than ever before, but they will not feel natural initially. Don't expect to alter your technique and run quickly and efficiently right away. You have probably run millions of steps improperly, so it will take time to adapt to correct technique.

Efficient runners increase stride length by increasing the power of push-off, not by elongating range of motion. Watch a professional runner, even at five-minute pace, and notice how narrow the angle between the legs stays. Even at very high speeds, the foot never reaches forward and the legs do not open very wide.

Landing with the foot directly beneath the hips places the leg in a position to develop propulsion immediately. This is the key value of this technique. As discussed earlier, waiting for the body to "coast" up over the foot causes a number of problems that this correct technique prevents.

Keeping the foot and leg directly beneath the hips enables basically horizontal running, as illustrated by the figure on the right in Figure 1.4. However, the figure on the left has reached forward with his foot, forcing an upward movement at push-off. This reduces the energy cost of push-off, the impact of the next landing, and the energy cost of controlling the landing (in terms of both support and balance).

Placing the foot down directly beneath the hips also maintains momentum and minimizes any braking effect caused at foot-strike. The large black arrow in Figure 1.5 shows the direction of the initial force transmitted by the ground at foot-strike. Clearly the out-in-front, forward foot-strike sets the runner up for significant braking forces,

FIGURE **1.4** HORIZONTAL RUNNING

whereas the foot-strike under the hips allows momentum to be carried cleanly through to the next stride. Accelerating back to running speed after braking increases both the energy cost of sustained fast running and local muscular fatigue in the quadriceps and hamstring muscles.

Remember, minimizing contact time between the feet and ground is a primary goal of efficient running since elastic recoil is such a critical component and minimal contact time between the feet and ground optimizes elastic recoil. Locating the foot-strike directly beneath the hips enables a short ground-contact time. An out-in-front foot-strike forces runners to wait until their bodies have coasted up over their hips, delaying push-off and unnecessarily increasing contact time between the feet and ground. Much of the energy stored at foot-strike dissipates during this split second of downtime, instead of being returned as elastic recoil propulsion.

Getting this foot-strike technique right must be the first step in improving your stride. Other techniques that increase running efficiency and reduce the risk for injuries can only be learned correctly after this critical adjustment is made.

Correct Foot-Strike Technique

The key to correct foot-strike placement is simply putting your foot down earlier during leg recovery. During recovery, the knee drives for-

FIGURE **1.5** FORCE OF GROUND AT IMPACT WITH INCORRECT (L) AND
            CORRECT (R) FOOT-STRIKE

ward and then the foot swings forward to catch up. Most runners allow the foot to swing forward past the knee. Instead, just before the foot catches up with the knee, pull back with the entire leg and put your foot down much earlier than you think you need to. I have seen thousands of runners swing the foot too far forward before foot-strike, but I have never seen a single runner put the foot down too early.

BODY POSITION AND BALANCE

Body position and balance are intrinsically related to the position of foot-strike. We use the natural angulation of the body as a yardstick for correct placement of the foot-strike. If your foot lands directly under your hips, as it should, your body will naturally lean slightly forward.

In contrast, most runners remain perfectly upright when they run or even lean slightly backward. This is the surest indication of out-in-front foot-strike placement. It's simple physics. If the foot is in front of the center of mass at foot-strike, something must move backward to maintain balance, and the torso usually takes that role.

With optimal foot-strike positioning, the runner's shoulders are *very slightly* in front of the hips, and the hips are *very slightly* in front of the average position of the legs. The forward lean should not be exaggerated, and the runner should lean from the toes while keeping the body in a straight line. Leaning forward from the waist is a common error that results in poor efficiency, muscular fatigue, and potential back injuries.

A slight forward lean allows balance with minimal energy cost. From this body position, the force of gravity pulling on the runner's torso counteracts the rotary forces created during push-off. Pulling the foot backward during contact with the ground (necessary for horizontal propulsion) also creates a rotary force that pulls the runner's upper body backward with each step. A perfectly upright body position requires the runner to expend significant energy counteracting this force, because gravity can't work with the runner to maintain balance from this torso position. Expending energy to press the torso forward from an upright position feels like running into a headwind. However, from this unbalanced body position, the force runners feel pushing backward on their torso is the very force they create against the ground at push-off. Figure 1.6 demonstrates how gravity pulls on

FIGURE **1.6** ROTARY FORCES

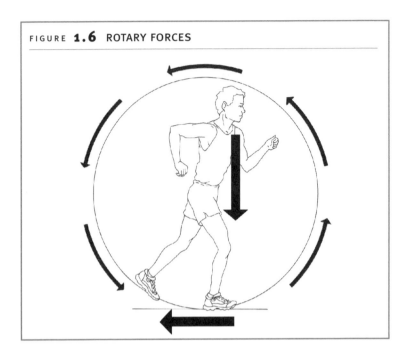

the torso of a forward-leaning runner to counteract the rotational forces of push-off and maintain balance.

Imagine a unicycle rider. If he pedals hard to create horizontal propulsion, the force of his wheel turning forward creates a rotary force that pulls the wheel out in front of his body and pulls his upper body backward. He can contract the muscles of his torso powerfully to counteract this force, or he can lean slightly forward, relaxing his torso muscles and allowing gravity to keep him in balance. Runners move more efficiently, just like a unicycle rider, with the same slightly forward body position.

Runners just learning the techniques of Evolution Running often feel like they are falling forward with each step. Some coaches actually tell runners they are using the force of gravity by "falling forward." A physics professor will tell you this is not actually true. A runner's center of mass begins the race a certain height off the ground and, therefore, with a certain potential energy. His or her mass ends the race the same height off the ground and with the same potential energy. However, the feeling of using gravity to propel does describe the feeling runners get when they first learn to run without braking. The braking associated with out-in-front foot-strike does give a runner a sense of greater control and balance. Of course, this feeling of control comes at a great cost in terms of both wasted energy and injuries.

One concept that helps many runners find the ideal balance point is feeling like they are leaning their weight forward onto their rib cage. We tell runners to lean on their navel. Once the under-the-center-of-mass foot-strike is mastered, this body position becomes automatic.

Head Position

Head position can affect body position significantly. If the head leans forward, the torso must lean backward somewhat to counterbalance the weight. Maintaining a very upright head position enables the efficient forward-leaning position. While you are learning a more efficient body position, it helps to focus your vision on an object that is slightly higher than eye level. Make sure to look at the ground only by rotating your eyes downward; avoid looking down with your head.

Arm Position

Another factor that contributes to an overly upright torso position is holding the arms in front of the shoulders. Many runners swing their arms forward in front of the body much farther than they swing them behind the body, which means the average position of the arms is in front. To counterbalance the weight of the arms, the runner must lean slightly backward. This leads directly to swinging the foot out for out-in-front foot-strike, which destroys the technique of efficient running.

To determine correct arm position, stand with your arms relaxed at your sides. Now bend your elbow to 90 degrees, but make sure to move your elbow back exactly as far as your hand moves forward. This is the correct average arm position for running. Your arms should move backward from this position as far as they move forward. In correct position and directly at your sides, the arms can be used to counterbalance the dynamic movements of each stride, and the torso will not have to move to balance the arms.

Much of the literature on running technique describes the ideal body position for efficient running as perfectly upright. One excellent book on training distance runners describes this ideal and offers pictures of three of history's greatest distance runners as evidence. However, when I drew a vertical line on the pictures through each of these runners' hip joints, their shoulders were all slightly in front of the line, indicating a slight forward lean. Look at side-view pictures of elite runners, and check them with a ruler and you will see that efficient runners lean forward.

Sprinter Michael Johnson's unique running style received a lot of attention at the 2000 Olympic Games. Television commentators discussed his "backward-leaning" running style. I videotaped his race, paused the tape, and held a ruler up to the screen through his hips and shoulders. This showed that Johnson's shoulders were, in fact, well in front of his hips, but he runs with his head in an exaggerated upright position. His head actually appears to lean slightly backward, which likely enables him to maintain balance efficiently with a more forward torso position. Again, appearances can be deceiving at first glance; look specifically at the position of the shoulders in relation to the hips.

If you find yourself completely upright or leaning slightly backward while running, put your foot down earlier during leg recovery. Never allow the foot to catch up with the knee. Make sure your arms are at your sides and not in front of your body, lift your chin, and focus your eyes on a spot on the horizon. Try to lean your weight forward onto your rib cage and establish that falling-forward feeling. If you can't establish that body position, you are almost certainly reaching forward with the foot.

FOOT-STRIKE TECHNIQUES

As mentioned previously, the key moment in a runner's stride-cycle is foot-strike—the moment the foot hits the ground. This is the moment speed is created and the moment that leads to almost all running injuries. Almost all of the modifiable goals of running technique relate directly to the moment of foot-strike. In a sense, every aspect of technique in an efficient stride-cycle is preparation for this moment.

The way a runner's foot actually hits the ground plays a huge role in efficient, injury-free running. There are three possible methods of foot-strike. The first, and most common, is the heel-strike. In this method, the heel hits the ground first, the foot slaps down, and the runner's weight eventually moves forward to the ball of the foot before push-off.

You hear runners describe this technique as their weight "rolling" forward, but to roll two objects together, one of them must be round.

I don't understand how two basically flat objects can be rolled together. The bottom of a running shoe is basically flat. While the earth is indeed round, in the context of the length of a running shoe, the ground is basically flat. Watch slow-motion video of a heel-striker who claims to "roll" forward and you will see that there is no rolling forward, but a foot slapping down forcefully.

The second method of foot-strike is flat-footed. In a flat-footed foot-strike, the heel and the ball of the foot hit the ground simultaneously. Even though this method is different than the heel-strike, for the purposes of this book I will collectively refer any method of foot-strike that places weight on the heel as a heel-strike.

The third method of foot-strike is landing with the weight on the balls of the feet. As we will see, this method provides a runner the best opportunity to run efficiently and injury free.

Whenever the heel touches the ground while bearing weight, the body's system of shock absorption and energy return gets bypassed. Efficient runners land on the balls of their feet and never allow their weight to be on their heels.

A forefoot landing maximizes use of the body's natural shock absorption system. Just as the elastic tissues in the feet and calves provide propulsion, they can absorb impact stresses. Allowing the heels to touch the ground and become weighted minimizes this function of the feet and calves.

The heel is made primarily of bone and is designed for support, not cushioning. Our heels were designed for walking, not running. Speed and injury resistance are not major factors in walking. When humans want to go fast they don't walk, they run. Using elastic recoil isn't important for walking. During walking, impact stresses are minimal and shock absorption is unnecessary. Reaching forward with the foot and landing on the heel are very efficient walking techniques, but they are not for running.

When a runner weights the heel at foot-strike, impact stress is passed directly from the heel up through the ankle to the shinbone, frequently causing shin splints and stress fractures. The shinbone transmits the stress to the knee, which also has minimal shock-absorption capacity, and can cause a number of different injuries. From there, impact stress travels up through the femur (thigh bone) to the hips to the low back, where it can cause an assortment of injuries. None of these tissues, from the heel all the way up to the low back, is designed to absorb the stress of a runner's foot-strike.

CORRECT FOOT-STRIKE POSITION

The most efficient runners never allow their heels to touch the ground until they walk up onstage during the awards ceremony. Forefoot landing is the only method of foot-strike that optimally stretches the elastic tissues of the foot and calf, engaging them for both shock absorption and then "free speed" in the form of energy return from elastic recoil.

Many runners in the process of adopting Evolution Running techniques make the mistake of running high up on their toes with the heels well off the ground. This mistake reduces efficiency because it does not allow the elastic tissues in the feet and calves to function properly. Staying high up on the toes also contributes significantly to calf and Achilles tendon overuse injuries. Don't move up on your toes, but keep your weight on the forefoot and off the heel.

Many runners doubt the effectiveness of a forefoot foot-strike until they have tried it. Perform the drills discussed in the next section to learn how to utilize your elastic tissues. Try the same drills with either of the heels-down foot-strikes and you will immediately feel the increased workload, which leads to premature fatigue, and the jarring impact, which leads to injuries.

Drills for Foot-Strike Placement and Elastic Recoil

Drills are a critical aspect of improving running technique. Drills remove the dynamics of propulsion and balance from the process of running and allow greater focus on one aspect of technique at a time. Using drills that build on each other, a runner can add one aspect of correct running technique at a time until the entire sequence of movements has been corrected.

TURNOVER

Stride Frequency versus Stride Length

Most runners, in a misguided attempt to run faster by artificially increasing stride length, take between 140 and 150 steps per minute.

RUNNING POSTURE

Stand with your feet close together, head up, and torso in a straight line.

Bend your elbows to 90 degrees, making sure to move the elbow back exactly as far as the hand moves forward. This is the arm position for ideal running posture. The arms should move forward and backward equally from this position, so this should be the average position in which the arms are held while running.

Bend your knees slightly and shift your weight forward onto the balls of your feet. The heels should be about one-fourth-inch off the ground. Relax in this position, especially your quadriceps (front thigh muscles).

Learn to balance yourself in this position without using excess energy.

Don't ignore this simple, but critical, aspect of running!

At any running speed, efficient runners use shorter strides with much higher turnover (more steps per minute).

Elite runners of any height and leg length generally run with a cadence of between 180 and 182 steps per minute. Watch the lead pack in a road race the next time you get the opportunity. You will be amazed at the incredible synchronicity of the runners' strides. Efficient runners of significantly different heights and leg lengths consistently choose almost identical turnover rates. Why would a 6'2" professional runner use the same turnover rate and significantly shorter stride length (proportionate to height) than a 5'4" runner?

The first answer (turnover rate) lies in the nature of the elastic responses of human tissue. At a given pace, longer strides mean more contact time with the ground. This reduces the benefit of elastic recoil, causing the muscles to contract more forcefully. Even though a taller runner's legs may be longer, her elastic tissues respond just like a shorter runner's. As discussed earlier, when human tissue is stretched and held, the stored energy dissipates and less energy is returned as elastic recoil. The taller runner must take strides that are proportionally shorter (compared to leg length) in order to keep contact time between the feet and ground short and enable energy return from elastic recoil.

TWO-LEGGED HOP

Stand in the running posture with your arms at your sides.

Begin to "bounce" on both feet, jumping just a couple of inches in the air.

Make sure that your knee angle stays constant and that all vertical movement comes from elastic recoil action in the feet and calves.

Concentrate on relaxing, especially your quadriceps.

Keep the movements quick and light.

Purposes of this drill:

- To develop the ability to create power from the elastic recoil of the feet and calves instead of from muscular contractions of the thighs

- To develop the skills for creating a quick contraction of the quadriceps at the moment of foot-strike, which prevents excessive bending of the knees and keeps thighs relaxed when contractions are unnecessary

- To increase strength, endurance, and elasticity of the muscles and connective tissues of the foot and calf

After getting the feel of this drill, try doing it while putting bodyweight on your heels. The effort level will increase tremendously, and you should feel incredible jarring from every impact. Which way do you want to run?

The second reason (stride length) is that a longer stride necessitates greater vertical displacement. If I wanted to throw a baseball 20 feet, I could basically throw it in a straight line without much arc. To throw the ball 50 yards, however, I would have to arc it upward, because gravity has a longer time to act on the ball. In the same way, running with long strides forces runners to move up and down more than shorter strides.

Longer strides require the muscles to contract more forcefully. To cover 20 percent more ground, even with optimal efficiency, 20 percent more force at push-off would be required. Factor in the need for vertical displacement and the loss of power from elastic recoil, and the increase in force required at push-off is staggering.

Contracting muscles more forcefully fatigues them far more than contracting them more frequently with less force. Each of our muscles is made up of thousands of muscle fibers. These muscle fibers fall into two basic categories (although there are also several subcategories): slow twitch and fast twitch. Fast-twitch fibers are tremendously powerful, but they fatigue very quickly. Slow-twitch muscle fibers have tremendous endurance, but they are not very powerful. Running with longer strides and slower turnover requires much more power at push-off than slow-twitch fibers can produce. This means the fast-twitch, "sprint" muscle fibers must contract to make up the difference, which leads to lactic acid accumulation and premature fatigue.

Running with a slow turnover requires increased vertical displacement, greater contact time with the ground, and more forceful contractions at push-off, all of which impair economy and lead to local muscular fatigue and greater risk of injuries. Improving this aspect of technique pays big dividends.

Our research shows that for triathlon race durations, optimal turnover is about 180 to 182 steps per minute, regardless of running speed. This is considerably higher turnover than most runners naturally use, especially on long, slow runs.

Learning to keep turnover higher on your easy runs is a critical part of efficient training. Good cyclists keep cadence relatively high even on an easy (heart rate Zone 1 or 2) ride. Keeping turnover high on easy runs is even more important than this, because slow-turnover running does not effectively train the elastic response you need to run your best on race day.

The Arms and Running Rhythm

The arms play an important role in running: They set a runner's rhythm. To a great degree, your arms dictate turnover and your legs dictate stride length. Keep arm movements short and quick. Avoid arm movements that increase torso rotation. Although the torso should rotate a small amount, many runners cross their arms in front of their torsos and exaggerate rotation. This leads to considerable wasted energy. Your arms should stay bent at about 90 degrees and should basically pump straight forward in front of the shoulder, with a relatively small amount of lateral movement.

As discussed previously, arm position also plays a significant role in body position. Your average arm position should be directly at your side, so make sure that your arms swing backward as much as they swing forward. Many runners swing their arms well forward of the torso but stop the backward movement when the arms are beside the torso. This means the average position of the arms is in front of the body, and the runner must lean slightly back with the torso to counterbalance the arms. This reduces the efficiency of foot-strike.

Monitoring Turnover

Learning and maintaining efficient turnover is the one step that will improve most triathletes' running more than everything else they could do combined. I recommend purchasing a metronome, which is a small electronic device that can be set to beep a certain number of times per minute. Modern metronomes are the size of a credit card, only slightly thicker, and cost about $35. This device, if used consistently, will improve your triathlon times more than a $1,200 set of race wheels.

I recommend going for a run with the metronome and adjusting it until the beeping matches your natural stride frequency. Gradually increase the speed of the metronome by two to four steps per minute each week, matching your foot-strike with the metronome's rhythm, until you can sustain 180 foot-strikes per minute. Remember that as turnover increases, stride length must decrease.

Efficient runners use quick, light leg-muscle contractions, not forceful ones. You will probably need to ease up on the power of your toe-off at first in order to increase turnover without increasing intensity. If you increase turnover by 25 percent and shorten stride length by 20 percent, you will still be running faster, but the toe-off will feel very light, almost passive.

Drills for Increasing Turnover

The next set of drills is another step toward integrating the new techniques into your stride. Be careful to patiently master each drill before moving on to the next.

INTEGRATING RUNNING TECHNIQUES

Efficient Stride

Now that we have developed a feel for using elastic recoil without weighting the heel at foot-strike and learned to run in place with a

RUNNING IN PLACE

Start from the correct running posture.

Alternately lift one leg at a time, shifting support from one leg to the other.

Lift one foot up directly toward the hips (just a few inches at first) while bouncing on the other.

Establish a quick rhythm (180 foot-strikes per minute is optimal).

Be careful not to raise your body from the knees using the quadriceps. The knee angle of the support leg should remain constant, and the quadriceps should remain relaxed. All of the power for the movement should come from the bouncing of the feet and calves.

Continue this motion and raise the nonsupport leg until the lower leg is horizontal.

Purpose of the drill:

- To further the goals of the previous drills (see Drills for Foot-Strike Placement and Elastic Recoil, page 28)
- To increase intensity by concentrating bodyweight on one leg at a time
- To force you to place your foot-strike directly below your center of mass, landing on the balls of the feet and using elastic recoil

foot-strike directly below our center of mass, we need to learn to use these skills for efficient running.

Beginning with the Running in Place with Heel-Flick drill, press your rib cage *slightly* forward. Rather than leaning from the waist, push your hips and chest slightly forward so that your body leans about one- to two-degrees forward, but remains in a straight line. This should produce a very gradual forward movement, about walking speed. Do not try to run, but instead establish a feeling of falling forward. Feel like you are running in place, with just slight movement produced by the angle of your lean.

Be very careful not to step forward with your foot. Work on adapting the running in place drill until you can comfortably perform it with high turnover, while leaning slightly forward and moving at a

---

SKIPPING IN PLACE

Begin running in place.

Insert an extra one-legged hop between each step.

Switch from right-left-right-left rhythm to right-right-left-left rhythm.

This drill increases the intensity of the elastic recoil and the calf muscle's contractions.

RUNNING IN PLACE WITH HEEL-FLICK

Begin the running in place drill, but begin kicking your heels up backward as if kicking yourself in the butt.

In addition to the goals of the previous drill, this drill emphasizes the importance of a quick and relaxed heel-flick and develops strength and endurance in the hamstring muscles.

---

very, very slow pace. Each step may be only about six inches forward. Do not try to run yet. The next section deals with propulsion, but master these elements before trying to incorporate it into your new stride.

Creating Propulsion

Creating propulsion is really what the sport of running is all about. So far, our discussion has centered on reducing wasted energy in your stride, or where *not* to spend your energy. Now we will concentrate on where you *should* expend energy and how to gain the greatest speed for the energy expended. Running at high speeds for sustained periods of time requires efficient production of horizontal propulsion.

The basic paradigm of how you should create propulsion is flawed for most runners. Not only is it difficult to execute the techniques they are attempting, but they are trying to execute inefficient techniques. Almost every runner thinks of developing running propulsion using one of two incorrect methods.

Incorrect Propulsion Techniques

The most common method runners use to develop propulsion is what I call the "upward thrust." After the body has coasted up over the foot (due to an out-in-front foot-strike), the knee is straightened forcefully, thrusting the body up and forward.

This technique wastes a tremendous amount of energy, leads to local muscular fatigue in the quadriceps, and slows turnover considerably. It also increases impact forces dramatically, which can lead to increased injury rate.

As indicated by the large black arrow in Figure 1.7, the direction of the force created by extending the knee is slightly forward, but mostly upward. Any increase in stride length is more than made up for by the decrease in turnover rate caused by the extended flight time during each stride. This results in slower running speed and increased energy cost. This up-and-down method of running, employed to some degree by most runners, is extremely inefficient. If your quadriceps ever fatigue during long runs at an easy to moderate pace, you probably subscribe to the upward thrust paradigm of creating propulsion.

A somewhat less common error of propulsion is the pull-through. These runners avoid the upward thrust push-off but create propulsion

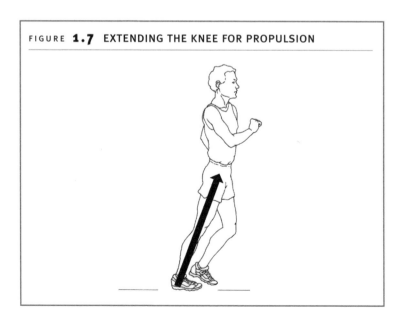

FIGURE **1.7** EXTENDING THE KNEE FOR PROPULSION

by bending their knee and pulling their body forward with the hamstring muscles. This running style is reasonably efficient: It does minimize vertical displacement and landing impact. The problem is the demand it places on the hamstring muscles (see Figure 1.8).

The hamstring muscles are relatively small and weak, and when they are almost exclusively responsible for propulsion, they fatigue easily. Learning to use the larger gluteus muscles along with the hamstrings enables runners to take advantage of the energy-efficient style and also prevents local muscular fatigue in the hamstrings by spreading the workload over greater muscle mass.

FIGURE **1.8** FLEXING KNEE

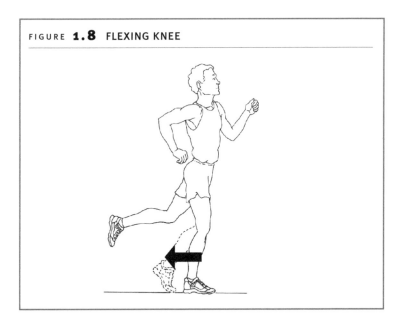

The pull-through style runner uses techniques that are a step in the right direction from the upward thrust method, and these runners are more likely to grasp and incorporate the techniques of Evolution Running quickly. If you suffer from hamstring fatigue or cramping during long or hard runs, while the rest of your body feels fairly comfortable, you probably use pull-through propulsion.

Creating Propulsion Correctly

We have discussed the two most common inefficient methods of creating propulsion. The most common method, the upward thrust, involves straightening the knee. The other incorrect method, the pull-through, involves bending the knee. Since straightening the knee is incorrect and bending the knee is incorrect, you might correctly conclude that knee angle should not change as part of the process of creating propulsion. This is the most important aspect of efficient propulsion.

I call the recommended propulsion technique the "foot-drag movement" (see Figure 1.9). It involves pivoting the leg backward from the hip with the entire leg as a fixed unit. The knee should be slightly bent, but its angle should not change from just before foot-strike, through the period of contact with the ground, to the follow-through. *Through the entire propulsion phase, the knee angle should be slightly bent and constant.* This technique accomplishes a number of the goals for efficient, fast, sustained running.

First, the foot-drag movement creates almost perfectly horizontal propulsion. Vertical displacement, and all the problems associated with it, can be minimized. Newton's Law states that "every action has an equal and opposite reaction." It follows that in order to create horizontal propulsion, we must pull straight back against the ground instead of pushing down into the ground. The foot-drag movement accomplishes this goal.

FIGURE **1.9** THE FOOT-DRAG MOVEMENT

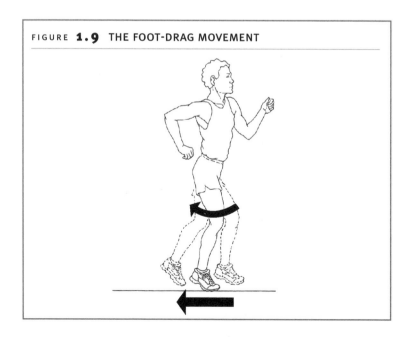

The foot-drag movement also takes advantage of the attachment points of the muscles on the back of the hips and thighs and spreads the work of propulsion among a much larger muscle mass than other methods of propulsion. Using greater muscle mass to accomplish a certain amount of work decreases the relative intensity of the work for each muscle. If more muscles are doing the same amount of work, each muscle is working less.

The hamstring muscles are unusual in that they cross two major joints. They attach above the hip, cross both the hip and the knee joints, and attach below the knee. Due to this unique attachment, they serve two major functions: extending the hip joint and flexing the knee joint. The gluteus maximus muscles, on the other hand, cross only one major joint, the hip. The glute muscles' only major action is hip extension.

The pull-through method of propulsion creates nearly horizontal propulsion, but it fails to engage the largest and strongest muscle in the body, the glutes. Which do you think would be stronger, your hamstring muscles or your hamstring muscles plus your glutes? That answer is obvious. If knee flexion is the primary producer of propulsion, the hamstrings have to create the force by themselves. By using hip extension instead of knee flexion to create propulsion, the hamstrings work in conjunction with the glutes. Therefore, each muscle is required to produce less force, which minimizes fatigue.

Pull-through runners frequently have extremely tight hip flexors, which prevents the hip extension that is so critical to creating high levels of horizontal propulsion without local muscular fatigue. If you often experience hamstring fatigue when you run, stretching your hip flexors will help you incorporate the foot-drag movement into your stride.

Propulsion Drill
The Pendulum drill on page 39 will help you learn to develop propulsion efficiently.

Movement of Foot at Impact
Most runners' feet are motionless, relative to their body, when they strike the ground. The average runner holds the foot out in front of the body during the flight phase, waiting for gravity to pull the body down into the ground. Very few runners think about this aspect of technique, but this error will prohibit efficient, injury-free running.

PENDULUM

Stand in the running position and hold on to a railing or a partner for balance.

Swing your leg, with the knee slightly bent, backward and then forward.

Pause and repeat.

Do not allow knee-angle to change during this drill.

Range of motion of the leg should be from a 45-degree angle forward to a 45-degree angle backward.

Maintain an upright posture and do not lean forward from the waist.

Keep the movement relaxed and feel the gentle contractions in your glutes and hip flexors.

As you gain a feel for the relaxation required for this drill, gradually speed up the movement while maintaining relaxation. Feel the leg swing without overcontrolling it.

This drill develops a feel for moving the upper leg from the hip, instead of focusing on the movements around the knee.

When the foot is held out motionless relative to the body until foot-strike, it is actually moving forward relative to the ground at a speed equal to running speed. Runners create force for propulsion against the ground, using the foot, in a backward direction. So runners using this technique and running 8 miles per hour ask their feet, which are moving forward at 8 miles per hour relative to the ground, to make an instantaneous 16-miles-per-hour change of direction—to accelerate from 8 miles per hour in one direction to 8 miles per hour in the opposite direction. Of course, that can't happen. This style of running causes excessive braking as the leg muscles contract to change the direction of force the foot applies to the ground. This slows the runners' momentum and requires reaccelerating with every step.

Combining Stride and Propulsion

Once you have mastered these individual elements of efficient stride and propulsion, you can begin reformulating your technique by putting

MAXIMIZE YOUR STRIKE

When an efficient runner's foot strikes the ground, it is already moving backward relative to the runner's body. Efficient runners recover their leg slightly in front of the hips and then forcefully pull it backward into the ground. This prevents braking, conserves their momentum, and eliminates the need to reaccelerate every stride. This also enables minimum contact time between the foot and ground, which ensures maximum elastic recoil.

them all together. From the Running in Place drill (page 33), lean your weight slightly forward and begin moving at walking speed. Begin to incorporate the foot-drag movement into your stride, pulling back from the hip and not the knee. Establish a feeling of pulling backward from the hip using the glutes instead of pulling back from the knee using the hamstrings. Extend the upper leg well behind the body, but keep the knees slightly bent. Concentrate on beginning the foot-drag movement before your foot hits the ground.

Once the foot begins to pull backward before striking the ground, you should feel no "braking" action when it does hit the ground. You should feel like the push-off is accomplished involuntarily and automatically as a result of you leaning forward and pulling the foot back into the ground. As you grow more accustomed to this style of running, you should feel that your glutes are working as hard as your thigh muscles. Feeling some soreness in the glutes is a sign that you are using them more. With training, this soreness will soon disappear and you will be running faster and more efficiently.

How many marathon runners do you know who have pulled out of a race because of hamstring cramps? Do you remember the video of the ironman athletes crawling to the finish line because their quadriceps had given out? How many times have you seen an athlete pull up lame because of glute fatigue? The thigh muscles will always give out first. The more you can use the glutes, the better.

Leg Recovery

Although by now you have likely made significant progress in improving your running efficiency, there are a few more elements of technique to consider. The mechanics of recovering the leg after follow-through are important to maintaining your desired pace of turnover and developing maximal efficiency. Incorporating a movement called the "heel-flick" will increase the speed of your leg recovery, as well as reduce the energy cost.

Imagine swinging a stick that is 10 feet long with a certain amount of force. Now imagine cutting the stick in half, holding the two 5-foot sections together and swinging with the same amount of force. What would happen? Obviously the swing would be faster. Even though the weight of the stick was the same, its center of mass was moved closer to your hands.

Heel-flick

The purpose of the heel-flick is to raise the center of mass of the leg closer to the hip. This enables faster leg recovery with less energy required.

Many runners accomplish this by contracting the hamstring muscles to lift their heel toward their buttocks. While this method does improve the speed and efficiency of the leg recovery, it also creates unnecessary work for the hamstring muscles, which are key muscles for propulsion. Because maximizing propulsion is a primary goal, runners should use the muscles that accomplish this only for propulsion. Learning to complete the heel-flick with relaxed hamstring muscles will allow you to run farther and faster.

Efficient runners use energy from the backward momentum of the leg and foot on the follow-through to swing their heel up toward the buttocks. In Figure 1.10, the figure on the left is just completing follow-through. Notice the backward and upward momentum of his foot and leg, which is represented by the black arrows. At the completion of the follow-through (shown in the second figure), he immediately begins to drive his knee forward while keeping the thigh muscles relaxed. This causes the heel and lower leg to swing upward using their momentum, without hamstring contractions. This places the runner in the position of the figure on the far right— the ideal position for a quick, efficient leg recovery.

Most runners pause at the completion of follow-through. However, this dissipates the backward and upward momentum of the lower leg and foot and then requires contraction of the hamstring muscles to lift the heel and lower leg into the ideal recovery position.

FIGURE **1.10** HEEL-FLICK TECHNIQUE

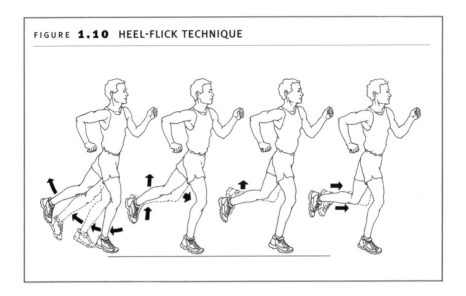

Instead, once mastered, this heel-flick movement will be quick, smooth, light, and relaxed. To train your body for proper heel-flick, focus on the following concepts.

- The forward knee drive begins powerfully, and immediately after follow-through.
- The foot is allowed to lag behind the knee on recovery.
- The thigh muscles are kept very relaxed during leg recovery. Only the hip flexor muscles, in the front of the hip and upper thigh, are working.
- After the foot leaves the ground, further propulsion is no longer possible. End the follow-through early and get the foot back in position for the next stride.

RUNNING TECHNIQUE AND INJURIES

Many runners, and even coaches, assume that injuries are an inherent part of running. They believe that if you run with enough volume and intensity to stimulate increases in strength and endurance, sooner or later you will suffer from serious injury. I passionately disagree with this philosophy! One common denominator of almost all great endurance performances is a long period of relatively uninterrupted training. Even small injuries can be incredibly disruptive to a training regimen. They should never be tolerated as normal!

I believe strongly that adjusting technique can dramatically reduce the frequency and severity of injuries. By minimizing vertical displacement and landing with your foot correctly oriented and in the right position relative to your center of mass, impact stress can be drastically reduced. By using proper technique to minimize impact stress, maximize shock absorption, and distribute the remaining stress optimally, injuries can become rare.

As discussed previously, runners moving their center of mass up and down during running not only waste energy, but also may injure themselves. The higher the center of mass travels during the flight phase, the more vertical velocity it will gain during descent, and the greater the impact stress will be.

Our bodies are designed with built-in shock absorbers. The muscles and connective tissues of the feet and calves are extremely elastic. Most runners bypass this shock absorption by allowing their weight to come down on their heels. The heel has almost no shock-absorbing capacity. It is made of bone, which is not elastic. Bone transfers shock very well, and stress can be sent to the ankle, shin, knees, hips, and lower back as a result. None of these tissues is designed to absorb impact stress, and the resulting trauma eventually creates an injury.

Many runners rely almost exclusively on the shock-absorption capabilities of their shoes instead of using their bodies' own built-in shock absorbers. Sometimes nature can do better than the shoe companies.

Fortunately, the techniques that minimize the risk for injury are the same as those that enable us to run fast and efficiently. Moving our weight off of bones and onto elastic tissues yields free speed from elastic recoil and makes best use of our body's shock absorbers.

Ways to Minimize Injury Risk

Minimize Impact Forces

Forces at the moment a runner's foot hits the ground create most running injuries. The harder the foot hits the ground, the greater the chance of injury. Adjusting running technique to minimize the impact stress reduces injuries dramatically.

Maximize Shock Absorption

The human body has tissues specifically designed to absorb impact stress. The muscles and connective tissues of the foot and calf are tremendously elastic and capable of absorbing impact stress. Using them properly is the key to minimizing injuries. This reduces downtime, during which fitness may decline quickly. Techniques that protect a runner from injuries may allow a runner to train with greater volume and/or intensity, potentially enabling greater fitness.

Foot-strike

The one step that will reduce running injuries more than anything is learning to run without putting weight on your heels. This change will both dramatically reduce impact stress and shift the remaining stress to elastic tissues that are designed to handle it.

The one caveat is that any change in technique will require time for the tissues to adapt to the new stresses. Few runners who have not had professional instruction on running technique use their calf muscles as much as they should. This improvement will place additional demands on the calf muscles. Volume and intensity of training will therefore need to be dramatically reduced and gradually rebuilt.

Weighted Running

Proper use of a weight vest reduces injuries, enhances running economy, and increases fitness. Weighted running provides a force overload specific to the demands of running on the tissues.

With any kind of strength training, tissues get thicker, stronger, and more elastic. This effect is specific to the movements involved. While strength training in the weight room is important and beneficial, it does not stimulate many of the tissues used during running. Using a weight vest will strengthen tissues in the foot, calf, and lower leg more directly than weight training does. Accomplishing this in the preparation and base periods of training, while volume and intensity are at their lowest, prevents injuries later when volume and intensity increase. Do not include weighted running in any long or fast workouts in your schedule.

Weighted running is an excellent tool for increasing running efficiency. Just as swimmers use fins to swim faster and increase the pressure of the oncoming water so they can feel hydrodynamic mistakes, weighted running makes technique errors more obvious. If you over-stride or land on your heel with an extra few pounds of weight added, you will feel the extra effort and wasted energy, which will help you naturally correct the errors. You will probably notice that without any intentional effort, you will shorten your stride, reduce vertical displacement, and increase turnover when wearing the vest. The vest almost forces you to run correctly, and then when you run without the vest, you will maintain your more efficient technique.

Runners use one set of muscles that act horizontally—creating forward propulsion—and another set that act vertically—they hold us up. Faster running overloads the muscles that act horizontally (glutes and hamstrings), but not the muscles that act vertically (quadriceps and calves). Weighted running increases intensity for the vertically acting muscles. This is important and useful for all runners, but especially for triathletes who must run with fatigued quadriceps after hard cycling.

With correct running technique, the quadriceps contract at foot-strike to keep your knee from bending: They simply catch your body-weight. The quadriceps should *not* contract to create propulsion at toe-off, because the propulsion they create is mostly upward, not forward. Weighted running teaches the quads to contract very quickly and powerfully at foot-strike and then to relax and not extend the knee at toe-off. By exaggerating the penalty for vertical displacement, and helping you to feel it when you are moving up and down too much, weighted running helps you run fast with less energy expenditure.

Athletes often fear injury from the use of a weight vest. If a runner is going to be injured by running a short, endurance-pace workout starting with an additional 2.5 lbs of weight, I believe he or she should look at running technique, and not the additional 1 or 2 percent added to their bodyweight, as the issue. Certainly runners who land on their heel with the foot in front of the body need to avoid anything that increases stress to the tissues, but runners who keep weight off the heel throughout foot-strike and land with the foot in the right spot have plenty of shock absorption available to handle a couple of additional pounds.

Begin with about 2 percent of your bodyweight and very gradually increase to 5 to 8 percent. Increasing resistance beyond 8 percent does not increase the benefit, but it does increase the stress.

Weighted running is not right for every athlete at every point in training, but it is a useful off-season tool for preventing injuries, increasing fitness, and maximizing efficiency. Use the weight vests conservatively and provide adequate recovery between sessions to optimize the benefits of weighted running while avoiding potential risks.

FREQUENTLY ASKED QUESTIONS

When I take more steps per minute, my landing feels light and my legs feel good, but I breathe much harder. How can this be more efficient?

First, you are probably running too fast when you increase turnover. Most runners overstride, using too much force at push-off. If you simply increase turnover by 20 percent, obviously the workload will be too high and breathing will be out of control. If you increase turnover by 20 percent, even with a 15 percent decreased stride length, you will still run 4.3 percent faster.

Lighten up the force of your push-off, allowing it to be a passive, automatic response. If you perform the foot-drag movement properly before foot-strike, the push-off will happen automatically. Consciously force yourself not to intentionally push off at all. Efficient movements in running are light and quick, not forceful. Try to establish the same feel as riding your bike at a very easy speed, in a super-easy gear, at high cadence.

Second, this style might not be more efficient for you, *right now*. Evolution-style running requires quick movements, which place greater demands on efficient neuromuscular patterning. Efficient runners use quick bursts of muscular activity with nearly complete relaxation between. Learning when to deactivate the muscles (when they should be relaxed) takes time. Perfecting these movements will take months. Be patient and keep working.

Third, in races with relatively long durations, as even the shortest triathlon has, every athlete will be peripherally, not centrally, limited. It will be the legs, not the heart or lungs, that give out. You will breathe hard during the race and your chest may hurt, but the respiratory muscles can continue to work despite great fatigue, and ultimately fatigue in the leg muscles will be what forces you to slow.

I've been using Evolution Running for about five weeks, and I like the style, but my hamstrings burn like crazy whenever I run—even at an easy pace. What can I do?

This hamstring burn is usually caused by one of two errors. You may be creating propulsion by bending the knee instead of extending the hip. At foot-strike, you are stopping the backward movement of the upper leg (femur) when the knee is under your hip and pulling back with just the lower leg. This requires the hamstring to create a very forceful contraction, which fatigues it.

The foot-drag movement is an extension of the hip, not the knee. The leg should pivot backward from the hip as a unit, without the knee angle changing. Only after the follow-through at the beginning of leg recovery does the knee angle decrease. The upper leg should move well behind the hip. This combines powerful contractions from the gluteus maximus muscle with the hamstring contractions, which reduces the workload of the hamstrings.

A second possible scenario has you contracting your hamstrings to lift your heel at the completion of follow-through before the leg recovery. Using muscular contractions to create movements that can be accomplished without energy expenditure using inertia is wasteful. Review the instructions and drills on the heel-flick movement and learn to relax your hamstring immediately after push-off.

I'm staying up on my toes when I run, but it kills my calves. What can I do?

A certain amount of calf strain is normal as you begin to call on muscles that have been underused while you run, but many people increase this unnecessarily by staying too high up on their toes. Evolution-style running keeps your weight on the balls of your feet, with no weight supported by the heel. Advanced runners' heels may remain only *slightly* off the ground—about one-fourth-inch off the ground at foot-strike. Concentrate on where your weight lands and don't try to keep your heels up in the air.

Also, remember to decrease your training volume and intensity when you are first adapting these techniques. Then build back up gradually.

I'm trying to increase my turnover to the 180 per minute you recommend, but there's just not enough time for toe-off. How can I get the same power?

The "toe-off" is a misnomer. Although efficient runners gain tremendous power from their calves, they show very little ankle-extension at push-off. They produce great power without great range of motion. Any attempt to gain power with a forceful push with any muscle at any point in the stride will only limit power by slowing the movement. The formula for determining power is:

POWER = FORCE x SPEED

Efficient runners gain power at the speed end of the spectrum, which requires minimizing force. Force and speed are inversely related, so high-force contractions are by definition slower. The extra time required to create force diminishes elastic recoil, which, ironically, increases the demand for a forceful contraction.

Forget trying to make your muscles contract powerfully. Perform the foot-drag movement correctly before foot-strike, then relax and let the muscles do the work themselves. They can make themselves toe-off more effectively than you can voluntarily make them do it. Let the powerful toe-off feel almost like a passive reaction to the rest of your stride. The resulting reaction will be quick enough to work with elastic recoil, diminishing the need for high-force contractions.

Also, don't confuse range of motion with power. The calf muscles, through both contraction and elastic recoil, produce enormous power at push-off with just a few degrees of ankle extension. The assumption that more power is generated with more degrees of ankle extension is incorrect.

I understand the philosophy of high turnover, but research shows that top runners do have long strides. How can I have both?

First, elite runners produce long strides through extremely powerful contractions at push-off and by storing energy from the previous stride and returning it as elastic recoil, not by moving their legs through a wide range of motion. The next time you watch professional runners, videotape them and pause when you have a good side view. You'll see that their upper legs never open more than about 100 degrees. You'll also see that they come forward only slightly with the foot, and that they pull the foot back underneath their hips before it hits the ground. They create powerful movements, which increase the distance they cover between strides, but they do so with a powerful toe-off that takes maximal advantage of elastic recoil.

Second, stride length is relative. An elite runner moving along at a four-minute pace takes both long and quick strides. You will not ever find an elite runner using long strides at the expense of turnover.

How should I breathe when running?

Efficient runners tend to time the rhythm of their breathing with the rhythm of their stride. At an easy pace, they inhale for four steps and exhale for four steps. At a moderately hard pace, they inhale and exhale for three steps each, and at a hard, steady pace, they inhale and exhale for two steps each. Taking slower, deeper breaths requires less energy than quick, shallow breaths. Learn to breathe by lowering your diaphragm as well as lifting the chest, and you will breathe more efficiently.

I have worked at implementing the techniques of Evolution Running into my stride. I like the soft landing, and I do seem to be faster, but my heart rate is higher than before. What does this mean?

When you incorporate more and larger muscles into your stride, each muscle works less, but your total energy expenditure might be higher initially while you learn to perform the movements. This will cause your heart rate to be higher at a given pace as you learn to make the movements more naturally. Remember that triathlon running is about avoiding muscle fatigue. Even while your heart rate is higher, these techniques will reduce muscle fatigue.

I took your clinic last month, and since then my hard runs have gone extremely well. I have not raced yet, but I am finishing the same workouts several minutes faster. I am having trouble doing slower runs. It feels so much more natural to run fast using these techniques. Is this a problem?

Learning to incorporate these techniques when running fast *is* more natural. Using them on slow, easy runs is more difficult, but it is extremely important. Many highly fit runners naturally use high turnover when running fast, but they use slower turnover for easy runs. This reduces the value of the easy runs. The elastic response is such a critical part of racing well that we want 100 percent of our run training to improve it. Slow runs at low turnover don't do this.

Concentrate on lightening your push-off. Keep the leg recovery quick, but let the push-off feel completely passive, like you are simply using the weight-bearing leg to brace the recovering leg. Use a metronome on easy runs and gradually increase turnover until you can run slowly at 180 steps per minute.

I learned Evolution Running last year and have had fantastic results. At the clinic, you said that I might not need orthotics anymore. I don't use orthotics, but my training partner says I need different shoes now. Is he just upset because I keep beating him, or should I switch shoes?

Most motion-control problems are due to asymmetry in the heel bone and become irrelevant with a foot-strike that keeps bodyweight off the heel. Most runners who switch from a heel-striking stride to Evolution Running find that they no longer need orthotics or motion-control shoes. Have your podiatrist or a qualified employee at a running store watch you run to find out what will be best for you.

2 Efficient Running on Hills

Imagine racing up a long hill stride for stride with a runner who is just a bit stronger than you. Your heart rate is redlined, your breathing is on the edge of out of control, and your legs are burning and feeling heavy. You know you won't last much longer at this effort level. As you crest the hill and the road slopes down, you squirt forward, as if propelled by a rocket, and gap your stunned opponent. By the end of the downhill, you have a 20-yard lead, your heart rate and breathing have returned to sustainable levels, and your legs feel bouncy again.

This doesn't have to be a fantasy. With a thorough understanding of ideal downhill technique, consistent concentration, dedicated hard work, and the courage to explore the limits of your leg speed, you can run faster down hills and expend less energy.

As important as efficient technique is on flat ground, it is even more important on hills. Most runners use poor technique on flat ground, but have even worse technique on hills. Learning to run hills efficiently and training your body for the unique demands of hilly courses enables triathletes to gain ground on an evenly matched opponent on every hill.

USE GRAVITY INSTEAD OF FIGHTING IT

If there is one place where an understanding of race strategy, physiology, physics, and running technique can pay off most, it is on downhills. The goals of Evolution Running—to minimize vertical displacement, to utilize elastic recoil, to take short and quick strides, to avoid braking, and to accomplish the heel-flick—may be even more beneficial on downhills than on the flats or uphills. Additionally, most runners' downhill techniques are even worse than their flatland techniques. Downhills are the perfect places to reap the rewards of efficient running technique.

The bad news is that fast downhill running can be very scary. Developing an efficient stride on downhills will take time and effort, and gradually pushing back the threshold of fear requires courage. Master these techniques on shallow to moderate hills first, and be very careful using them on steep hills.

The good news is that there is a substantial amount of time *and* energy to be saved with good downhill technique and attitude. Running downhill slowly takes more energy than running downhill quickly once you learn not to fight gravity, but to flow with it smoothly.

The following are two key concepts to efficiently running fast down hills.

> **Gravity Propels:** Gravity will provide much or all of the propulsion required to run fast downhill. Efficient downhill runners expend their energy on limb movement, support, and balance, but they avoid using much energy in either braking or propulsion. Gravity will provide plenty of power if you can avoid fighting against it and keep it under control.

> **Fear Slows:** You can maintain control at very high running speeds. A runner picking up too much speed and falling face-first down a hill is not a likely occurrence. Although efficient downhill runners fear this every time they run fast down a hill, they have trained their bodies to maintain control, and they have trained their minds to push past the fear. Every runner has a threshold of controllable downhill speed and a threshold of comfortable downhill speed. The comfort threshold is usually a much slower pace than the control threshold. Training your

body and mind to increase both of these thresholds pays huge dividends come race day.

LEARN TO ROLL DOWN HILLS

Running down hills slowly requires much more energy than running down them quickly. The wheel model provides the best insight into optimal downhill biomechanics. On a flat road, the wheel's center of support is directly under its center of mass and yields perfectly horizontal movement, exactly parallel to the road (see Figure 2.1).

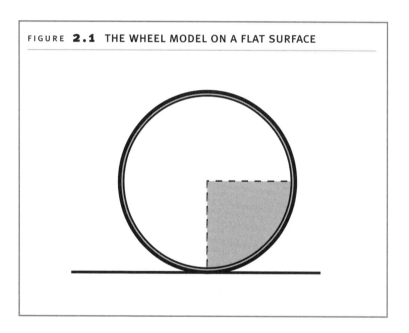

FIGURE **2.1** THE WHEEL MODEL ON A FLAT SURFACE

When a wheel rolls downhill, however, these dynamics change. The orientation of its center of support and center of mass rotates with the grade. The wheel's center of support falls behind its center of mass, at an angle proportionate to the grade of the slope. In addition, the wheel rolls parallel to the slope instead of perfectly horizontally (see Figure 2.2).

Taking the analogy a step further, cyclists tend to pedal with less power down gradual hills, and they stop pedaling completely on the way down steep hills. The greater the assistance of gravity, the less force for propulsion is required from the athlete.

FIGURE **2.2**   THE WHEEL MODEL ON A DOWNHILL SURFACE

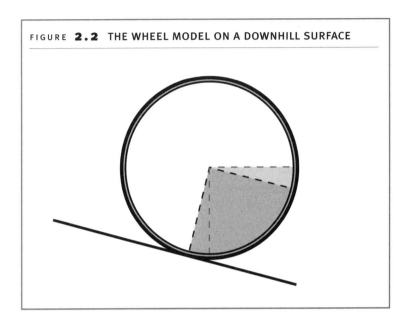

To diagram optimal theoretical downhill running technique, we simply rotate the diagram of optimal flatland technique in proportion to the grade of the hill. Notice that on downhills, the foot-strike is actually positioned behind the hips and the entire body leans forward in a straight line from the toes to the head. This is a very difficult movement to perfect because it feels like you are falling forward. Efficient downhill runners do, in fact, fall forward down the hill, but in a controlled manner with minimal braking. Leaning forward with the hips and shoulders and trusting your leg speed and balance takes time, but the rewards are amazing.

Efficient downhill runners lean forward almost as much as the grade of the hill, so they maintain almost the same body position, relative to the ground, as they have in the flats. They develop propulsion relatively parallel to the ground.

Avoid Stair-Stepping

Most runners use what I call the "stair-step technique" to run downhill, which creates horizontal propulsion and allows gravity to pull them down to the ground. The muscles must contract forcefully for propulsion (instead of allowing gravity to do the work), which prevents physical recovery during downhills (see Figure 2.3).

FIGURE **2.3** STAIR-STEP RUNNING

Stair-step running dramatically increases landing impact and therefore requires more forceful contractions to "catch" bodyweight at impact, which increases the risk of injuries. This stair-step pattern of "brake-propel-brake-propel" slows a runner and uses much more energy than Evolution Running. If you feel like you run faster down hills, but hit the ground harder, you are definitely a stair-stepper. Save that technique for when you are actually going down steps. Learn to "roll" down the hills and you'll run much faster, use less energy, and protect yourself from the damage of hard landings.

Correct Rolling Technique

With optimal technique, the runner's center of mass always travels in a line almost parallel with the slope of the ground (see Figure 2.4). The additional force of gravity, due to the hill, is used to provide propulsion instead of cause a harder landing. Remember, it takes more energy to fight gravity and slow down than it does to run downhill quickly and smoothly, working with gravity.

The real key to this technique is putting your foot down *behind* your hips. Although it sounds simple, it will take you awhile to establish the correct placement, and it will take a long time for this foot-strike position to feel natural. Put your foot down much earlier during

FIGURE **2.4** CORRECT DOWNHILL RUNNING

leg recovery than you do now. When you get it right, you'll feel your-self squirt forward at foot-strike without any attempt to provide propulsion. Your natural reaction to this feeling will be to reach for-ward with the other foot to regain "balance." Fight that tendency. Maintaining balance does not have to mean slowing down. Put the other foot down behind your hips and squirt forward again. Learn to stay light on your feet, turn your legs over very quickly, and avoid braking. Let gravity do the work of propelling. Expend your energy supporting your bodyweight, maintaining balance, and turning your legs over extremely quickly.

LEARN TO "BOUNCE" UP THE HILLS

If there's one time when even the worst heel-strikers land on the balls of their feet and keep their weight off their heels throughout the stride-cycle, it is when they are running up a hill. On moderately steep hills, runners can't land on their heels even if they want to. The slope of the hill simply doesn't allow it.

One benefit of Evolution-style running is that you run up hills using the same muscles that you use in all your training. Heel-strikers train their calf muscles only when running uphill. Imagine a 40-mile-per-week runner trying to run hard up a hill in a race when she has trained those muscles only about 1 mile per week. And aren't hills where we ask the most of our muscles in races?

Many of the same Evolution Running techniques as discussed in Chapter 1 apply to uphill running. The force dynamics of running hard up a hill should not differ drastically from the force dynamics of flatland running. The difference should be in direction of force, not magnitude of force.

Most runners make a huge mistake here. They push forcefully up the hill, allowing the slope to reduce turnover and using more forceful contractions to "muscle" to the top.

Most triathletes realize that maintaining cadence during uphill cycling is critical. They watch beginning cyclists struggle up the hills at 60 rpm and wonder why they don't shift gears. Then they run up the hill doing the same thing as the cyclists they just scoffed at.

Maintaining turnover when running uphill is important for all the same reasons as it is in cycling, plus one big additional reason. As discussed in Chapter 1, reduced turnover (and the longer contact with the ground that comes with it) dissipates the energy stored in the muscles and prevents optimal energy return via elastic recoil. The muscles are already required to create substantially greater force to propel the athlete uphill. If you also subtract the power of elastic recoil, muscling up the hills becomes extremely taxing. Even if optimal speed is maintained, it comes at a great metabolic cost, which will be paid back with reduced speed later in the race.

Efficient runners allow uphills to reduce their stride length instead of turnover. They maintain the same efficient 180 to 182 steps per minute used on flat ground and continue to gain power from elastic recoil. Optimal speed is maintained and muscular fatigue is minimized by using this approach on hills.

The differences between efficient flatland running and efficient hill running stem from the fact that minimizing vertical displacement is not a goal for uphill running. The slope of the hill demands vertical displacement. Optimal vertical displacement for uphill running ensures that the runner's center of mass travels on a line nearly parallel to the slope of the hill. The adaptations to Evolution Running required to run efficiently uphill are described in the following paragraphs.

On flat ground, efficient runners create propulsion from hip extension, not from knee extension. When running up hills, efficient runners use hip extension to provide horizontal propulsion and knee extension to provide vertical propulsion.

The foot-drag movement is critical running uphill, for the same reasons as with flatland running. Pulling the foot back and down prevents braking and stores energy for elastic recoil. A key difference is the direction of movement of the foot-drag. With flatland running, the foot is pulled almost directly backward into the ground. While going up hills, the foot is pulled back and down into the ground at a steeper angle, using a combination of hip extension and knee extension. At the moment of foot-strike, the knee is slightly bent, but it is in the process of straightening. Extending the knee and using the quads creates the upward force required to move upward as well as forward. Over flat ground, this wastes energy and slows turnover, but up hills it is necessary and efficient.

When running up hills, you will not have very much downward vertical displacement before foot-strike to help prestretch the tissues for elastic recoil. Concentrate on pulling your foot forcefully down into the ground—actually feeling like you are kicking the ground. Get this right and you'll feel the same bounce as on flat roads.

To enable the backward and downward foot-drag, the knee must be brought up much higher during leg recovery, and it remains bent to a much more acute angle until the foot-drag/knee-extension movement begins. Driving the knee powerfully upward puts the leg in position to drive downward into the ground, prestretch the muscles, and provide both upward and forward propulsion (see Figure 2.5). Using the gluteus maximus, hamstring, and quadriceps muscles together is critical.

When running up hills, try to maintain the same body position, relative to gravity (not relative to the road surface), as on flat roads. This will require leaning your body forward and will produce an even greater feeling of falling forward, up the hill, because your angle with the ground will be more acute.

Just as with flatland running, do not let your foot extend in front of your knee. The knee should drive farther forward and upward, and the foot-strike should move slightly in front of the hips, but not in front of the knee.

FIGURE **2.5** KNEE DRIVE IN UPHILL RUNNING

Practice running efficiently up hills. When you do, concentrate on the following:

- Maintain the same high turnover used in flat-ground running.
- Pump your arms with short, quick movements.
- Drive your knees powerfully toward the top of the hill.
- Pull your foot back down into the ground with a powerful motion.
- Don't just allow gravity to pull you down—feel as if you actually kick the ground.
- During foot-strike, drive the opposite knee toward the top of the hill.
- Minimize contact time between feet and ground—feel the "bounce" of elastic recoil.
- Maintain the same body position with respect to gravity that you use for flatland running.

TRAINING FOR HILL RUNNING

In addition to modifying technique, specific training for running on hills will make a major difference in your race performance. The muscles and connective tissues face different stresses when you are running on hills than when running over flat ground, and they must be trained to handle those stresses optimally.

Strength training is even more important for hill running than for flatland running. Efficient runners use the quadriceps very little running over flat ground, but it is used significantly when running uphill. The hip flexors also must travel through a much greater range of motion and need to be trained to handle the additional stress. After a comprehensive strength-training program is completed in the off-season, weighted running and hill-based running workouts are the best ways to strengthen and prepare these muscles.

Although a runner with perfect technique won't hit the ground any harder running downhill than when running on flat ground, no human has perfect running technique. Our hips will not travel on a line *perfectly* parallel to the ground, and we will likely land with much greater impact. Smart runners prepare their bodies for this before a hilly race.

As discussed in Chapter 1, weighted running overloads the muscles that act vertically in the running stride. Using a weight vest for an easy, hour-long run trains the slow-twitch fibers in those muscles. Generally, the muscles that are more active on hills never get any sustained work during flat running. They work hard running up hills and then rest, work hard up hills and rest—every workout for these muscles is an interval workout. However, weighted running on flat terrain provides a steady, low-intensity workout for these muscles.

Make sure that most of your race-pace workouts take place on terrain that is very similar to the courses of your priority races. If your key races are hilly, some of your aerobic-capacity workouts should be conducted as hill repeats instead of on the track. Doing lactate threshold training on hills provides an excellent workout and can be very good for working on technique as you try to maintain heart rate on downhills.

We all tend to focus on uphills, but work just as hard on improving your downhill running. One of my clients raced the Columbia Triathlon several years ago. The Columbia course is brutally hilly; athletes often refer to it as the "Beast of the East." She got off her bike in the lead, but was passed in the first mile on an uphill by a woman in her age group who was running much faster. On the next downhill, she caught her and retook the lead. For 4 miles they exchanged the lead on almost every uphill and downhill before my client finally opened a gap on a downhill that she could hold to the finish. That she got passed on every uphill reveals who was in overall better condition. However, in this race, the trophy went to the most efficient downhill runner, not the strongest athlete.

During hilly workouts and races, think about your technique until it becomes 100 percent natural. Drive your knee up the hill, lean forward, pull your foot down powerfully into the ground, and keep your turnover up when the road climbs. Lean forward with your rib cage, put your foot down behind your hips, and let gravity pull you down the hills. Specific work on your hill-running technique will pay huge dividends on the day of a hilly race.

PART TWO

Training

3 Planning a Season

In this chapter, we will look at how to develop an effective annual training plan. The annual plan should be the starting point for any attempt to organize training. Developing the annual plan is really about prioritizing and budgeting resources. During different times of year, different types of training should be prioritized. The annual plan does not give workout specifics but provides a skeletal framework that lists priorities chronologically and ensures that training stays focused and that each month builds on the previous month's training. Different types of workouts are prioritized at different times of the season based on when the priority races are.

If I were going to drive from Washington, D.C. to Los Angeles, I would never pull out of the driveway with just a map of Washington, D.C., head west, and see what happened. I *would* have a detailed map of Washington, D.C., but I would also have an atlas that showed the major routes across the country and a detailed map of California. Most triathletes pull out of each season's driveway with just a local map. Each month's training is an extension of last month's, but it is generally just an increase in mileage without an idea of where it is all leading. Without an annual plan, it is unlikely that each step will build optimally on the last. Even experienced athletes are likely to leave out an important step if they "shoot from the hip" with training plans.

SETTING GOALS

You always hit what you aim for. If that happens to be nothing, you'll get it every time.
—Zig Ziglar

The first step in planning a season is setting goals. Our goals need to be very specific, objective, and measurable. As coach Joe Friel explains in his book, *The Triathlete's Training Bible* (VeloPress, 1998), "Clearly defined goals improve one's ability to achieve them." Don't make the mistake of selecting goals that could leave you not knowing if you attained them or not after your priority race.

Behold the turtle. He makes progress only when he sticks his neck out.
—James Byrant Conant

We need to remain balanced. Select goals that make you reach, that stretch you, and that push you, but that are also realistically attainable. Certainly the goal of winning the Hawaii Ironman® during your first season isn't going to happen, but aggressive goals often push triathletes beyond what they thought was possible.

The opposite of mediocrity is not winning. Recognizing a challenge, taking it head-on, and refusing to consider an easier, less gratifying path—that to me is escaping mediocrity.
—Ashley Powell

Our goals must focus on things within our sphere of control. If you decide to win your age group at a certain race, you might train exceptionally well with full motivation, drive, and discipline, and have a fantastic race, only to miss your goal because a really fast athlete you've never seen before shows up on race day.

We need to set long-term and short-term goals. Long-term goals are achieved over a number of years, while short-term goals may be achieved this season. Each season's goals should build on the previous season's goals, as well as work toward the long-term goal. A second-year triathlete may set as short-term goals finishing an international-distance race four minutes faster than last year and finishing strong in a half-ironman. A long-term dream goal might be finishing an ironman-distance race.

> *Only those who risk going too far can know how far*
> *one can go.*
>
> —T. S. Eliot

Make sure your goals are stated as positives. A good goal for a first-time ironman racer might be "to pace and fuel myself properly so that I run the entire marathon." This is a much more positive goal than "to keep from having to walk the marathon."

Serious triathletes need to internalize each season's goals and keep telling themselves that this is what they have chosen to do and they will do it. I often have triathletes who are seeking to qualify for the Hawaii Ironman® put a picture of the race on their bathroom mirrors so they are reminded of their goal and their commitment every morning. This is a very effective way to trigger the subconscious mind and keep you on track with your goals. See the section on "self-talk" in Chapter 10 for more information about this technique.

PRIORITIZING RACES

Triathletes race fairly often for a number of reasons: Racing is fun. Races provide some of a triathlete's best workouts. The only way to gain race experience is to race. The psychological and physiological dynamics of racing are different than training.

One key to having great races is prioritizing them. If everything is a priority, then nothing is a priority. Many athletes train hard all year and have a string of fairly good races, but they know they never really had the day their bodies are capable of. Better race prioritization will solve this.

We generally prioritize races on a three-tiered system. "A" priority races are those at which you really want to excel. Preparation for these races is very specific to the demands of the course and expected conditions. In the weeks and months leading up to this race, all preparations are specifically focused on peaking that day. An extended taper—a period of rest designed to create maximal performance on race day—will interfere with training, but it will maximize performance at an A race.

"B" priority races are those in which you would like to perform well, but not at the cost of interfering with progress toward an A race. Generally, tapers before these events are somewhat shorter than optimal because a B race is not worth missing weeks of training for. Training leading up to B races is not specific to the course or conditions. Two of the biggest races in the eastern United States are the Columbia Triathlon and the Blackwater Eagleman. Columbia, known as the "Beast of the East," is extremely hilly. Blackwater is pancake flat. Since the two fall only a few weeks apart, one has to have priority. Many athletes who choose Blackwater as an A race go to Columbia having trained hard, but not in the hills. Triathletes can have good, solid performances at B races, but they won't be at 100 percent of their potential.

"C" races are workouts. Smart triathletes don't care how they perform in C races, but they use them to gain race experience. They use the race environment to have a really good workout and to test their preparations for more important races. Usually a C race constitutes all of the high-intensity workout for the week before and the week following the race. Dropping the intensity from those midweek workouts is generally the only "taper" for C races.

LIMITERS

Limiters are specific physical or mental qualities that need to be improved so you can reach your goals in your priority races. We determine limiters by analyzing the demands of the courses of our priority races, including terrain and distance, and combining those results with our own personal strengths and weaknesses. Although limiters are often personal weaknesses, they do not have to be. Lance Armstrong's limiters for racing in the Tour de France are sustained climbing and time trialing—two disciplines he excels at. However, these abilities are so heavily emphasized in the Tour de France that prioritizing them is required to reach his goals, regardless of how well he already does them. If you were a terrible climber on the bike, but the bike segments of all of your priority races were pancake flat, then climbing would not be a limiter.

Different qualities limit different runners. The following sidebar lists common limiters for triathlon runners. Rate yourself on a scale of 1 to 10 for each quality. Then rate how important each quality is for the specific courses of your priority races, also on a scale of one to 10. Your primary limiters will be qualities that rated seven or higher on both scales.

Determining your limiters is a critical step in developing a customized training program. Two athletes at the same level, training for the same race, may have very different training priorities. Make sure to thoroughly analyze your own limiters at the beginning of each season and revisit this analysis regularly. Limiters may change within a season, so stay on top of your current situation.

Every triathlete should consider economy in all three sports a limiter. With other limiters, there comes a point at which more is not better. A triathlete who can run 100 miles won't do better in a triathlon than one who can run 50 miles. When do triathletes become so efficient that they don't want to be more efficient?

COMMON RUNNING LIMITERS

Basic Abilities

Economy (technique and tissue elasticity)

Endurance

Muscular Strength

Advanced Abilities

Muscular Endurance (quadriceps, hamstrings, and/or calves)

Power (raw speed)

Anaerobic Endurance (aerobic capacity and/or lactate tolerance)

Other Important Factors

Mental/Psychological Strength

Injury Resistance

Body Composition

Available Time to Train

General Health

Fueling/Hydration

Thermal Regulation

TRAINING BASIC ABILITIES

Joe Friel popularized his "basic abilities triangle" in the *Training Bible* book series. This is a simple, yet effective way to picture periodization (see Figure 3.1). At the corners of the triangle are endurance, force, and speed skills. These are the basic factors that should be emphasized early each year, during the Base period of training.

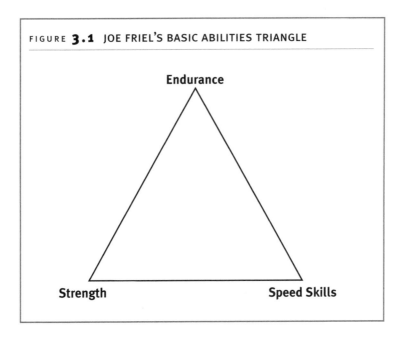

FIGURE **3.1** JOE FRIEL'S BASIC ABILITIES TRIANGLE

Endurance

Strength   Speed Skills

Endurance: The first step in developing a triathlete's racing abilities is to make sure you can go the distance. Endurance training builds the slow-twitch muscle fibers that make an athlete faster at every intensity level. Many changes, including basic strengthening of connective tissues, increased size and number of blood vessels in the muscles, increased number of alveoli in the lungs, and increased size of the heart itself, occur in response to this training.

Force: Running fast means creating significant force against the ground with every stride. Force, or muscular strength, plays a key role in racing quickly. Stronger athletes run faster and more efficiently than weaker athletes. This type of training is best accomplished very early in the training season. Force is a relatively stable adaptation that remains after strength training is stopped. Force is developed with strength training in the weight room and then with specific workouts for swimming, cycling, and running to train your stronger muscles to transfer their new strength to the specific movements that will be required for racing.

Speed Skills: Speed skills refer to economy or efficiency in all three triathlon segments. As described in Chapter 1, increasing efficiency is even more critical than increasing work output for sustained, fast running. The best time to focus on speed skills is early in the base phase of training. Performing a few minutes of drills before every run, thinking about technique during workouts, and carefully monitoring turnover are key elements of improving efficiency.

TRAINING ADVANCED ABILITIES

Each of the edges of the triangle represents a more advanced ability that should be emphasized after maximizing the qualities emphasized at the corners (see Figure 3.2).

Muscular Endurance: A combination of force and endurance, muscular endurance is the most common limiter for intermediate, advanced, and elite triathletes. A triathlon runner needs to create significant force on each stride and sustain that for the duration of the race. Improving muscular endurance is almost always a critical component of training. This involves elevating lactate threshold, improving lactate tolerance, and maximizing glycogen storage.

Training for muscular endurance begins in the Base period with short interval efforts in Zone 3 early in the Base period, increasing to Zone 4 late in the Base period, and sustained work in Zones 4 and 5a during the Build and Peak periods of training. Muscular endurance is maintained during the Race period.

Anaerobic Endurance: Anaerobic endurance is the combination of speed skills and endurance—the ability to repeatedly produce high levels of short-term speed without fatigue. This

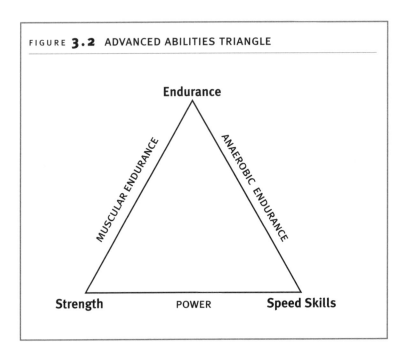

FIGURE **3.2** ADVANCED ABILITIES TRIANGLE

Endurance

MUSCULAR ENDURANCE

ANAEROBIC ENDURANCE

Strength   POWER   **Speed Skills**

ability is very important for short-distance racing, but its importance decreases as race duration increases.

Aerobic capacity training falls into this category. Hard, steady efforts sustained for up to six minutes with recovery periods are the primary method of stimulating improvements in aerobic capacity. This type of training should be emphasized, for athletes whose racing goals require it, in the Build and Peak periods.

Power: Power is the combination of force and speed skills. Powerful athletes can create high-force contractions very quickly. Power workouts involve short duration, very high intensity efforts with long recovery periods in between. Triathlete runners don't require sprinting ability, but this type of training can be used to teach the muscles to fire and relax with perfect timing to maximize economy. These workouts also increase elasticity of the muscles and connective tissues.

Determine your level in each of these six abilities in all three sports, and determine which of these abilities are required for the courses of your priority races. Abilities that your key races demand, but on which you rank yourself relatively low, will be your limiters. Prioritizing workouts that improve your limiters is the essence of effective training.

Longer races will always tend to emphasize the basic abilities while shorter races tend to emphasize the advanced abilities.

PERIODIZATION

Once you have determined your limiters, it is time to build a plan that addresses them at the appropriate points in the season. Develop training systematically so that each month's workouts focus on different priorities and build on the previous month's training. This is a key factor in producing optimal results. "Periodization" means maximizing training adaptations at appropriate times so that the benefits of each type of training come together and overlap optimally on race day. When an athlete gets this just right and peaks on the day of an important race, the results can be amazing. Those days where we just fly and know that we can keep going do not often happen by chance.

Some physiological adaptations to training take longer than others. Fortunately, these adaptations also generally take longer to reverse. Qualities that train slowly also detrain slowly. An athlete can work on certain types of training early in the year and reduce emphasis on these workouts later—the benefits will last until race day. Figure 3.3 shows how short-term and long-term adaptations can be overlapped so that the benefits of a number of different layers of training can all come together on race day.

After these basic abilities are well developed, decreasing emphasis on the workouts that stimulate slow-changing qualities enables the athlete to prioritize differently. Now, as a priority race approaches, you can concentrate on workouts to stimulate changes that train and detrain more quickly. This way, on race day, you benefit maximally from many different layers of training.

Most athletes, after their first well-planned season, talk about how "everything came together at the last minute." This occurs because they have worked on slower-changing characteristics first, shifted to emphasizing medium-changing characteristics at the right time, and then shifted focus to fast-changing characteristics for the last few weeks before the big day. Racing your best at your most important races doesn't happen by chance.

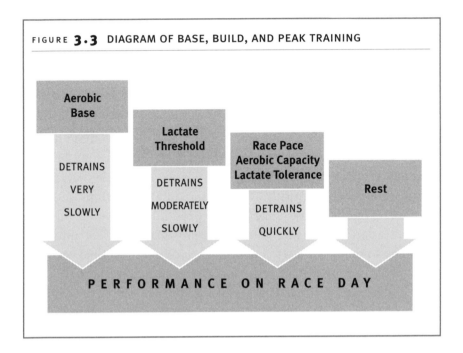

FIGURE **3.3** DIAGRAM OF BASE, BUILD, AND PEAK TRAINING

Many athletes think of periodization as starting off with low-intensity training and building to higher-intensity training. While this pattern occurs frequently with training for short, fast races, periodization is really about training in ways that will improve general fitness early in the year and becoming more and more race-specific as the priority race approaches.

TRANSITION PERIOD

At the end of a long, hard, grueling season, a triathlete's mind and body need a rest. However, few athletes realize this and take time off appropriately. The season winding down may have been a breakthrough year and the athlete does not want the excitement, challenge, and fun to end. Or, she may have had an awful season and yearn for just a few more weeks to make up for it or want to get an early start for next year. Regardless of the athlete's feelings, a Transition period in training is essential for meeting the goals listed in the following sidebar.

During this period, it is vital to get completely away from consistent, structured training in swimming, cycling, and running. Find

> ### GOALS OF THE TRANSITION PERIOD
> Relax and get away from the sport.
>
> Get your body and mind 100 percent recovered and refreshed.
>
> Get back to "chomping at the bit."

other activities that will relieve the mind of stress and allow the body to fully repair and recover to a degree that was never possible during the season. Give yourself two to six weeks completely off from any serious training and next year's training will go better.

Few serious athletes take the Transition period easy enough and get away from triathlon training as much as they should. Getting out of shape now won't hurt you next year. In fact, recharging the batteries to 100 percent requires getting far away from race shape. Basic conditioning can and should be maintained, but this needs to be done at far less volume and intensity than in-season training. Good activities include skiing, hiking, in-line skating, tennis, and other crosstraining activities.

By the middle of the Transition period, you should be dying to get back to hard training—completely "chomping at the bit." Be patient and follow the plan. You are storing up physical and mental energy that will be required later during sustained hard training.

PREPARATION PERIOD

The Preparation period prepares the body to start training again. This period, lasting three to six weeks, comes after long Transition periods and includes relatively light training designed to prepare you for harder training in the next period. Workouts during this phase are designed to prepare your body for heavier training in the Base period. Workouts are not intended to make you faster during this time.

Focus on consistent, moderate-distance workouts at endurance intensity. This is an excellent time of year to include significant crosstraining. You are trying to develop basic endurance in the muscles, heart, and lungs. This does not have to be specific to swimming, cycling, and running.

Strength training begins during the Preparation phase, but at a light level. These workouts are not really designed to increase strength, but to prepare the muscles and connective tissues for the heavier lifting in future phases.

See the following sidebar for a list of goals for this training period.

GOALS OF THE PREPARATION PERIOD

Reintroduce your body to training.

Develop general fitness that is nonspecific to racing.

Prepare your body and mind for the training to come.

BASE PERIOD

The Base period is perhaps the most critical period of training for any athlete. Without the pressure of upcoming races, this is the time to focus on adaptations that are both learned and unlearned slowly. During this time frame we make changes that will stay with us once this type of training is de-emphasized. The basic abilities, endurance, force, and speed skills are prioritized during this period (see the following sidebar).

I often tell my athletes, "What you do in January to be your fastest in May and June is very different from what you do in January to be your fastest in February." This is a major difficulty coaches have with athletes who "know what works for them." These athletes are often shortsighted and have only learned what works for peaking. Their thinking is often just on the short term, and they do not realize that the long-term plan should look quite different.

GOALS OF THE BASE PERIOD

Increase your endurance with relatively long, easy workouts.

Increase your force with strength training.

Increase your speed skills by altering technique and through economy and strength-transfer workouts.

The Base period is the time to prioritize basic endurance training and strength training, and to make changes in technique. Training volume can be quite high and can also gradually increase during this period because training intensity is kept under control.

The Base period, which generally lasts 12 weeks, is the longest of all the training periods. The most common mistake athletes make is prioritizing high-intensity training too early in the year. After developing a good base, it is amazing how quickly speed can be improved. Exercise patience!

THINGS TO ACHIEVE DURING THE BASE PERIOD

Increase the ability to run a long distance at an easy pace.

Develop an optimal level of strength in the muscles, bones, and connective tissues.

Reach optimal race weight.

Prepare the body for the higher-intensity training that follows.

Make changes in technique.

Maximize fuel storage in the muscles.

For planning, break your Base period into thirds. Each four-week segment will increase in volume and intensity from the previous four weeks.

Base 1: During the first four weeks of the Base period, focus on endurance, force, and speed skills. Strength training, long easy workouts, and skills practice are the components of your training. Volume is moderately high.

Base 2: During the next four weeks of the Base period, continue with the priorities of the first four weeks, while increasing intensity of weight training and volume of endurance work. Also add a light muscular endurance workout each week. This workout, often a tempo workout in Zone 3, is designed to prepare your body for harder training in the next phase rather than make you faster.

Base 3: During the final four weeks of the Base period, continue to increase volume to its highest level. Endurance workouts will become quite long, and weight-training sessions should continue to increase in intensity. Muscular endurance work shifts from Zone 3 tempo to cruise intervals: four- to six-minute efforts in Zone 4 with one- to two-minute recoveries in between.

BUILD PERIOD

The Build period is where training becomes more race specific, both in terms of the specific requirements of your priority races and your own specific strengths and weaknesses. This is the time when you will see the disciplined work you did during the Base period really start to pay off. See sidebar for a list of goals for this training period.

Intensity increases during the Build period and volume remains high. For sprint- and international-distance athletes, volume should decrease slightly from the Base period, but it remains relatively high. For ironman-distance athletes, volume peaks during the Build period.

GOALS OF THE BUILD PERIOD

Increase your intensity while maintaining relatively high volume.

Increase your muscular endurance, anaerobic endurance, and power.

Place greater emphasis on race-specific limiters.

Refine your psychological skills and race nutrition program.

The Build period is when you should focus most heavily and most specifically on your greatest limiters—whatever qualities are most likely to keep you from achieving your goals in priority races. Attack these with full force during this time.

During the Build period, training volume and intensity are both high. Overtraining and injury are more likely to occur now than at any other time of the year, so take steps to prevent them. Monitor your body closely and moderate hard workouts, or include additional rest days if necessary. Remember that the quality of individual breakthrough workouts is what will make you faster, not just an accumulation of stresses. Take care of your body during this time. Pay attention to sleep, nutrition, and stretching. Details on these are available elsewhere in this book (see Chapters 7, 12, and 13).

Including Low-Priority Races

A number of low-priority C races will fall during the Build period and should be included in your training. C races can provide valuable race experience, excellent workouts, and a gauge of the effectiveness of the training program you are following. You will probably not race at your best during this period, because race preparation is not complete and because you will not complete a full taper.

Consider these races key workouts. Allow enough rest beforehand that you can get an effective workout and recovery afterward, but do not allow full rest (as a taper would) because that will interfere with your preparation for higher priority races. If everything is a priority, nothing is a priority.

Analyze the volume and intensity of the race and count those minutes as training. Often a weekend race will provide almost enough intensity, especially in terms of muscular endurance training, for two weeks of training. Fill in enough quality training during the week before the race to maintain the planned workload, but allow full recovery during the week afterward.

For planning, break your Build period into two sections.

Build 1: In the first Build phase, training volume is maintained at a relatively high level, although it is slightly decreased from the Base period. Muscular endurance training increases during this phase, primarily as long, steady blocks of lactate threshold training. For athletes racing sprint-, international-, or half-ironman-distance races, speed endurance training may begin in the Build period. These workouts could be high-intensity track sessions, specific hill work, or interval or repetition workouts conducted on roads or trails. Begin these workouts conservatively to reduce the risk of injury and overtraining. For ironman-distance athletes, volume will continue to increase with basic endurance and muscular endurance as the primary priorities.

Build 2: In the second Build phase, volume is slightly decreased and intensity continues to accelerate. Strength training should be at a maintenance level during this phase to allow your body's resources to be directed toward sport-specific limiters.

PEAK PERIOD

The Peak period is when athletes put the final touches on their race preparation—the icing on the cake. Physiological adaptations that change most quickly are emphasized at this point in training. Generally, quality is emphasized over quantity and athletes focus on the one area of preparation that will most affect performance. See sidebar for a list of goals for the Peak period.

GOALS FOR THE PEAK PERIOD

Sharpen your economy while maintaining fresh muscles.

Emphasize short-duration, race-pace efforts.

Finalize planning for nutrition, pacing strategies, and logistics.

Fine-tune your psychological skills.

Volume decreases significantly during this phase and intensity is moderate to low. The goal of this period is to increase efficiency and endurance at race pace, so one or two weekly race-pace workouts will be your highest priority. Make sure to allow 48 to 72 hours of recovery in between.

Perform a moderate muscular endurance workout for the swim and your weakest event (bike or run) and a race-pace brick workout each week during this phase. Include plenty of rest. This is the time to focus heavily on one or two workouts per week and be sure not to be tired for those. Give yourself every opportunity to have good key workouts during this phase. Additional rest days and very light days are critical. It is almost like a mini-taper for every key workout. Do not overtrain during this phase.

RACE PERIOD

The time you've been waiting for is at hand, and all your hard work preparing for the race is about to pay off. During each nonrace week during this phase, perform a race-simulation workout. This workout includes quick transitions between sports and efforts at race pace, but it should be nowhere near race duration.

Every athlete should also do several economy workouts during this period. This is the time to keep training volume and intensity low, but keep a few short-duration, high-intensity efforts in the mix to keep your movements sharp and efficient. See information about tapering in Chapter 15.

Planning your season so that all the different layers of training come together on the days of your highest priority A races gives you the best chance of racing to your abilities. More details about periodization are available in Joe Friel's book, *The Triathlete's Training Bible*.

R E F E R E N C E S

Friel, Joe. *The Triathlete's Training Bible*, 2nd ed. Boulder, CO: VeloPress, 2004.

C H A P T E R

4 Choosing the Right Training Intensity

The most critical factor in endurance training is intensity. In any structured training program, each workout should have a specific purpose. To achieve the ideal response from the body, the stimulation must be specific to the desired adaptation and must allow quick recovery for the next key workout. Intensity, more than any other variable, determines the body's response to the training stimulus.

This absolutely does *not* mean that harder is better. The optimal training schedule for any athlete provides the lowest volume and intensity that will stimulate the desired adaptation, not the highest the athlete can sustain. This is a major paradigm shift for many endurance athletes who grew up hearing, "No pain, no gain." If mile repeats at 5:08 stimulate increased aerobic capacity, then that is how fast those workouts should be performed—even if the athlete can run repeats at 4:55. Being "tough" and always going harder and harder will not yield ideal results. Tough guys never seem to get any faster, they just get tougher—and it seems like fast guys are always winning the races.

Training efficiently means balancing the cost and benefit of each workout. Every workout has a cost, in terms of recovery. Every workout also increases fitness. Efficient workouts provide training benefits that are worth the recovery cost. Every athlete, at any point in time, has certain recovery resources. Smart athletes develop habits to maximize these resources, but they will always be finite and need to be budgeted.

Maintaining optimal intensity during every workout is a key aspect of managing resources (such as those listed in the sidebar) and minimizing risks. These are all limited resources, and running at the right pace during each workout makes the best use of them. This allows you to benefit maximally from each workout and gets you ready sooner for the next key workout.

Remember that it is the quality of the individual workout that makes an athlete stronger and faster, not just an accumulation of stresses. Many athletes train medium hard all the time. On their hard days, even if they put in 100-percent effort, they don't get 100-percent speed because they are a little tired from yesterday's workout or from the accumulation of weeks of training without quite enough recovery.

If you should be running 800s at 2:42, but you keep hitting 2:46 because you are fatigued from yesterday, that is bad training. Your legs don't respond to or improve from your 100-percent effort, they just pound out 2:46 800s. What the body responds to is not your 100-percent effort, but your 2:46 output, which is submaximal. Therefore,

RECOVERY RESOURCES

Stored Glycogen: Glycogen is the form of carbohydrate stored in our muscles and liver that serves as the primary fuel for endurance exercise. Hard or long workouts expend tremendous amounts of glycogen and demand full fuel tanks at the beginning of the workout. Maintaining optimal intensity makes best use of this limited resource.

Muscles: Muscles sustain damage during running workouts. Lactic acid accumulation damages the muscles chemically, and impact stress damages the muscles mechanically by producing tiny tears called microtrauma.

Connective Tissue: Every workout, but especially a run workout, stresses and damages connective tissues. These tissues need to heal and rebuild adequately between workouts. Injuries are an ever-present risk in any workout, especially run workouts. During high-volume or high-intensity workouts, the risk of injuries increases.

the workout's benefit will be submaximal. This means you're training yourself to run slow even though you're working hard.

MUSCLE-FIBER RECRUITMENT

Each muscle in our bodies is composed of thousands of muscle fibers. These muscle fibers come in three basic types, and each of our muscles is composed of some combination of the three. The percentage of each type depends on individual genetics.

Slow-twitch muscle fibers are our endurance fiber. They can keep going all day long, but they are not big, fast, strong, or powerful. Slow-twitch muscle fibers are able to burn either fat or carbohydrate for fuel, depending on the intensity.

Fast-twitch muscle fibers are our sprint fibers. They are big, fast, strong, and powerful, but they fatigue very quickly. Fast-twitch muscle fibers cannot burn fat for fuel.

Our muscles also have an intermediate fiber that produces more power than slow-twitch fibers and has greater endurance than fast-twitch fibers. These fibers are called fast oxidative glycolytic (FOG) fibers, and I refer to them as speed endurance fibers.

When a muscle contracts, each fiber either contracts with its full force capability or remains relaxed. When an athlete picks up a 1-lb dumbbell, very few fibers contract. However, those that do contract do so just as powerfully as when the athlete picks up a 70-lb dumbbell.

After aerobic plateau, which requires several minutes at the beginning of each workout (and after each shift in intensity during a workout), the athlete's body will recruit muscle fibers according to the power or speed requirement of the activity. The endurance fibers will be recruited first. At low intensity, only a few endurance fibers will be recruited. As intensity increases, the speed endurance fibers will be recruited next, and finally the sprint fibers.

We should train each type of muscle fiber together as a group for two reasons. First, muscle fibers within each category respond to similar training stimulus. All the slow-twitch fibers improve from long, slow workouts. All the FOG fibers improve from steady, fast running. All the fast-twitch fibers improve from short durations of very fast running.

Second, muscle fibers within each category share similar recovery characteristics, so training them together in groups enables us to optimize stimulation without overtraining. Slow-twitch muscle fibers can withstand enormous training volume and recover relatively quickly for the next workout. FOG fibers are able to withstand moderate volume and require several days to recover for the next workout. Fast-twitch fibers overload very easily and require minimal training volume and extended recovery time between workouts. Training at the optimal intensity zone for each workout will enable you to stimulate the desired adaptations in each type of muscle fiber, as well as allow for full recovery before each of those muscle fibers is called on again.

TRAINING INTENSITY ZONES

Seven zones for training intensity are described in the following paragraphs. Each intensity zone stimulates a specific desired adaptation that will enable you to race more effectively. Make sure that every workout has a specific purpose and maintain the appropriate intensity level to achieve that end.

Zone 1: Active Recovery

Sometimes an easy workout promotes recovery better than a day of complete rest. The key is maintaining a *very* low intensity. The goal is to maintain an intensity high enough to stimulate increased circulation to deliver nutrients to the muscles and to remove toxins, and hard enough to stimulate growth hormone release (which speeds recovery), but not high enough to demand more recovery. This is an extremely low-intensity level that doesn't even seem like training.

FIGURE **4.1** MUSCLE FIBER RECRUITMENT, ZONE 1

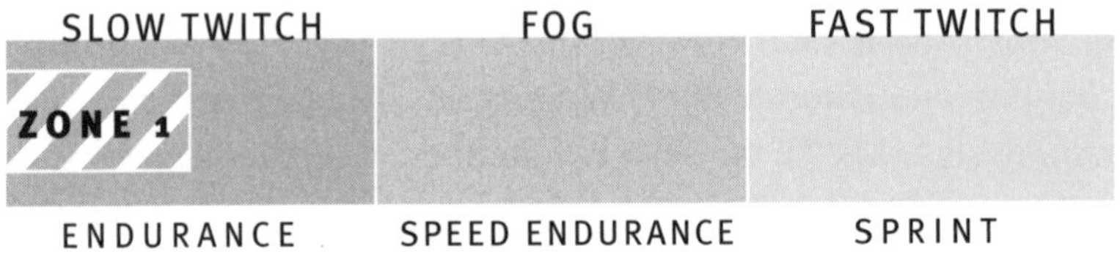

SLOW TWITCH	FOG	FAST TWITCH
ZONE 1		
ENDURANCE	SPEED ENDURANCE	SPRINT

Many athletes and coaches will tell you that "recovery run" is an oxymoron. While I agree with this in general, the effectiveness of using running for active recovery is very much an individual thing. Some athletes can go for a short, easy run and recover very quickly for the next workout. Others find that easy runs, over time, run them into the ground and/or increase overuse injuries. How much this has to do with individual physiological differences versus differences in the ability to maintain correct active recovery intensity is unclear. Certainly both are factors. When in doubt, use swimming or cycling as active recovery workouts.

Zone 2: Basic Endurance Training

Aerobic threshold (AeT) is the workout intensity at which almost all of the endurance muscle fibers are being used, but none of the speed endurance or sprint fibers are active. Basic endurance training is best accomplished at or slightly below aerobic threshold. Basic endurance training forms the backbone of any good triathlon run-training program. This training should comprise a higher percentage of most triathletes' training programs. Most triathletes spend too much time running medium hard and would do better to slow down for most of their training.

Running at a basic endurance pace, in heart rate Zone 2, trains the endurance, or slow-twitch, muscle fibers. These fibers have tremendous capacity for distance, but not much capacity for speed. They do

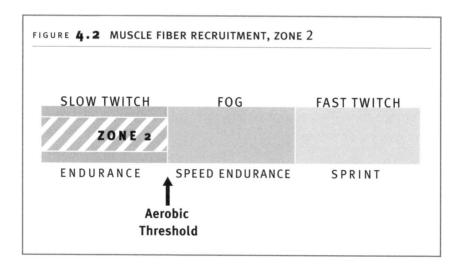

FIGURE **4.2** MUSCLE FIBER RECRUITMENT, ZONE 2

SLOW TWITCH   FOG   FAST TWITCH

ZONE 2

ENDURANCE   SPEED ENDURANCE   SPRINT

Aerobic
Threshold

most of the work in any triathlon. Endurance fibers generally produce 65 to 75 percent of the energy in an elite athlete in an Olympic-distance race and well over 90 percent in an ironman-distance race. Slower athletes rely even more on the slow-twitch muscle fibers.

These fibers can withstand and benefit from enormous training volume if intensity is appropriate. However, at higher intensities, muscle fibers that lack the endurance capabilities of the slow-twitch fibers are recruited. These fibers cannot withstand training volumes appropriate for the slow-twitch fibers. Training just a little too fast during basic endurance workouts reduces the positive effects while adding cost in terms of recovery time.

At basic endurance intensity, the muscles burn a relatively even mixture of fat and carbohydrate for fuel (individual differences in genetics and training affect this somewhat). Since fat is such a concentrated energy source, containing about 2.25 times as much energy per gram as carbohydrate, even the leanest athlete has enough fat stored to run many, many miles.

When intensity increases above basic endurance pace, the muscle shifts over to burning more carbohydrate and less fat. This happens for two reasons. First, the body must begin recruiting some of the speed endurance muscle fibers, which do not burn fat effectively. These fibers compete with the endurance fibers for available oxygen, so the endurance fibers then lack adequate oxygen to burn fat and also begin to burn more carbohydrate. This depletes muscle and liver glycogen storage unnecessarily. Many athletes run their basic endurance workouts just slightly too fast, depleting resources and delaying recovery for tomorrow's workout. Doing basic endurance workouts too fast won't make you faster.

Training at the appropriate Zone 2 intensity for running will include long runs, long bricks, and moderate-duration midweek endurance runs. Warm-ups for higher-intensity runs also take place at basic endurance intensity.

Zone 3: Tempo Training

In Zone 3, the body is recruiting all of the endurance fibers and some of the speed endurance fibers. At this intensity, fuel use has shifted significantly away from fat and the muscle burns mostly sugar (carbohydrate). At this intensity you aren't really going hard enough to

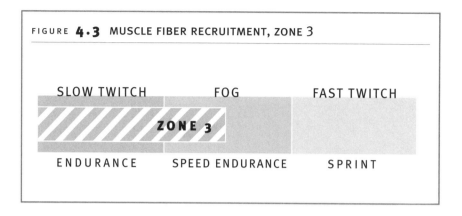

FIGURE **4.3** MUSCLE FIBER RECRUITMENT, ZONE 3

SLOW TWITCH   FOG   FAST TWITCH

ZONE 3

ENDURANCE   SPEED ENDURANCE   SPRINT

make yourself faster, but you are going fast enough to deplete yourself for the workout tomorrow that *is* designed to make you faster.

This intensity zone can be effective for maximizing carbohydrate storage in the muscles and preparing the body for the demands of higher-intensity training. Zone 3 training should only be used early in base training, when there are no high-intensity workouts to interfere with, or during the Build and Peak periods when you are training for races that will take place at this intensity (race-pace training). Zone 3 training has its place, but most athletes spend too much time at this intensity.

Zone 4: Lactate Threshold (LT) Training

Whenever an athlete exercises at any intensity, even walking, lactic acid (lactate) is constantly being produced. Fortunately, our bodies also constantly recycle lactate by actually burning it up and using it for fuel. As intensity increases, lactate production also increases. Lactate threshold is the highest intensity at which an athlete recycles lactate as quickly as it is produced, so that lactate does not accumulate. Muscle and blood levels of lactate are moderately high at lactate threshold intensity, but they do not increase over time. Increasing pace just slightly at this point will cause lactate to accumulate, which increases discomfort, damages the muscles, and delays recovery for tomorrow's workout.

You may have heard the terms *lactate threshold, anaerobic threshold* (AT), and *ventilatory threshold*. These terms refer to three different ways of measuring the same intensity and may be used interchangeably.

Lactate threshold training, in the right doses at the right time of season, is important for almost every triathlete. For most athletes, lactate

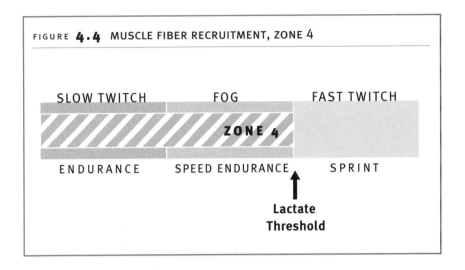

FIGURE **4.4** MUSCLE FIBER RECRUITMENT, ZONE 4

threshold training has the best cost-to-benefit ratio of any type of training. Its intensity is high enough to stimulate adaptations that dramatically increase speed endurance, but because lactate is not accumulating, damage to the muscles and blood vessels is minimal, and the recovery cost of the workout, if conducted properly, is modest.

At lactate threshold intensity, the body recruits all of the endurance muscle fibers and all of the speed endurance fibers, but does not recruit the sprint (fast-twitch) fibers. Just as the endurance fibers can sustain much higher training volumes than the speed endurance fibers, the speed endurance fibers can withstand much, much greater training volume than the sprint fibers.

At lactate threshold intensity, the speed endurance fibers create a lot of lactic acid, but only at a rate at which the endurance fibers can burn it up and use it for fuel. Sustaining this intensity trains the speed endurance fibers to work more aerobically, so they produce less acid, and trains the endurance fibers to burn more acid, both of which push the threshold to a higher level (and greater speed).

LT training is the only effective endurance training for the speed endurance fibers. At lower intensities they are not recruited. At higher intensities, sprint fibers are recruited, which results in lactate accumulation. This reduces the duration that the athlete can sustain the intensity and dramatically delays recovery.

Most athletes and coaches overestimate LT intensity and, when running at the correct pace, feel like they are not going hard enough.

This creates a major problem, either limiting potential training volume or inducing overtraining. Training 1 percent over lactate threshold, at an intensity at which lactate accumulates slowly, causes much greater damage and requires much greater recovery time than the same duration at lactate threshold. Reducing training volume or suffering overtraining are poor trade-offs for the slight benefits of the 1-percent increase in intensity. For a 20- to 30-minute segment, a run at this slightly elevated intensity does not feel that much harder. However, lactate accumulates slowly, but continually, and does damage in the muscles that the athlete cannot necessarily feel. Five minutes into a segment at 101 percent of lactate threshold, lactate levels in the muscles and blood will be only slightly higher, but later in a long set they may be dramatically higher. Muscle damage and recovery time may increase enormously. A well-trained athlete can sustain LT intensity for 75 minutes or more with 100-percent effort, such as in a race.

Training Techniques

There are two basic formats for LT training: cruise intervals and tempo segments. Cruise intervals alternate four- to six-minute segments at lactate threshold with one- to two-minute recoveries. Tempo segments are hard and steady segments of 12 to 60 minutes at or slightly below LT pace. Each has specific uses and benefits.

Cruise intervals are very effective for introducing higher-intensity training during late Base periods. The recovery cost of cruise intervals is relatively light, and the damage from accidentally running slightly above LT intensity is not as great.

Relatively long tempo segments are the core of LT training. These efforts are hard and steady. The legs will feel a mild to moderate burn, and breathing will be hard but controlled. Athletes who time their breathing to their steps probably inhale for two steps and exhale for two steps at this pace. It is important to maintain a steady effort for LT tempo segments. Most athletes tend to run up hills at above LT intensity and relax on the downhills, allowing their effort to fall below the desired intensity.

Training slightly below LT and training right at LT have different benefits and detriments. Both are important to efficient training. Steady efforts right at LT are effective for increasing speed at LT, while longer efforts slightly below LT increase endurance at LT. An athlete may have an LT of 6:00 per mile and be able to sustain that intensity for 75 minutes. Training right at six-minute pace (high Zone 4) will increase her LT speed to 5:50. Longer segments at 6:20 pace (low Zone 4) will enable her to sustain a 6:00 pace for longer than 75 minutes.

High Zone 4 is right at to slightly below LT. Heart rate is sustained approximately zero to four beats below LT, and speed stays within 3 to 5 percent of LT. I generally use 12- to 20-minute segments at this intensity to increase speed at LT.

Low Zone 4 is somewhat below LT, with heart rate sustained approximately five to eight beats below LT and with speed about 4 to 6 percent below LT. At this intensity, most of the speed endurance (FOG) fibers are still recruited, but there is a safety zone against lactate accumulation. During the Build period, I have athletes perform tempo segments of 20 minutes all the way up to an hour at this intensity.

Training in the lower end of Zone 4 increases the endurance of the FOG fibers and enables the athlete to sustain LT wattage, or speed, longer. This is an incredibly efficient training intensity. The cost, in terms of recovery for tomorrow's workout, as well as the psychological cost, is relatively low. Most athletes enjoy this training, and prescribing very long sets may increase compliance with intensity. If I'm doing a 40-minute segment, it is not so tempting to run too fast.

All athletes like to think they are more motivated than the rest. They will train harder, be more consistent, and more disciplined. Coaches like to think the same about their clients. Remember, though, no matter how passionate and motivated the client is, this is a finite resource. Budget it wisely. Correct use of LT training, generally a little on the conservative side, plays a big role in sustaining motivation.

Maintaining appropriate intensity for these workouts is critical. Zone 4 is very efficient training. Understand that if the optimal intensity is 171 to 177 beats per minute, this is recommended because that intensity produces the best results, not so that you can finish the 40-minute segment. Joe Friel frequently recommends "the least amount of work that will produce the desired results." Remember the tendency of every athlete to want to go as hard as possible for whatever the duration. That does not produce the best results.

Zone 5a: Super-Threshold Training

Zone 5a is often referred to as super-threshold pace. Intensity is slightly above lactate threshold, so acid is accumulating in the muscles and in the blood. At this intensity, acid accumulates gradually, so the intensity still can be sustained for a long period of time.

Many athletes mistakenly train in Zone 5a when they intend to be in Zone 4 doing lactate threshold training. This is a costly mistake because the recovery time from Zone 5a training is much greater than from Zone 4 training. Since acid accumulates very slowly in Zone 5a, the difference between 4 and 5a is negligible when sustained for short periods of time. However, when sustained for moderate to long durations, the acid accumulation in Zone 5a does significant damage to the muscle cells and requires significantly more recovery time (see Figure 4.5).

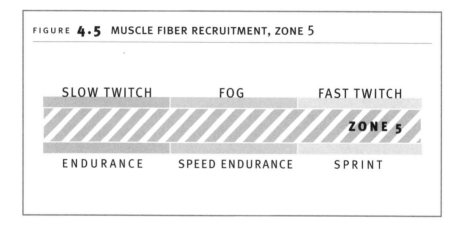

FIGURE **4.5** MUSCLE FIBER RECRUITMENT, ZONE 5

SLOW TWITCH   FOG   FAST TWITCH

ZONE 5

ENDURANCE   SPEED ENDURANCE   SPRINT

Zone 5a training is excellent for improving lactate tolerance. The muscles are trained to continue to produce speed efficiently despite the buildup of acid. This is a benefit, but it comes at a great cost in terms of the volume and intensity of other workouts.

AEROBIC CAPACITY TRAINING: MAXING THE VO$_2$

Maximal aerobic capacity (VO$_2$max), the amount of oxygen consumed in one minute of maximal aerobic exercise, is widely considered the standard test for aerobic conditioning. Improving VO$_2$max is a crucial step in maximizing endurance performance in any event lasting four minutes or longer. The higher an athlete's VO₂max, the greater the contribution of the aerobic system to energy production. This translates into greater endurance at any intensity.

Each muscle fiber type has both aerobic and anaerobic capabilities. Endurance fibers are mostly aerobic, but they do have some anaerobic metabolism. Speed endurance fibers are more balanced. Sprint fibers are mostly anaerobic, but their aerobic abilities can still be important in racing. Aerobic capacity workouts improve the aerobic capabilities of the sprint muscle fibers.

Stimulating these adaptations requires maintaining an intensity that is high enough to demand recruitment of the sprint fibers, but low enough to enable the athlete to sustain the intensity for a duration that will stimulate aerobic adaptations in those fibers, instead of only anaerobic adaptations.

Aerobic Capacity Pace

To improve aerobic capacity in a well-trained athlete, training should take place at about 95 percent of VO₂max. While the results of a VO₂max test can be useful in pinpointing optimal training pace for aerobic capacity training, research shows that field testing also determines optimal intensity very effectively.

Since field testing incorporates psychological as well as physiological variables, and since it is more practical, it is used most frequently. Perform a six- to eight-minute time trial on a track. Make sure you are well rested before the time trial. Monitor your speed and heart rate during the test, checking splits every quarter mile. The highest intensity that can be sustained for six minutes produces optimal results. We refer to this as six-minute time trial pace (TT6).

The intensity (heart rate and/or speed) determined by the field test is that at which all aerobic capacity workouts should be conducted. It is not correct to go faster when performing shorter intervals or repetitions, and it is not correct to perform intervals as quickly as possible. *Training beyond the optimal intensity has no additional benefit to the aerobic system, yet it comes at a great cost in terms of the body's recovery resources. Energy to increase output above six-minute race pace is derived almost 100 percent from anaerobic sources and, therefore, will not increase aerobic capacity.* When in doubt, err on the conservative side with aerobic capacity training. It can be a powerful tool, but a little bit goes a long way.

The pace determined by your field test could feel too easy for several reasons. You could have improved conditioning or economy since your last test. You could have used less than full effort in the test. Or you could be accustomed to performing track workouts too fast for an endurance athlete. Before you increase your interval pace, prove that you need it with a faster field test.

Duration and Work-to-Rest Ratios

To increase aerobic capacity, an athlete needs to spend considerable time performing near maximal oxygen consumption. Raising exercising VO_2max involves both an intensity component and a duration component. Even when performing at a very high intensity, it takes 1:40 to 2:00 to elevate oxygen consumption to the levels necessary to increase aerobic capacity optimally. So, running six sets of two minutes at aerobic capacity pace and running for 12 minutes near VO_2max are quite different. There are two ways to maintain oxygen consumption near VO_2max for extended durations in a workout: repeat training and interval training.

Repeat Training

Repeat training involves relatively long repetitions with basically full recovery between sets. Since approximately two minutes are required to optimally elevate VO_2, repeats need to be considerably longer than two minutes. In a sense, the benefits are only *starting* at the two-minute point when oxygen consumption has climbed to near maximal levels.

A sample workout using repetition training would be four repetitions of four minutes each at six-minute time trial pace. Obviously this is an extremely taxing workout. Since each repetition yields about two minutes of performing near maximal aerobic capacity, this workout will provide about 10 minutes near VO_2max. This type of workout should be used primarily during late Build and Peak periods. It is also effective in developing lactate tolerance and in preparing an athlete psychologically for the demands of racing. However, be conservative with this training because it is extremely costly, both physically and psychologically.

Interval Training

A second way of maintaining elevated VO_2 for extended periods is interval training. Performing shorter repetitions at the same intensity (six-minute time trial pace) and minimizing recovery between repetitions leads to increasing VO_2 throughout the set. Reducing the recovery causes the athlete to begin each repetition at a higher VO_2 than the previous rep, so that through most of the set the desired near-maximal oxygen consumption is attained much earlier in each repetition. In the workout example from the previous section, the athlete performed at TT6 for 20 minutes, but only about half of that time was spent near VO_2max. An athlete performing a set of short-rest intervals may keep VO_2 elevated for a much greater percentage of the set duration. *Be careful not to perform at a higher intensity during shorter intervals. Going above TT6 will not increase aerobic gains, but it will increase the recovery cost dramatically.*

The classic aerobic capacity workout is five sets of three minutes at TT6 pace with a three-minute recovery jog in between. This is a hard workout that needs to be built up to.

Another very effective aerobic capacity workout is called "30/30s." This workout involves 30-second repetitions at TT6 pace with a 30-second recovery jog between each repetition. This is an extremely efficient workout. The benefits are extremely high, and aerobic capacity and high-speed endurance may be increased dramatically, but the cost of the workout (recovery cost and psychological cost) is relatively low since lactic acid doesn't accumulate to a great degree because of the short repetition duration. The acid can be recycled during the recovery periods.

As repetitions get longer, work-to-rest ratio must increase. Even with a short work repetition, such as 30 seconds, there is not enough time for a huge drop-off in VO_2. With a longer, perhaps two-minute repetition, a 1:1 work-to-rest ratio is not great enough. I generally limit interval recovery to about a minute between repetitions and consider anything over a minute to be almost full recovery. Even after a hard repetition, oxygen consumption decreases dramatically with significantly more than a minute for recovery, and the next repetition will require the full two minutes to elevate to near VO_2max.

Another effective workout that combines lactate threshold training and aerobic capacity training involves running a segment at LT, followed immediately by a segment at TT6 pace. This type of workout is effective because oxygen consumption is already considerably elevated at the beginning of the TT6 repetition, so the athlete reaches the near-max oxygen consumption much more quickly than when starting from rest or from basic endurance pace. For more details about these workouts, see Appendix A.

Getting Started

Begin aerobic capacity training conservatively. It will probably be a significant increase in intensity for most athletes. I recommend starting with short-rest intervals, like 30/30s, for about eight to 12 minutes of "on" time and building volume slowly but consistently. Gradually shift to sets with longer repetitions. Monitor your recovery response carefully because it varies considerably between individuals. Many athletes, even those who tolerate high training volume very well, break down easily with aerobic capacity training.

Zone 5c: Anaerobic Capacity Training

Zone 5c intensity is significantly faster than TT6 pace. This type of training has two purposes: The first is to improve your sprint. Since triathlon running is endurance based and requires steady, sustained efforts, this is not a triathlon-training objective. The second purpose is improving running economy, which is a major goal of triathlon training.

ECONOMY TRAINING: MAXING THE GAS MILEAGE

As discussed in great detail in Chapter 1, economy or efficiency plays a major role in fast distance running, especially after hard cycling. Technique plays an important role in improving economy, but training does as well. Physical training can help increase the strength, endurance, and elasticity of your tissues properly, as well as train your muscles to contract and relax at exactly the right moments during high running speed running. Remember that 1 percent of an hour is 36 seconds. A 1-percent improvement in economy goes a long way toward a triathlon run-split personal record.

Developing optimal strength is critical to efficient running. Strength training in the weight room will be covered in Chapter 11.

Reaching ideal race weight also affects running economy. Details on that will be covered in Chapter 7.

Economy training involves very fast runs over short distances, interspersed with relatively long periods of slow running to allow nearly complete recovery between repetitions. Economy workouts should not be fatiguing at all. The major variables in a repetition workout are pace, duration of repetitions, and duration of recovery period.

BENEFITS OF ECONOMY TRAINING

Increases the elasticity, strength, and quickness of muscles and connective tissues.

Improves the ability to relax each muscle group at the appropriate time during the running stride.

Helps to embed correct mechanics, especially the all-important relationship between stride length and turnover.

Determining Economy Pace

Economy pace is the highest speed at which you can run with good efficiency. As you speed up from easy running paces, you actually become more economical. A runner might increase speed by 4 percent and use only 3 percent more oxygen. This trend will continue to very fast running speeds. As you go faster, you gradually become slightly more efficient. However, at economy pace, this trend reverses. Running 1 percent faster than economy pace increases energy expenditure by much more than 1 percent.

Pace is critical because it must be fast enough to force proper mechanics and to powerfully prestretch the tissues. Running faster than the correct economy pace changes running technique from a fast but efficient style to a sprinter's style, which trades efficiency for maximal speed. Running repetition workouts too fast increases the likelihood of overtraining and overuse injuries and actually trains the body to run inefficiently. That is the opposite of what is intended.

Economy pace is 5- to 8-percent faster than TT6 pace. A triathlete who runs a mile all out in six minutes should run economy reps between 5:33 and 5:43. (Calculated as the range between six-minute miles divided by 1.08 [8 percent faster] and six-minute miles divided by 1.05 [5 percent faster].) More experienced and more fit runners should stay on the slower side of this scale. Beginner and intermediates will be able to run at the faster end.

Be disciplined with economy-pace sessions. Experienced runners can perform these workouts anywhere, but until you have a feel for the pace and can reproduce it consistently and accurately by feel, use a track or marked section of road and check your watch. Running too fast may actually reduce your economy. Even though these are very fast sessions, running faster than economy pace is not better. These sessions are not designed to develop you into a sprinter, but to make you more efficient at triathlon race pace.

An economy workout should generally have you running between two and six minutes at economy pace. Ideal duration of repetition is 20 to 45 seconds with a work-to-rest ratio of at most 1:4. Do not cut recoveries short. These workouts are designed to increase economy and should not become interval workouts. There is *no* benefit to reducing recovery, but there are detriments.

Economy workouts should be very easy. If they are not, you are running too fast, doing too many repetitions, or allowing inadequate recovery between repetitions. Include economy workouts in your training relatively frequently, but when in doubt, do less in each workout.

Economy workouts are ideal during a pre-race taper because they provide enough intensity to maintain red blood cell count and keep your stride sharp and efficient, yet the recovery demands are minimal.

Economy training is important for athletes competing at any distance. Many long-distance athletes argue that they don't need the speed developed by these workouts. Economy workouts should not be performed with the intent of increasing speed. Athletes competing in aerobic events of any duration will benefit from increasing economy. At which distances is an athlete interested in wasting energy?

Hill repetitions may be used as economy workouts when training for hilly events. Be careful to keep turnover extremely high when doing economy work on hills. Start conservatively with relatively few short repetitions. Remember that different muscles are used in different ways running on hills versus flats. Make sure that all of your training includes a variety of terrains, while emphasizing terrain similar to that of your most important races.

LACTATE TOLERANCE TRAINING: DELAYING THE INEVITABLE

At any intensity an athlete's body produces lactate (lactic acid). At speeds faster than lactate threshold, it accumulates for as long as pace is maintained. Some triathletes must slow down as soon as they feel that familiar burn in their legs. Others can continue to run hard, pushing through the pain. The goal on race day is for lactate to accumulate slowly, causing complete fatigue at the finish line, but not before. While lactate accumulation always slows an athlete, the muscles can be trained to perform better under these conditions. Lactate tolerance training increases the body's ability to buffer lactate in the muscles and blood, keeping pH moderate even at high lactate levels. These workouts also enable the muscles to work more effectively in an acidic environment. These changes enable an athlete to sustain paces well beyond lactate threshold until a race's finish.

There is no magic formula for lactate tolerance workouts. At intensities of Zone 5a or higher, lactate is accumulating. In fact, most organized track workouts meet the goals for lactate tolerance training even if their intent was to increase aerobic capacity. To increase lactate tolerance, an athlete must subject the muscles to increasing levels of lactate with recovery periods that are inadequate to return lactate level to normal. There are a number of ways of doing this.

Be extremely careful with lactate tolerance workouts. They can sharpen the edge of an athlete just coming into peak form, or they can drive the athlete into overtraining. When in doubt, do less lactate tolerance training. A little bit goes a long way.

MONITORING INTENSITY

Ensuring that you train at optimal intensity for each workout is probably the most important factor in maximizing the benefits of your training. There are a number of different ways to monitor your training intensity, each with its own unique benefits and potential pitfalls.

Perceived Exertion
Perceived exertion is the most basic method of measuring intensity. How hard does it feel? For an experienced athlete, even when using

more technology to monitor intensity, staying in touch with perceived exertion is critical. Perceived exertion is an excellent means of monitoring intensity because it is always available and convenient, it takes into account an array of different variables that might affect fatigue, and it is the key factor when racing.

The potential pitfall of training by perceived exertion is its subjectivity. Athletes who train only by perceived exertion tend to train faster on days when they feel good, which is not efficient. Optimal training intensity is the same on a day when you feel strong as it would be on a day when you feel average or less than your best. Controlling intensity is a key to having better days for all your workouts.

Experienced athletes have learned precisely how each intensity level should feel and perceived exertion can be a very effective means of monitoring intensity. However, until the athlete has learned specifically how aerobic threshold, lactate threshold, aerobic capacity pace, and economy pace feel, using perceived exertion is simply training by intuition. Training by perceived exertion is completely different from "training by feel." Training by perceived exertion must involve a knowledgeable and experienced athlete who knows what the most efficient training intensities are and uses how the body feels to monitor intensity. Many athletes train by feel, using intuition instead of running at the optimal intensities. Stay away from training by intuition.

Whenever you train, tune in to how your body feels. How hard am I breathing? How much force am I using to push off the ground? What is my turnover? What, if any, is the level of burning in my legs? How heavy do I feel? When I ask my legs to accelerate, how do they respond? Which muscles in my legs feel fatigue? Learn to associate these different feelings with your levels of exertion. For instance, if your legs begin to show signs of fatigue at a lower respiration than normal, that is important. Stay tuned into how these factors interrelate.

Speed

Running speed is another important measure of training intensity. One of the major benefits of training by speed is its objectivity. Seven-minute miles are seven-minute miles. Also, speed is ultimately what wins races. The purpose of training is to make us faster, not to enable us to hold a higher heart rate, greater blood lactate levels, or higher perceived exertion.

The potential detriment of training by speed is that intensity at a given running speed may be quite different in different environmental conditions. Seven-minute miles uphill, into a headwind, on soft ground, or on a 100-degree, 100-percent humidity day is quite different from the same pace under different conditions. In addition, the same pace, under ideal conditions, may be a quite different intensity for the same athlete on different days. On a day when you didn't sleep well the night before, the day after a hard track workout or long run, or the first day back from an extended rest period, seven-minute miles will require different effort levels. When training by speed, always tune into other methods of monitoring intensity.

Several companies have developed global positioning systems (GPS) that essentially function as a speedometer for runners. These can be very effective tools if used properly. As with all technology, don't rely too heavily on this feedback. Use this technology, and all the other tools for objectifying intensity, to train and continually recalibrate your sense of perceived exertion.

Heart Rate

Heart rate has become the most widely accepted means of monitoring intensity—and with good reason. Heart rate is a relatively inexpensive, convenient, and effective means of monitoring intensity. Athletes wear a strap around their chest that tracks the electrical activity of the heart and transmits a signal to a wrist unit (or a handlebar-mounted unit for cycling) that tells how many times per minute the heart is beating. Heart rate will generally follow a consistent pattern—increasing as intensity rises and decreasing as intensity falls. Athletes can then train by heart rate zones, with each zone keeping them near the optimal intensity for each type of training.

As with any technology, one pitfall is overreliance on the heart rate monitor. Many athletes think that heart rate is the end-all and the be-all of training and racing. It is not. I knew one man who had a terrible race after the battery in his heart rate monitor died. Had he tuned into perceived exertion while he trained with his heart rate monitor, he still would have been able to race effectively with a dead battery. Another athlete I coached set a 40-kilometer personal record by over a minute, but was furious that he hadn't averaged the heart rate he had hoped for.

Smart athletes use a heart rate monitor in conjunction with other measures, especially perceived exertion and pace, to learn how their body functions. The heart rate monitor can become an incredible teacher for you if you stay tuned to other factors while watching heart rate and don't approach its use legalistically. Pay attention to heart rate and how it reacts in different situations, but don't become a slave to your heart rate monitor.

PHYSIOLOGICAL TESTING

Physiological testing by a qualified technician provides the best means of developing specific, individualized training intensities. A properly conducted test using a metabolic analyzer provides data that can be used to produce heart rate zones specific to your unique physiology. Unfortunately, the equipment to perform this testing is quite expensive and often technicians have the expertise to perform the test properly, but not to analyze the results to their full benefit.

Testing may be inconvenient and moderately expensive, but it does provide a greater degree of precision for determining training intensity. If you have access to a lab facility, I recommend testing. Have tests performed on the bike and the run separately, because the zones may be very different. Make sure that you are fully recovered from training before the test. Any workouts the day before the test should be very light. Don't eat or consume caffeine for three hours before the test, but be well hydrated. More information about physiological testing is available at *www.Fitness-Concepts.com*—my company's Web site.

DETERMINING TRAINING INTENSITIES

To develop heart rate zones, you need to know your lactate threshold heart rate. If you have access to a good lab, testing is the ideal way to determine it, but if you don't, you can approximate it using a time trial.

Make sure you are well rested and find a course where you can run uninterrupted for an hour. Flat to gently rolling terrain works well. A track is ideal. Warm up for at least 20 minutes with several surges of about one minute to approximate one-hour race pace. Run as hard as you can for one hour, averaging your heart rate for the last 30 minutes. The heart rate you could sustain in a workout for the last 30 minutes is

TABLE **4.1**   RUNNING HEART RATE ZONES

Find your lactate threshold (LT) heart rate (bold) in the "Zone 5a" column. Then read across left and right for training zones.

ZONE 1 ACTIVE RECOVERY	ZONE 2 BASIC ENDURANCE	ZONE 3 TEMPO TRAINING	ZONE 4 LACTATE THRESHOLD	ZONE 5A SUPER-THRESHOLD	ZONE 5B ANAEROBIC ENDURANCE	ZONE 5C ANAEROBIC CAPACITY
93–119	120–126	127–133	134–139	**140**–143	144–149	150–156
94–119	120–127	128–134	135–140	**141**–144	145–150	151–157
95–120	121–129	130–135	136–141	**142**–145	146–151	152–158
95–121	122–130	131–136	137–142	**143**–146	147–152	153–159
96–122	123–131	132–137	138–143	**144**–147	148–153	154–160
96–123	124–132	133–138	139–144	**145**–148	149–154	155–161
97–124	125–133	134–139	140–145	**146**–149	150–155	156–162
97–124	125–134	135–140	141–146	**147**–150	151–156	157–163
98–125	126–135	136–141	142–147	**148**–151	152–157	158–164
99–126	127–135	136–142	143–148	**149**–152	153–158	159–165
99–127	128–136	137–143	144–149	**150**–153	154–158	159–166
100–128	129–137	138–144	144–150	**151**–154	155–159	160–167
100–129	130–138	139–145	146–151	**152**–155	156–160	161–168
101–130	131–139	140–146	147–152	**153**–156	157–161	162–169
102–131	132–140	141–147	148–153	**154**–157	158–162	163–170
103–131	132–141	142–148	149–154	**155**–158	158–164	165–172
103–132	133–142	143–149	150–155	**156**–159	160–165	166–173
104–133	134–143	144–150	151–156	**157**–160	161–166	167–174
105–134	135–143	144–151	152–157	**158**–161	162–167	168–175
105–135	136–144	145–152	153–158	**159**–162	163–168	169–176
106–136	137–145	146–153	154–159	**160**–163	164–169	170–177
106–136	137–146	147–154	155–160	**161**–164	165–170	171–178
107–137	138–147	148–155	156–161	**162**–165	166–171	172–179
108–138	139–148	149–155	156–162	**163**–166	167–172	173–180
109–139	140–149	150–156	157–163	**164**–167	168–174	175–182
109–140	141–150	151–157	158–164	**165**–168	169–175	176–183
110–141	142–151	152–158	159–165	**166**–169	170–176	177–184
111–141	142–152	153–159	160–166	**167**–170	171–177	178–185
111–142	143–153	154–160	161–167	**168**–171	172–178	179–186
111–143	144–154	155–161	162–168	**169**–172	173–179	180–187

TABLE **4.1** (CONTINUED) RUNNING HEART RATE ZONES

Find your lactate threshold (LT) heart rate (bold) in the "Zone 5a" column. Then read across left and right for training zones.

ZONE 1 ACTIVE RECOVERY	ZONE 2 BASIC ENDURANCE	ZONE 3 TEMPO TRAINING	ZONE 4 LACTATE THRESHOLD	ZONE 5A SUPER- THRESHOLD	ZONE 5B ANAEROBIC ENDURANCE	ZONE 5C ANAEROBIC CAPACITY
112–144	145–155	156–162	163–169	**170**–173	174–179	180–188
113–145	146–156	157–163	164–170	**171**–174	175–180	181–189
114–145	146–156	157–164	165–171	**172**–175	176–182	183–191
115–146	147–157	158–165	166–172	**173**–176	177–183	184–192
115–147	148–157	158–166	167–173	**174**–177	178–184	185–193
116–148	149–158	159–167	168–174	**175**–178	179–185	186–194
117–149	150–159	160–168	169–175	**176**–179	180–186	187–195
117–150	151–160	161–169	170–176	**177**–180	181–187	188–196
118–151	152–161	162–170	171–177	**178**–181	182–188	189–197
118–152	153–162	163–171	172–178	**179**–182	183–189	190–198
119–153	164–163	164–172	173–179	**180**–183	184–190	191–199
120–154	155–164	165–173	174–180	**181**–184	185–192	193–201
121–154	155–165	166–174	175–181	**182**–185	186–193	194–202
121–155	156–166	167–175	176–182	**183**–186	187–194	195–203
122–156	157–167	168–176	177–183	**184**–187	188–195	196–204
123–157	158–168	169–177	178–184	**185**–188	189–196	197–205
123–158	159–169	170–178	179–185	**186**–189	190–197	198–206
124–159	160–170	171–179	180–186	**187**–190	191–198	199–207
125–160	161–171	172–180	181–188	**189**–192	193–200	201–209
126–161	162–172	173–181	182–189	**190**–193	194–201	202–210
126–162	163–173	174–182	183–190	**191**–194	195–201	202–211
127–163	164–174	175–183	184–191	**192**–195	196–202	203–212
127–164	165–175	176–184	185–192	**193**–196	197–203	204–213
128–165	166–176	177–185	186–193	**194**–197	198–294	205–214
129–165	166–177	178–186	187–194	**195**–198	199–205	206–215
129–166	167–178	179–187	188–195	**196**–199	200–206	207–216
130–167	168–178	179–188	189–196	**197**–198	199–207	208–217
130–168	169–179	180–189	190–197	**198**–201	202–208	209–218
131–169	170–180	181–190	191–198	**199**–202	203–209	210–219
132–170	171–181	182–191	192–199	**200**–203	204–210	211–220

Source: *The Triathlete's Training Bible*, 2nd ed. by Joe Friel (Boulder, CO: VeloPress, 2004).

approximately your lactate threshold heart rate. Do not use a race for this test. Athletes run harder in a race, and using an LT that is too high is a prescription for overtraining, not improving. Check your results against the chart in Table 4.1 to find your heart rate zones. Lactate threshold heart rate is the number in bold, and the zones listed in that row represent your heart rate zones.

FATIGUE

No discussion of training intensity would be complete without touching on the causes of fatigue. The ultimate purpose of all training is to push back the thresholds of fatigue with regard to duration and/or speed. The roots of fatigue will be different for races of different durations, on different terrain, in different environmental conditions, and for different athletes. Determining the most likely causes of fatigue for you in your priority races will help you tailor your training to improve limiters and maximize success.

Ventilatory Distress

In very short endurance efforts of two to six minutes, the lungs' ability to move enough air to oxygenate the blood may be a performance limiter. The duration of the shortest triathlons is long enough that this will never be a factor. While we will breathe very hard at times during races and our lungs may hurt, they are unlikely to be a limiting factor in triathlons.

Acid Accumulation

Every athlete knows the burn that accompanies acid accumulation in the muscles. New research indicates that it may not actually be lactic acid accumulation that causes fatigue, but acidity in the muscles definitely contributes to fatigue. At sprint and international distances, this is the most likely cause of fatigue for athletes, and for well-conditioned athletes, acid accumulation can contribute significantly to fatigue at the half-ironman distance.

Fuel Depletion

Almost every triathlete knows what running out of fuel is like. The dreaded "bonk" brings our progress to a halt and causes severe effort and pain at even very slow paces. Certainly triathletes need to avoid bonking. Most triathletes think their engines function like a car's. When a car has one one-hundredth of a tank of gas left, it still produces full horsepower. The human body doesn't work that way. Performance begins to decline slightly a long time before we bonk. Make a greater effort to fuel optimally and you will race faster. See Appendixes E and F for more information on fueling.

Dehydration

Water is our body's most critical nutrient. Just as performance declines with moderate glycogen depletion, before we can even feel it, we slow down from dehydration long before we feel dehydrated. Most triathletes do a relatively good job of hydrating on the bike during training and races, but they do a terrible job on the run. I recommend taking water with you on any run lasting more than 40 minutes. Just as you fill a water bottle for a short easy spin, fill a fuel belt for most of your run workouts. Consume 20 ounces of water per hour per 150 pounds of bodyweight.

Muscular Fatigue

Acid accumulation, fuel depletion, and dehydration are common causes of fatigue in triathlons, but our muscles can also fatigue for unknown reasons. Even when a well-trained athlete stays below lactate threshold and consumes adequate fuel and water, the muscles will eventually fatigue.

Again, training intensity is the most critical factor in determining your body's response to training. Training at the appropriate intensity will improve your results more than anything else. Make the effort to learn how hard you should be going for each workout, and you will race faster this year.

CHAPTER

5 Building Your Plan

In this chapter we will discuss how to develop monthly training schedules based on your annual training plan. Each workout will have a specific purpose. This is a missing piece in most athletes' training. Most athletes aim to build up mileage and intensity to accumulate as much training stress as possible, but they do not develop workouts around specific training objectives.

During each training phase, each athlete will have specific training priorities. These priorities will shift from training phase to training phase, and even through the cycles of a given training phase. Each month's training should build on the last month's training according to a specific progression. This allows athletes to peak on command and plan when their best performances will be. Human performance runs in cycles. When an important race approaches, we can work with those cycles and manipulate them so that we peak on the right day, or we can ignore them and cross our fingers that our performance will be up when the race arrives.

BREAKTHROUGH WORKOUTS

Training should be prioritized around "breakthrough" workouts. A breakthrough workout is one designed specifically to address a limiter and to challenge and overload your body by increasing volume and/or intensity well beyond the norm for your training program.

Efficient training is all about making your breakthrough workouts, usually only one or two per week, as effective as possible, so designing a schedule is really about determining breakthrough workouts and then programming other weekly workouts to support them. A well-designed schedule gives you the best chance of having an excellent workout every time a breakthrough is scheduled. Effective schedules provide a mini-taper prior to every breakthrough workout, which ensures that you are ready to accomplish the goals of the workout without overtapping your mental or physical resources.

PRIORITIES BY PHASE

Each phase of your training year will be characterized by different priorities, and the workouts during that phase should be structured accordingly. In the Transition phase, fun, relaxation, and getting your mind and body fully rested and recovered from the season are your priorities. Stay away from any high-intensity training and keep workouts loose and unstructured. Training volume should be very low.

The purpose of the Preparation phase is not to make you stronger and faster but to prepare your body for the work ahead, which will make you stronger and faster. Emphasis should be on the basic abilities of endurance, force, and speed skills. Volume should increase from the Transition phase, but it should still be relatively light. This is the best time of year to work on major changes in your technique.

The Base period is when serious training really begins. The basic abilities of endurance, force, and speed skills should receive serious focus, and volume and intensity begin to increase gradually. Endurance workouts should stay in Zone 1 to 2 and will gradually lengthen. Weight training is used to increase strength. Strength-transfer training (i.e., hand paddles, big gear pedaling, weighted running) is used to teach the muscles to use their newfound strength for sport-specific movements. Speed skills should be emphasized with drills in each sport—focusing on cadence/turnover and concentrating on correct movements.

In the Build period, workouts become more specific to the demands of the race. Triathletes with priority races at sprint and international distances begin ramping up the intensity. Half-ironman triathletes increase the duration of their long workouts and add race-pace segments. Ironman-distance triathletes continue to increase their long workouts. During Build periods, the advanced abilities of muscular endurance, anaerobic capacity, and power should be addressed if they are limiters. This is the time of year to monitor your intensity and recovery most carefully, because overtraining is most likely to occur now.

During the Peak and Race periods, race-pace workouts, rest, recovery, and economy are the priorities.

PRIORITIES BASED ON LIMITERS

The workouts to be included and prioritized in your specific training schedule are chosen based on your limiters. The schedule needs to be built around key breakthrough workouts that challenge and improve your limiters. Other workouts need to be scheduled and designed to support those workouts, not interfere with them.

Preparation Period

During the Preparation period, developing consistency is the key. Begin weight training, but don't be aggressive with it yet. Schedule three weekly runs on nonconsecutive days. Begin using a metronome and gradually try to increase your turnover without increasing intensity (that means reducing stride length proportionately).

Base Period

Every athlete should include one relatively long run, specific work on technique (including drills), and strength training during the Base period. How these workouts are prioritized depends on the athlete's specific limiters.

If economy is a limiter, pay particular attention to your technique. Perhaps you should arrange for regular lessons from a qualified instructor or use video for feedback. Also emphasize use of a metronome and include a few very short (30–40 seconds) repeats at economy pace with full recovery.

If endurance is a limiter, extend the long run and gradually increase total running volume. Based on your injury history, consider adding a fourth weekly run. If force is a limiter, prioritize strength-training workouts and add one or two weighted running sessions per week.

If injury resistance is a limiter, Base period is the time to implement a program that will keep you injury free throughout the season. Details on that are available in Chapter 13. Triathletes for whom getting to race weight is a limiter should prioritize that now. More information about that is available in Chapter 7.

Build Period

During the Build period, triathletes should focus on muscular endurance and other advanced abilities that are limiters. Include a weekly lactate threshold workout. Continue to emphasize economy.

Ironman-distance triathletes and triathletes with endurance limiters should continue to emphasize basic endurance workouts. Force-limited athletes should continue a maintenance strength-training program and include force training within their swim, bike, and run workouts. Sprint- and international-distance triathletes should include aerobic capacity training if anaerobic endurance is a limiter. Bricks should be prioritized for athletes who run significantly better in open races than in multisport races. During this period, every triathlete should begin implementing race-day nutrition plans during some workouts. Remember that we must train our gut to digest and absorb fuel during intense exercise just like we train our legs and lungs.

Peak and Race Periods

In the Peak and Race periods, recovery between workouts needs to be the greatest priority. You will be doing some hard breakthrough workouts, and the quality of those individual sessions is key—not just a buildup of volume and intensity.

This is the time to emphasize race-pace workouts. Make sure to allow 48 to 72 hours of recovery between them, and don't make these killer workouts. The goal is to make you efficient at race pace, not to overly fatigue you.

If thermal regulation is likely to be a limiter on race day, this is the time to make that a priority. More details on this type of training are available in Chapter 14. Peak and Race periods are also the time to prioritize sharpening mental skills. More information about that is available in Chapter 10. Sprint- and international-distance triathletes with anaerobic endurance limiters should continue to focus on lactate tolerance workouts.

CREATE WEEKLY PATTERNS

After you have determined your specific priority workouts by training period, the next step is developing weekly patterns. Do this one month at a time. Develop your specific schedule from the annual plan for each four-week cycle after completing the previous cycle. Feedback from the previous cycle is important in developing your next schedules. For instance, if an athlete scheduled a 90-minute basic endurance run in the last month of base training (March) expecting it to be really tough, the long runs on April's schedule should probably not exceed that. However, the athlete may find that after proper base training, the 90-minute run was no problem at all and may want to increase it in April, even though the intensity of other workouts also increases.

Some athletes prefer to use training cycles that don't match the seven-day work week. Instead they simply apply the same principles to 10-day cycles. Most athletes, however, have work or school Monday through Friday and the rest of their lives scheduled according to a seven-day week, so unless there is a reason to do otherwise, we usually plan training according to the seven-day weekly cycle.

The "hard/easy" principle has changed the way endurance athletes approach training. Although we tend to think in terms of hard day, then easy day, many athletes find it more effective to use blocks of hard days and blocks of recovery. Never placing two quality workouts back to back limits the number of quality sessions you can get in. Fortunately for triathletes, changing exercise mode allows us to squeeze hard sessions in different sports more tightly together without risking injury or overtraining.

Generally triathletes will swim two to four times per week, bike three to five times per week, and run three or four times per week. Workout frequency needs to be higher in the sports that are limiters and during periods when you are working to improve economy in one of the sports.

Triathletes vary as to how they adapt to running frequency. Some athletes, even good runners, do best not running on consecutive days. Remember that the potential for injuries and overtraining is a limiter for a lot of triathletes. Better to have three good run workouts and stay healthy than to be too aggressive and suffer downtime.

Lay out Monday through Friday on a page with spots for A.M. workouts and P.M. workouts (and possibly lunchtime workouts). Cross out any times you are not available to train. Write in prescheduled workouts that you always attend, such as a Masters Swim workout.

Now add in your highest priority workouts first, filling in lower priority workouts where they will not interfere with the key workouts. Make sure that the days before your two or three highest priority workouts are relatively light. You want to be fresh and strong for your most important breakthrough workouts.

If you will be doing a long ride and a long run on weekend days, do the run on Saturday if at all possible. Riding on legs tired from running yesterday is better than running on legs tired from riding yesterday. Also, triathletes who do long runs the day after long rides tend to suffer more injuries, presumably from running for so long on legs already tired from yesterday's ride. Due to its greater intensity and higher impact, the long run should be prioritized—even if cycling is a greater limiter for you.

Some of the most effective weekly patterns I have found are listed in Table 5.1.

BUILD A FOUR-WEEK SCHEDULE

Coaches and athletes have found that four-week training cycles generally produce the best results. Volume and intensity increase gradually for three weeks, followed by an easy week designed to allow full recovery from the three-week buildup. Three-week cycles, with a two-week buildup followed by a recovery week, work better for some athletes at certain points in the season, particularly beginning and Masters athletes.

Now that you have decided on a weekly pattern, it is time to develop your monthly schedule. Sticking with the same weekly pattern, gradually increase the volume and intensity of breakthrough workouts from week 1 to week 2 and week 2 to week 3. Week 3 of each monthly schedule should be pretty tough. For the fourth week, reduce volume dramatically, generally to between one-half and two-thirds of week 1 and include almost no intensity. Make sure you have at least one day during the fourth week with no workouts, but don't drop a workout in a sport in which economy is a major limiter for you. Frequency is an important factor in economy, so include those workouts, but make them light.

TABLE 5.1 WEEKLY TRAINING PATTERNS FOR TRIATHLETES OF VARIOUS DISTANCES		
	SPRINT AND INTERNATIONAL	HALF-IRONMAN	IRONMAN
MONDAY	Swim long and easy	Swim long and easy	Swim long and easy
TUESDAY	Hard Run Easy Ride (optional)	Hard Run Easy Ride (optional)	Hard Run Easy Ride (optional)
WEDNESDAY	Hard Swim Hard Ride	Hard Swim Hard Ride	Hard Swim Long, Hard Ride
THURSDAY	Moderately Hard Run Easy Ride (optional)	Moderately Hard Run Easy Ride (optional)	Moderately Hard Run Easy Ride (optional)
FRIDAY	Swim long and easy	Swim long and easy	Swim long and easy
SATURDAY	Long Run or Brick	Long Run or Brick	Long Run or Brick
SUNDAY	Long or Hard Ride	Long or Hard Ride	Long or Hard Ride

The recovery week at the end of each cycle is tremendously important. It provides a constant, built-in protection against overtraining. The recovery week renews your resources and keeps you sharp, both physically and mentally. By the end of week 4 you should miss hard training and be chomping at the bit to get back to it. Your muscles, joints, and connective tissues should have healed, and you should have no soreness. Hopefully you took advantage of the extra time available due to your reduced training volume and got some extra sleep.

BUILD INDIVIDUAL WORKOUTS

You will find specific workouts listed according to the limiters they address in Appendix A and Appendix B. Always begin a new type of training conservatively. When in doubt, do less and do it well. General workout ideas designed to address various aspects of training are discussed in the following sections.

Basic Endurance Training

Basic endurance training, which is done at Zone 2 intensity, is the backbone of every effective triathlon training program. Basic endurance training includes specific long runs, long rides, and long bricks, as well as shorter midweek workouts. In addition, the warm-up and cooldown for every workout will be at basic endurance intensity. Endurance-limited athletes can extend their warm-ups to address endurance to some degree in every workout.

Lactate Threshold Training

Lactate threshold (LT) workouts are incorporated differently into each athlete's schedule based on limiters and priorities, but LT training is a key component of almost every triathlete's race preparation.

Improving LT speed and endurance are primary goals of preparing for races that are between 30 minutes and five hours in duration. The muscles' fast oxidative glycolytic (FOG) fibers—also known as speed endurance fibers—will produce a significant percentage of speed at these distances, and acid accumulation in the muscles is likely to be a major factor limiting performance.

However, LT training is still an important component of training for events that are shorter or longer than the previously mentioned range. Even though training the fast-twitch fibers will be critical for sprinting, the FOG fibers still play an important role in events that last less than 30 minutes. And, even though the slow-twitch fibers produce the majority of the energy needed to race an ironman-distance event, and the FOG fibers will not be recruited for sustained durations, LT training (especially very long segments at the lower end of intensity) maximizes glycogen storage and vascularity, as well as increasing central adaptations such as the heart's stroke volume.

The reality is that most athletes at some point, even in an ironman race, exceed aerobic threshold intensity and recruit the FOG fibers for moderate durations. Athletes will likely recruit their FOG fibers on a particularly steep hill even if they are disciplined and pace appropriately, so we do want these fibers trained even though they are relaxed for much of the race. While training the slow-twitch fibers at aerobic threshold (AeT) intensity should always be the priority in preparation for ironman and longer races, LT training, on the conservative end, still has value.

Incorporating LT Training

LT workouts are incorporated into the schedule differently based on the athlete's goals, limiters, and the time of season. If muscular endurance is a primary limiter, LT segments could be included in both midweek workouts and the long weekend efforts during the Base period.

Begin with cruise intervals (see Chapter 4 for more information on this) late in the Base period. Include sets of four minutes, done in low Zone 4, with two-minute recoveries. Start with three to five sets. Add a set in week 2 and another in week 3, then decrease to less than week 1 in the fourth (recovery) week. Continue to increase the number of repetitions and/or the duration at LT (to five or six minutes) in each training cycle during the Base period. Also gradually progress the intensity from the low end of Zone 4 to the top of Zone 4, being careful not to exceed LT.

After cruise intervals have been part of your workouts for several cycles, you may want to move into tempo segments. When moving from cruise intervals into tempo segments of LT training each season, I generally begin with about 15 minutes in low Zone 4. For well-conditioned athletes, I increase this rather aggressively, often following the pattern 15 minutes, 20 minutes, 25 minutes, and 10 minutes for a four-week schedule.

Aerobic Capacity Training

Aerobic capacity (AC) workouts are an important component of a training program for many intermediate, advanced, and elite athletes. I do not recommend these workouts for first-year triathletes. Get a year of endurance and LT training under your belt before beginning AC workouts.

Faster athletes who are not endurance limited for their priority races are most likely to benefit from AC workouts. Generally, a well-conditioned intermediate athlete racing at sprint or international distance, an advanced athlete racing at half-ironman or shorter distances, and many elites racing at any distance will benefit from AC workouts.

AC workouts will be placed in the Build, Peak, and Race periods. Start with relatively short intervals, such as 30/30s (30-second repetitions at six-minute time trial pace followed by a 30-second recovery jog). Build the volume for one cycle before progressing to a more aggressive workout. The sprint (fast-twitch) fibers have not yet been stimulated at all, so the more conservative workouts will still improve aerobic capacity at this time.

Monitor your recovery carefully when adding AC workouts. Make sure to include relatively light days before and after, and I recommend not running either the day before or the day after. As mentioned in Chapter 4, do not run faster than a six-minute time trial (TT6) pace for any AC workouts.

Lactate Tolerance Training

Lactate tolerance training is the icing on the cake. Make sure to include this type of training only for four to six weeks before an A-priority race for which lactate tolerance is a limiter (this should fall into the late Build, Peak, or Race phase). Most triathletes should avoid lactate tolerance training, as it will interfere with other workouts more than it will help. With all workouts—but especially lactate tolerance workouts—when in doubt, leave it out.

Who Needs Lactate Tolerance Training?

Lactate tolerance may or may not play a role in triathlon, depending on the event duration, terrain, and the fitness level of the athlete. Determining whether lactate tolerance will likely be a limiter is an important step in developing the annual training plan for a serious intermediate or advanced triathlete. If an athlete will be able to sustain intensity beyond lactate threshold for much of the duration of his A races, increasing lactate tolerance will be beneficial. If not, spending training time and energy on increasing speed at threshold (either LT or AeT) instead of on building lactate tolerance will make for faster race times.

In sprint-distance triathlons, most serious athletes will race slightly above lactate threshold, so lactate tolerance will play a significant role. In international-distance triathlons, beginners and intermediates generally perform below threshold, so lactate tolerance is not a significant factor on relatively flat courses. High-level athletes will race beyond lactate threshold, so this training will be an important factor.

On relatively flat courses at international distance, lactate tolerance is likely to play a significant role in race outcomes only for very high-level triathletes. On hilly courses, however, athletes should produce greater wattage on climbs and recover on descents. When climbing, speed will increase almost proportionately to increased wattage. When descending, additional wattage primarily increases displacement of air, so high-energy expenditures are not efficient. Because every triathlete will spend significant time over threshold wattage on a hilly course, lactate tolerance will be a factor in these events.

At ironman and half-ironman distances, the race is long enough that intensity will be below lactate threshold. For these athletes, lactate tolerance training uses resources that should be dedicated to other types of training.

Periodization: Later is Better

If you have determined that lactate tolerance training will be beneficial for you, keep in mind that lactate tolerance is an adaptation that both trains and detrains very quickly. Because of that, and due to the enormous recovery cost of these workouts, they should generally be emphasized for just four to six weeks before A-priority races in which lactate tolerance is likely to be a limiter. If started earlier than this, lactate tolerance workouts will interfere with other key workouts—such as threshold workouts and aerobic capacity workouts—more than they will benefit you on race day. Lactate tolerance workouts in March (did anyone say training races?) might be fun, and they will certainly improve lactate tolerance for group rides and training races in early April, but they will reduce the benefit of other key workouts that should be prioritized until the Peak phase. Lactate tolerance workouts demand enormous physiological and psychological resources from the athlete. Don't underestimate that! Budget those resources wisely.

In addition, most athletes turn aerobic capacity workouts into lactate tolerance workouts by using an intensity that is too high and either reps that are too long or reps with insufficient recovery. This quickly leads to overtraining. There is a time for lactate tolerance workouts, in which harder is better, but this is inappropriate and detrimental earlier in the season.

Creating Lactate Tolerance Workouts

There is no magic formula for lactate tolerance workouts. To increase lactate tolerance, an athlete must subject the muscles either to extended periods of moderately high lactate accumulation or to very high levels of lactate for moderate durations. There are a number of effective ways of doing this.

Most hard group bike rides are effective lactate tolerance workouts. Most organized running track workouts, performed at too high an intensity, are perfect lactate tolerance workouts—even if their intent was increasing aerobic capacity and economy. When producing effective lactate tolerance workouts, we break every rule used for developing aerobic capacity and threshold workouts with an optimal cost-to-benefit ratio. While we usually strive for maximal stimulation of aerobic function for minimal lactate accumulation (both lactate level and duration), now we strive to increase muscle lactate levels and sustain them for greater durations.

Combining Stimulation. Generally, lactate tolerance workouts will be designed to improve (or maintain) aerobic capacity or lactate threshold while stimulating increased lactate tolerance. Combining workouts this way enables the week to be opened up for more easy and/or rest days. This is an important point about lactate tolerance workouts. They are extremely costly and will provide quick benefits, but they are also a quick road to overtraining or injury. Athletes need more recovery after this type of workout than any other.

Group fartlek workouts are a method of lactate tolerance training that many athletes find more appealing than structured workouts. Fartlek is a Swedish word meaning "speed play." The workouts are similar to structured track workouts in benefit, but they are run by feel instead of by the clock. Several athletes of similar ability alternate periods of two to four minutes of very hard work (aerobic capacity pace or higher) with recoveries of only about one minute. With each repetition lactate levels climb higher, and the recovery periods never allow the muscles to clear out much of the lactate.

Inserting a one-minute surge at approximately aerobic capacity pace every five minutes during an extended lactate threshold segment can be used to increase lactate tolerance while providing a maintenance benefit for economy and threshold.

Lactate crisscross workouts—alternating two minutes at two to three beats above LT with two minutes two to three beats below LT—increase tolerance while maintaining threshold.

Interval workouts combine aerobic capacity training with lactate tolerance training by increasing intensity beyond the six-minute time trial pace. I often have the athlete increase intensity to near 100-percent effort for about half the usual number of repetitions. A cyclist who has built up to six three-minute hill repeats at TT6 intensity for an aerobic capacity workout might instead do three of four all out when training for lactate tolerance.

Two to three long (seven to nine minutes) repetitions at full effort with full recovery between reps works well to increase tolerance and maintain aerobic capacity. Another method of combining an aerobic capacity workout with a lactate tolerance workout is reducing the rest interval between reps. For instance, a runner who does 800s at TT6 pace with a 400-meter jog for recovery could do 800s at TT6 pace with a 200-meter jog recovery. Again, volume must be reduced.

A structured lactate tolerance workout for a runner is repeating 400s with only 15 seconds recovery between reps. This is an extremely demanding workout that can be used to improve lactate tolerance and maintain aerobic capacity, economy, and lactate threshold during Peak phase.

Design with Specificity. When tailoring lactate tolerance workouts to your needs (and when deciding whether or not to include them), reanalyze your limiters. Determine to what degree force, threshold, aerobic capacity, and economy will be limiters in A-priority races. Use a method of training lactate tolerance that stimulates other limiters in a manner relatively specific to the demands of competition. Athletes that struggle with maintaining discipline and structure in their workouts will probably not do well with structured lactate tolerance workouts, but they will love the freedom of fartlek lactate tolerance workouts.

Lactate tolerance training is a powerful tool, but a little goes a long way. Make sure to reduce volume, incorporate fewer breakthrough workouts each week, and allow significant additional recovery time when adding these workouts.

Remember also to put them off for as long as possible until just before priority races. With lactate tolerance workouts, we are stimulating changes that occur very quickly and reverse very quickly.

We are also placing enormous demands on the body's recovery systems, so other workouts must be compromised.

Economy Workouts

Economy workouts are very effective and very efficient. Include economy sets often. Despite their high speed, your body will recover from these workouts very quickly and easily because the reps are so short and because of the full recovery between reps. Again, at what point are you efficient enough that being more efficient would not make you faster on race day?

Economy sets can be included with almost any workout. I frequently include them with most high-intensity breakthrough workouts, either tacking them on after the main set or using them to complete the warm-up. Long runs can include economy sets as well, although I usually don't include economy work in a long run that is expected to be relatively challenging or in the first hour of any long run.

Economy work should be included to some degree in every training period, but it should be most heavily emphasized during the Base period. Include one or two economy sets per week in each sport. Don't underestimate this! Remember the goal is to get faster, not just stronger.

REMINDERS

Develop your training schedules three or four weeks at a time, and follow the priorities and objectives developed in your annual training plan—unless something unexpected dictates otherwise. Make sure that work and recovery are balanced within each week and within each month. The body needs to be recovered enough for each priority workout to be maximally effective.

6 Brick Workouts

ultisport running differs from open running. Therefore, triathletes should approach many aspects of training and preparation differently. The most important difference in preparation is "brick" workouts. Brick workouts are designed to ease the transition from cycling to running. Triathletes who fail to consistently incorporate bricks into their training routine have trouble running immediately after cycling. Many athletes have gotten very strong on the bike and very strong on the run only to find that they cannot run anywhere near their capabilities after the bike portion of a triathlon.

PREPARING TO RUN AFTER BIKING

Brick workouts incorporate the skills needed for running directly after cycling. Where the term brick came from is a mystery. Some say that it came from the first two letters of brick—B for bike and R for run. Others say it came from the way your legs feel after a hard bike—like bricks.

Long or hard bricks should generally be added during the Build phase, but many athletes begin incorporating light bricks into their routine in the Base phase to prepare their legs for the more serious bricks to come.

Minimizing the time between the bike and run is a priority for brick workouts (as it is for triathlons). Whenever practical, set up a transition area and incorporate transition practice into each brick.

Even when this is not practical, begin the run as soon as possible after you finish your ride. I frequently do brick workouts out of my car after driving to an ideal training venue. You should be able to put your bike on top of the car, lock it, change shoes, grab a water bottle, and go in about two minutes.

There are a number of different types of brick workouts, each with its own specific purpose and its own place in your training program. Each brick workout very specifically targets a particular limiter of running after cycling.

TARGETING BRICK WORKOUTS TO LIMITERS

Targeting workouts specifically to your limiters is the basis of all effective training, and this holds true for bricks. Choosing the appropriate brick workouts to improve your endurance, muscular endurance, force, or speed will help you run well on race day.

Endurance-limited athletes need to prioritize long, easy workouts. Often the best choice for these athletes is not a long brick, but a Saturday long run followed by a long-ride brick on Sunday. This allows the endurance-limited athlete to do a longer run and ride than would be reasonable if the two were done as one long brick, and yet preserve the benefits of running after the bike. Do not be tempted to increase your run off the bike in a long-ride brick. Keep it to 15 or 20 minutes. After a long run on Saturday, the risk of injury goes up dramatically with a moderate-length run on Sunday when you are already fatigued from cycling.

Most intermediate to elite triathletes competing in half-ironman or shorter races are muscular endurance limited. These athletes will do best combining long bricks at basic endurance pace with lactate threshold and/or race-pace bricks. A key workout for an international-distance triathlete might be as follows: Ride 90 minutes in Zone 2 followed by 30 minutes in Zone 4. Transition as quickly as possible, then run 20 minutes at race pace (RP), and cool down with 20 minutes easy jogging.

Race duration plays a major role in choosing the appropriate brick workout. Each race distance provides the triathlete with unique challenges, and different preparation is required for each.

For sprint-distance racing (and international distance for advanced triathletes), coming off the bike and running fast right away is crucial. Giving away too much time "finding your legs" is not allowed. There simply aren't enough miles left in the race to make up for lost time. Brick workouts for these race durations should focus on enabling the athlete to come off the bike with legs full of lactic acid and get to goal pace right away. Race-pace bricks or brick interval workouts are key during the Build, Peak, and Race training phases.

For half-ironman racing, the challenge is running relatively fast for a very long time. A well-trained triathlete will push the pace somewhat for the entire duration of the race. Bricks for half-ironman racing focus on muscular endurance. It isn't jumping off the bike and running fast right away that is important, but running efficiently and giving your legs time to acclimate to running without giving up too much time.

Endurance bricks should be prioritized in the Base period, gradually giving way to race-pace and/or LT bricks in the Build period. As indicated previously, endurance bricks can be combined with race-pace or LT bricks by extending the duration of the basic endurance phase of the bike that comes before the higher intensity segments.

Every ironman athlete, from the beginner right to the Hawaii Ironman® champion, is endurance limited. Ironman-distance racing is about not falling apart, not about being so strong that you can push hard the entire distance. Muscular endurance bricks could have their place for high-level athletes, but endurance bricks will take priority.

Many ironman-distance athletes, without realizing it, do almost all of their training at faster than race pace. Again, even for the top pros, an ironman-distance race is about not falling apart. What is your average pace per mile in an ironman marathon? It probably is not nearly as fast as your pace on most long runs. This is a huge mistake. For an athlete hoping to run a 3:30 ironman marathon, eight-minute mile pace feels ridiculously slow, but that is the ideal intensity for most of your running. A primary purpose of ironman-distance training is to reduce the amount of glycogen you burn at race pace by training the muscles to burn more fat and less sugar. This is best accomplished at very low intensities. A second major purpose of endurance training is to get the legs accustomed to running the way they will on race day. Training at this pace maximizes neuromuscular efficiency most effectively.

Most ironman-distance triathletes should do a short run after almost every long bike workout. Frequency is the best way to adapt legs to running while fatigued to that degree, but doing a long run after the long ride may cause you to dig deeper into your reserves than you want to. Doing a long run on Saturday and a long-ride, short-run brick workout on Sunday works well. I frequently have an athlete follow this pattern through the Base period and switch to an endurance brick (long ride and long run) in the Build period. Sometimes we alternate a Saturday long-run/Sunday long-ride brick weekend with a Saturday swim-only/Sunday endurance brick weekend.

TYPES OF BRICK WORKOUTS

Lactate Threshold Bricks

LT bricks for sprint- and international-distance racing will usually be conducted high in Zone 4. Generally these workouts incorporate an extended warm-up in Zone 2, followed by a steady segment of Zone 4 riding, a transition, a steady segment of Zone 4 running, and a cool down of Zone 2 running. The Zone 2 riding segment may be extended, but the running cool down should not. After a fatiguing workout like an LT brick, extended endurance running poses a significant risk for injury. Also, be careful not to exceed Zone 4 intensity during these workouts. The slight additional benefit is not worth significantly delaying recovery.

LT bricks improve muscular endurance. These become a key workout for athletes once endurance is built and riding and running for race duration are no longer a problem. These workouts are very efficient, having among the best cost-to-benefit ratios of any workout. The pace is high enough to stimulate changes in the muscles that make you faster, but it still allows relatively quick recovery for the next workout. Be very careful not to do these workouts too hard. Riding and running at 95 percent of LT intensity still produces excellent results. Riding and running at 101 percent of LT intensity dramatically delays recovery. Any benefits of the additional 1 percent of intensity are not worth the cost.

Race-Pace Bricks

Race-pace bricks are very hard workouts for sprint- and international-distance racers that have a wide variety of benefits. Obviously, working hard on the bike and run increases fitness, but race-pace bricks do much more. They are among the only ways to develop pacing skills. However, make sure to keep the duration of both the bike and run segments well below race duration. The full effort of racing should only be approached on race day. I generally recommend keeping duration between one-half and two-thirds of the duration of the race's bike segment and between one-third and one-half of the duration of the race's run segment. Do these well, but avoid overdoing them. Choose quality over quantity.

Race-pace bricks should be incorporated in the Build, Peak, and Race periods. These are stressful workouts, so make sure to include adequate recovery. A race-pace brick counts as one intense bike session and one intense run session.

Brick Intervals

Brick intervals are among the hardest workouts a triathlete can do. They can be enormously productive if you get adequate recovery before and after the session. Brick intervals are powerful medicine, so remember that a little goes a long way!

Take a trainer to the track and alternate periods of hard riding followed immediately by hard running. Recover and repeat. Details of workout design are available in Appendix B. These workouts can be excellent physically and psychologically, but when in doubt, be conservative.

Long Bricks

The long brick is a breakthrough workout that should not be attempted too often. Most triathletes should perform these approximately every other week at most. This workout consists of a long ride (four to six hours) followed by a long run (90 minutes to two hours). These workouts develop deep fuel reserves, train the mind to maintain concentration for long periods, and give the athlete a taste of the effort required on race day. These workouts train every aspect of race day management, and if they go well, they can provide a huge confidence boost. Make sure that you are rested and logistically prepared for these. Treat them with respect and they will prepare you for race day.

Make sure you implement your fueling and hydration strategy exactly as you plan to on race day. Remember that we must train the stomach to digest and absorb calories at a faster rate just as we train the lungs to move more air and the legs to work harder and longer.

Brick workouts are a key to maximizing race-day run performance. Make sure to tailor your brick workouts to your limiters. Take these seriously and you will run faster off the bike.

PART THREE

Additional
Preparation
Factors

7 Reaching Optimal Race Weight

The primary force a runner must overcome is gravity. Gravity pulls at a triathlete throughout the run segment in direct proportion to bodyweight. Determining and achieving optimal bodyweight is a key to performing well on the run. Losing just a pound or two of unnecessary bodyweight will help you run faster with fewer injuries.

In addition to the increased pull of gravity, additional body fat slows the runner by interfering with thermal regulation. Fat insulates the body against heat loss. While this might be beneficial to an Eskimo, it is not beneficial to a triathlete during the run. The insulation of fat causes our bodies to direct more blood to the skin for cooling instead of to our legs to deliver oxygen to the working muscles. This can be an enormous factor on a very hot day, but it can play a significant role on any triathlon run.

We have discussed elsewhere in this book what a difference 1 percent can make to a serious athlete—36 seconds per hour. Bodyweight reductions provide almost proportional benefits to a runner. A 1-percent reduction in bodyweight yields almost exactly a 1-percent increase in running speed. A 150-pound runner will race 1-percent faster if he is 1.5 pounds lighter.

When I started training for my first triathlon, I was a 230-pounder (at 5'8" tall) who couldn't jog once around a track without stopping. Today I weigh in the high 150s, and I couldn't imagine doing a triathlon wearing a 70-pound backpack. My wife Melissa and I have lost a combined 160 pounds and have both gone on to win triathlon national championships.

When I was in college, body fat reduction is what first interested me in exercise physiology, nutrition, psychology, and biology (I majored in each for at least a year). I had tried every "diet" published in the magazines. I even lost 60 pounds once by just eating next to nothing—and I gained 70 pounds the next year. I knew there had to be a better way, and I hoped that by studying the chemistry of our bodies I could figure it out. What I figured out has worked for me, worked for my wife, and worked for many athletes I have coached. I think it will work for you.

DETERMINING IDEAL RACING WEIGHT

Racing triathlon to one's full potential requires being relatively lean (although being too light can come at the cost of fitness). I often ask clients, "If two cars are identical except one has a six-cylinder engine and one an eight-cylinder engine, which is going to win a race?" Obviously the car with eight-cylinder engine will be faster, *even though it is heavier.* For athletes, the key is losing the excess bodyweight, but not the cylinders. Carrying excess body fat under the skin will slow you down, but so will lost strength if you lose too much weight. Be sure that you lose weight from the chassis and not the engine. Athletes with too much body fat will not race their best, but neither will depleted athletes.

Maintaining protein intake is critical during periods of body fat reduction. Consuming adequate protein helps prevent fat storage, helps maintain muscle mass, and maintains the metabolic rate. Each of these is important to reducing body fat and racing to your potential.

Estimating your percentage of body fat can be useful in determining race weight. Understand that each method of body fat testing is an estimate and not a true measurement and that each method has its own pitfalls. Don't put too much emphasis on a body fat percentage estimate, but use it as one tool in determining your optimal race weight. Males will generally race their best at about 6 percent body fat and females at about 12 percent (females have more fat stored around their organs, so their body fat percentage will be higher even when they are lean and have little fat stored under the skin). While these are the ideals that will help you perform to your absolute potential, not every triathlete wants or needs to be this lean.

With or without measurements, athletes generally know when they are not as lean as they should be. Stand undressed in front of a mirror. An extra layer of fat around the midsection or hips will make you run slower. Grip the skin just next to your navel. There should be skin and only a thin layer of fat. Can you see the rough outline of your abdominal muscles? You don't need a ripped "six-pack," but you should be able to see the basic shape of those muscles.

GETTING TO RACE WEIGHT

If you have determined that you would race better a few pounds leaner, you need to develop a plan to make it happen. *Be patient! Body fat cannot be lost quickly.* If you do lose weight quickly, much of it will be lean tissue. Fast weight loss impairs performance and drastically reduces resting metabolic rate, which will lead to weight regain. Remember that, in the long term, *not eating makes you fat.*

Athletes with fewer than 10 pounds of extra body fat to lose should plan to drop 1 pound of body fat every two to four weeks. Athletes with more than 10 pounds to lose may be able to drop body fat slightly more quickly initially—in the range of 1 pound of body fat every one to two weeks. Take it slow. If an athlete with 15 pounds to lose takes half a year to lose it, and then is able to stay lean forever, isn't that six months well invested? I certainly think so.

What caused you to be less lean than you want to be? It is probably not as simple as the "calories in/calories out" paradigm would lead you to believe. That paradigm says that if you have too much body fat, you don't exercise enough (laziness) and eat too much (gluttony). I bet very few people reading this book are either lazy or gluttonous! You probably exercise fairly consistently and try to eat a basically healthy diet. You probably eat a hot fudge sundae or a candy bar every now and then (rarely), but so do athletes who are extremely lean. That occasional splurge, as long as it truly is occasional, is not the problem.

COMMON MISTAKES MADE BY ACTIVE PEOPLE TRYING TO REDUCE BODY FAT

Eating carbohydrates in a way that causes them to be stored as fat.

Eating in such a way as to make themselves hungry.

Conducting basic endurance training at a pace that is too high to burn fat most effectively.

Failing to eat enough protein.

Eating too much fat.

Failing to eat when they are hungry.

I have designed a system that will allow you to develop habits that work *with* your body, not against it, to reduce body fat. You will learn to manage hunger and satiety responses and eat when you are hungry. You will not feel deprived. Discipline and willpower are not the answers.

Expect this to be an up-and-down process. Remember that perfection is not the goal—developing patterns that work for you is. After trying to eat well and exercising hard without complete success, you may feel that perfection is the price of leanness, but it is not. Missing a workout or eating a little bit of junk food occasionally won't ruin your efforts. What we want to do is gradually reshape your attitudes about getting lean, your exercise habits, how you choose your foods, and when you eat which foods.

THE INSULIN RESPONSE

Before reading the following sections, keep this information in mind. Carbohydrate is necessary in the muscle for effective fat burning to occur, so carbohydrate stored in the muscles is good. However, carbohydrate can also be stored as fat in the fat cells, which enlarges them. When, how, and what type of carbohydrate you eat will dramatically affect where and how carbohydrate is stored.

The human body tries to maintain control over all its functions. It has thousands of built-in self-correction systems to keep it running smoothly. Blood sugar is one of the functions over which the body maintains tight control. Our endocrine systems react strongly to keep blood sugar within certain normal parameters. If blood sugar becomes either too high or too low, alarms are set off, and the body reacts powerfully to bring blood sugar levels back to normal.

Insulin is a hormone secreted by the pancreas to help maintain optimal blood sugar level. Insulin's job is to remove sugar from the blood and store it, either as glycogen in the muscles and liver or, more frequently, as fat. Insulin is good. It helps maintain balance in the body. However, when triggered at the wrong times and in great amounts, insulin will make you fat. Preventing frequent and intense insulin responses is the single most critical step in reducing body fat for many people.

Insulin also has a negative effect on resting metabolic rate. Depending on the frequency and the severity of the insulin response, it may reduce the number of calories burned at rest by as much as 8 percent! Over time, this could add up to a significant amount of extra body fat.

Carbohydrates are very simple molecules that digest quickly and easily. Even the most complex carbohydrate is nothing more than strings of sugars loosely tied together. Digestion of carbohydrates begins right in the mouth with an enzyme called salivary amylase, which is located in the saliva. By the time carbohydrates even reach the stomach, digestion is well under way and much of the carbohydrate you just ate is already sugar.

When you eat carbohydrates by themselves, they digest too quickly and the sugar enters the bloodstream all at once, sending your blood sugar level soaring. This sets off an alarm, and the pancreas secretes insulin into the bloodstream to take some of the sugar out. This is a good response, preventing a dangerous situation, but it comes at a cost.

As Figure 7.1 shows, when you eat a carbohydrate, blood sugar may increase quickly. When blood sugar rises beyond the level the body is comfortable with (represented by the upper dotted line), the body secretes insulin to take sugar out of the blood and store it, either in the muscles as glycogen or in the fat cells. While insulin prevents dangerously high blood sugar levels, our bodies tend to overreact, storing too much sugar.

Severe insulin responses cause excess fat storage and low blood sugar. Low blood sugar causes a number of problems. The first is lethargy. Even mild activities seem exhausting. Another symptom of low blood sugar is mood swings, but the greatest problem caused by low blood sugar when trying to reduce body fat is hunger. There are a number of different triggers for hunger and satiety. When blood sugar

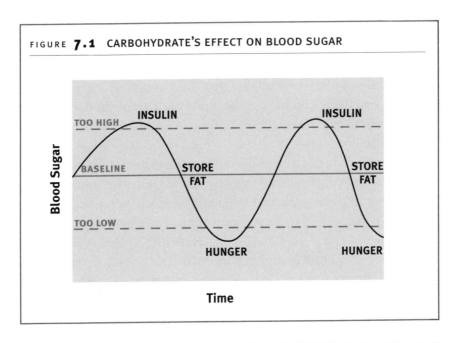

FIGURE **7.1** CARBOHYDRATE'S EFFECT ON BLOOD SUGAR

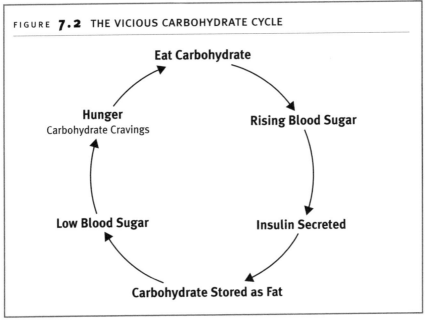

FIGURE **7.2** THE VICIOUS CARBOHYDRATE CYCLE

is the trigger, guess what specific cravings are usually manifested? You guessed it, carbohydrate. This sets up a vicious cycle—eating can make you hungry and reduce energy levels. Repeatedly triggering the insulin response causes fat storage, hunger, and lethargy. Nobody intentionally makes him- or herself fat, hungry, and tired, but many people unknowingly do so several times every day.

PREVENTING THE INSULIN RESPONSE

The way you consume carbohydrate may be making you fatter than you want to be, but carbohydrate is not the enemy. Depending on how you structure your food consumption, carbohydrate may be stored mostly as fat (bad), stored mostly as carbohydrate in the muscles (good), or not stored at all (good). Managing the insulin response is a critical aspect of this. Carbohydrate in the bloodstream provides energy right now. Carbohydrate in the muscles gives energy for tomorrow's workout. *Depleting carbohydrate will not make you lean.*

The key is structuring meals and snacks so that you can consume carbohydrates in your diet, but keep from suddenly elevating your blood sugar level. Three strategies come into play here. The first is choosing carbohydrates that digest more slowly and therefore enter the bloodstream gradually. The second is combining carbohydrate with other types of food that digest more slowly—essentially "time-releasing" carbohydrate. The third is consuming concentrated carbohydrates—such as sugar, pasta, rice, cereal, bread, corn, rice, and potatoes—only after workouts. When consumed immediately after workouts, calories from concentrated carbohydrate sources are likely to be stored in the muscles as fuel for tomorrow's workout instead of in your fat cells.

Glycemic Index

The glycemic index (GI) of a food is a measurement of how quickly the carbohydrate in that food enters the bloodstream compared to pure glucose. Glucose has a glycemic index of 1.0. A food that has a GI of 0.7 enters the bloodstream 70 percent as quickly as pure glucose.

Figure 7.3 shows blood sugar curves for two different feedings. First, the subject consumes 75 grams of pure glucose and blood sugar is monitored. At a different time, the subject is fed enough of a certain food to provide 75 grams of carbohydrate. Again, blood sugar is

FIGURE **7.3**   GLYCEMIC INDEX

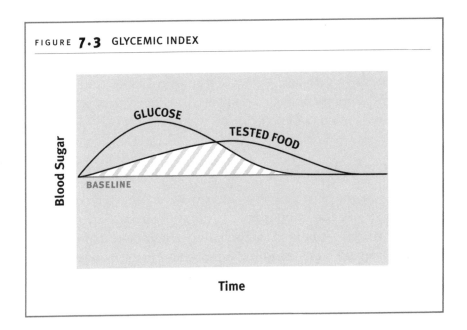

monitored. Blood sugar after this feeding is represented by the "tested food" curve. The GI of the food is the percentage of the glucose curve that is overlapped by the tested food curve. If the shaded area covers 70 percent of the area under the glucose curve, the food's GI is 0.7.

For someone trying to lose body fat, a diet comprised largely of low-GI foods prevents excessive insulin secretion and ensures that the carbohydrates in the diet are available as fuel instead of being stored as fat.

See Appendix D for a list of the GIs of common carbohydrates. Carbohydrates with a GI of 0.4 or lower may be considered low-GI foods, which are the best choices. Carbohydrates with an index between 0.4 and 0.7 may be considered moderate-GI foods and are good choices. Carbohydrates with a GI over 0.7 will tend to trigger an insulin response and should be eaten primarily right after workouts or in combination with lower-GI foods (to create a combined GI of less than 0.7).

Combining Foods

Protein is the friend of an active person trying to decrease body fat. Consuming protein with carbohydrate helps ensure that the carbohydrate is not stored as fat.

Choosing low- to moderate-GI carbohydrates is a useful strategy for reducing insulin secretion, but properly combining foods in meals and snacks can be just as powerful. Learn to make this strategy a natural part of your lifestyle, and you will become leaner.

Carbohydrate is a very simple molecule that digests rapidly and easily. Protein, on the other hand, is a very large, complex molecule that digests much more slowly. Remember that when you eat different types of food together, they move through the digestive tract together, being digested and absorbed at the same rate. If you eat protein and carbohydrate together, the protein dramatically slows the carbohydrate's digestion. Instead of a large amount of carbohydrate entering the bloodstream all at once and driving the blood sugar level up dramatically, the carbohydrate trickles slowly into the bloodstream. Protein "time-releases" the carbohydrate. As digestion occurs, blood sugar is gradually burned off almost as quickly as it enters the bloodstream, which prevents quick increases in blood sugar level and the resulting insulin response. Blood sugar remains just slightly elevated for a long period of time. This creates the perfect situation: good mood, feelings of energy, minimized hunger, and a slow, steady supply of sugar to be burned with fat to provide the body with energy for daily activities.

Fat digests very slowly, just as protein does, so logically it could be combined with carbohydrates to prevent dramatic blood sugar fluctuations. While this will prevent the insulin response, think carefully about the logic behind consuming fat to be sure that the carbohydrate you eat will not be stored as fat. You will just store fat calories as fat calories instead of storing carbohydrate calories as fat calories, and you get fat for a different reason. Fat is the most calorie dense of all biological fuels. It has about 2.25 times more calories per gram than either protein or carbohydrate. Better to stick with low-GI carbohydrates and combine them with protein in a relatively low-fat diet.

EAT A MODERATELY LOW-FAT DIET

Despite the popularity in the press recently of some dangerous high-fat fad diets, eating fat makes you fat. Of all the calories we consume, fat is the most likely fuel to be stored in our fat cells for a number of reasons.

- Fat has the highest caloric density of any fuel in our normal diets by a ratio of more than 2:1.
- Fat has the lowest thermic effect of any calories we eat. This means dietary fat can be saved as body fat very efficiently. Fewer calories are lost as heat storing fat than any other fuel in our diets.
- Our metabolic rates adjust upward with increased caloric intake of either protein or carbohydrate consumption, but not with fat consumption.
- People consistently eat higher-calorie self-selected meals when offered higher-fat foods—and people consistently have lower activity levels after consuming high-fat foods.
- People who eat a higher-fat diet become more efficient at storing fat due to proliferation of lipogenetic (fat-storing) enzymes.

You can store fat by improperly eating carbohydrates, but the best way to get fatter is to eat fat.

These facts spurred the low-fat eating revolution of the 1980s and 1990s. People would avoid every gram of fat—to the exclusion of getting enough protein and to the point of increasing carbohydrate dramatically. "I avoided the 3 grams of fat in the chicken breast, and it only took me one (2,400-calorie) box of fat-free cookies to do it."

While this was a move in the right direction, the pendulum had swung to the opposite extreme. Eventually we learned that extremely low-fat diets are neither necessary nor effective. Research shows that extreme low-fat diets are very difficult to follow. Fat has a pleasant texture, helps control appetite, and tastes good. Even very motivated dieters on extremely low-fat diets have very low compliance rates. Also, research has shown that extremely low-fat diets impair the release of human growth hormone. This hormone is important for anyone trying to lose weight, but especially for active people trying to reduce body fat.

A diet that gets 20 to 25 percent of its calories from fat is far better than a diet that derives 30 percent or more of its calories from fat. However, a 5- to 15-percent fat diet is not better than a diet composed of 20 to 25 percent fat. Most people have little problem adjusting to getting between 20 and 25 percent of their calories from fat, and that is good enough.

Volumes have been written on low-fat eating. While we don't need to run from every gram of fat, we should try to avoid excess fats that don't add to the pleasure food brings.

See the following table for a list of lower-fat food selections. In addition, these are a few more ways to reduce dietary fat to moderately low levels.

- Use skim dairy products. Whole milk gets over 50 percent of its calories from fat.
- Be careful with "reduced-fat" anything. According to U.S. law, a reduced-fat product must have 25 percent less fat than the regular product. Reduced-fat peanut butter, for instance, has only a small percentage of the fat removed. It is "reduced" to about 70 percent of calories from fat, and a large amount of sugar is added. Reduced-fat peanut butter will make you fat. Products such as peanut butter and cheese, which are extremely high fat, can still be loaded with fat—even after the fat content has been "reduced."
- Use applesauce or yogurt for butter or oil in baking.
- Skip the cheese on sandwiches and hamburgers.
- Use fat-free mayonnaise.
- Avoid creamy soups and sauces.
- Use Parmesan and Romano cheeses. Stronger flavor means less is required.
- Replace cream cheese with low-fat cream cheese, skim ricotta, or skim cottage cheese.
- Use nonstick sprays and nonstick pans instead of oil for cooking.
- Beware of adding fat during cooking! Many low-fat foods can become fatty after they are cooked.
- Trim all visible fat from meats before cooking, and drain grease carefully after cooking.

Try to reduce dietary fat, but don't look at this as *the* answer to getting leaner. Low-fat eating is one effective strategy for reducing body fat, but we learned in the 1980s and 1990s that it is definitely not "the secret."

TABLE **7.1** MAKING BETTER FOOD SELECTIONS

HIGH-FAT CHOICES	LOWER-FAT CHOICES
Muffins	"Normal" breads and cereals
Biscuits	Bagels, English muffins
Cornbread	Pasta
Waffles	Rice
Pancakes	Corn
Granola	Oats
French fries	Baked potatoes
Croissants	Pretzels
Chips, crackers	Saltines
Oil-popped or microwave popcorn	Air-popped popcorn
Salmon, swordfish, trout	Halibut, cod, haddock, sole
Mackerel, anchovies, sardines	Flounder, red snapper, tuna, shrimp, crab, mussels, scallops, clams, oysters
Dark-meat poultry or poultry with skin	Skinless white poultry meat
Many cuts of beef	Chuck, round, or flank sirloin
Most pork products	Canadian bacon, pork loin
Hot dogs, cold cuts	Organ meats
Duck	Chicken or turkey
Eggs	Egg whites, Egg Beaters (or similar low-fat products)
Cream sauces	Broth or bouillon sauces
Mayonnaise	Salsa, mustard, ketchup, horseradish
Butter and margarine	Soy, teriyaki, or Worcestershire sauce

EXERCISE: NATURALLY CHANGING YOUR BODY'S CHEMISTRY

It is important to remember that the chronic changes in resting metabolic rate and in how the body selectively burns and stores different fuels that result from exercise are much more important than the energy cost of exercise (the calories it burns).

Everybody knows that exercise should be an important part of any weight-loss plan. Most weight-loss programs make some reference to exercising as a benefit. The problem is that most weight-loss programs are derived from the calories in/calories out paradigm and fail to provide adequate emphasis or instruction on effective exercise for body fat reduction. They provide no information on why exercise is beneficial, what type of exercise best suits different individuals, how to perform the exercise, how hard to exercise, how frequently to exercise, or how long to exercise. Just like everything else, there are good ways and bad ways to exercise to get leaner. The right way for you to exercise to get leaner may be very different from the way that naturally lean people exercise.

Without an understanding of why they are exercising, many people underestimate how critical exercise is to long-term weight loss. Many become frustrated when they work out very hard and the exercise bike tells them they burned only 250 calories: "I could just skip one sandwich and not do the workout. Everything would be the same. It's not worth it. It's easier to just eat less." This may be true in the short term—in the context of a single workout or a single day—but chronic changes in how the body burns and stores energy also result from exercises and make enormous differences over time. My body at rest burns about 310 calories per day more than the average male of my height, weight, and age. Is 310 calories a big deal? No, it's a sandwich. But over the course of a year, this accounts for 113,150 calories—or 32.3 pounds of fat. I come from a genetically overweight family and once weighed 70 pounds more than I do now, so I am confident that my accelerated metabolic rate can be attributed to exercise. I have seen similar changes in resting metabolic rate in scores of athletes I have worked with.

Optimizing Your Workouts

Many people exercise too hard to burn fat yet not hard enough for maximal increases in fitness. Driven by the calories in/calories out formula, they go as hard as they can for the duration of each workout in a misguided effort to maximize the energy cost of each workout. Every workout ends up being medium hard. This approach poses a number of problems. First, the tendency to go moderately hard makes increasing workout duration difficult. Long, easy workouts are the cornerstone of a weight-loss exercise program. Long, medium-paced workouts are not easy at all, but they are a great way to learn to hate exercise. Second, the "moderately hard" approach ignores the weight-loss benefits of very high-intensity exercise, which is that performed at a higher intensity than can be maintained for extended durations. Most people benefit dramatically from slowing down for 75 percent of their exercise volume and speeding up for the other 25 percent. Medium-hard workouts try to accomplish two things at once and don't optimize either.

Exercise has many benefits for weight management, and the energy cost of the exercise is just one. From a long-term perspective, the energy cost of exercise is actually a minor benefit. Even if you exercise two hours a day, your body burns far more calories during the other 22 hours than during your workouts. A balanced exercise program has an enormous effect on how your body manages fuels—including fat—both during workouts and when at rest.

Muscle Mass and Metabolism

Never eat more than you can lift.
—Miss Piggy

Exercise increases muscle mass. Muscle burns most of the total calories burned in a day, even for sedentary people, and it is the only tissue in the body that can burn fat (yes, your muscles burn 100 percent of the fat you burn!). Muscle, even at rest, is extremely metabolically active. It requires an enormous amount of energy for maintenance.

Imagine if you couldn't turn off your car's four-cylinder engine, but it sat idling in the driveway all night. You would burn a lot of gas driving around for an hour a day, especially if you drove fast, but even more would be burned during the remainder of the day and overnight. Now think about an eight-cylinder engine. It burns more gas driving around town, but it also burns much more gas idling in the driveway. Increasing your muscle mass will help you burn many more calories during workouts as well as at rest. It will give you an eight-cylinder metabolism.

An effective strength-training program is a key to increasing your resting metabolic rate. A pound of muscle burns between 35 and 75 calories per day at rest, just for maintenance. For every additional 5 pounds of muscle you add to your frame, your resting metabolic rate will increase by 175 to 375 calories per day. That's like burning the calories required to run 1.5 to 3 miles, just for existing! Multiply that by 365 days, and you burn an additional 63,875 to 136,875 calories each year. How many hours would you have to exercise to burn that many calories if the energy cost of exercise were the only benefit?

Aerobic Conditioning

If a pound of muscle burns 35 to 75 calories per day at rest, we obviously want to add more 35 to 75s to our body. We also want to make them closer to 75s than 35s. We want every pound of our muscles to burn as many calories as possible, all the time. This can have a huge effect on metabolic rate—as much as 300 calories per day for a normal person.

Research indicates that the mitochondrial density of a muscle determines its level of metabolic activity—and therefore how many calories are burned at rest. Mitochondria are tiny parts of each cell that serve as the sites for most energy metabolism. Think of them as the powerhouse of the cell. The best way to stimulate your muscles to make more mitochondria is through intense aerobic exercise. We'll look at how to optimize this type of training later.

Thermic Effect of Food

Everything a person eats must be digested, absorbed, and transformed into a form that can be used for fuel or stored. Most of these transformations involve many steps, and each step wastes some energy. This energy is released as heat and is referred to as the "thermic effect" of food. For those trying to lose body fat, this wasted energy is good.

Releasing heat is one way the body adjusts to increased calorie intake. When you eat more, your body wastes more calories, which prevents you from gaining weight. Research shows that this process does not function optimally in sedentary people. The thermic effect of food is much greater in people who exercise. This is another way that sedentary people become more calorie efficient—enabling greater fat storage and reducing fat burning.

Insulin Secretion and Sensitivity

Insulin's job is to remove sugar from the blood and store it, either as fat or as carbohydrate. In general, people trying to lose body fat do not want to store sugar; they want it to stay in the blood until it is burned. People who exercise regularly tend to secrete less insulin.

If calories must be stored, we certainly want them to be stored as carbohydrate in the muscles. Exercise increases the sensitivity of the insulin receptors on the muscles, which means that calories are more likely to be stored as carbohydrate in the muscles than as fat.

Increased Fat Burning

Our bodies use a number of different types of fuel. Each fuel is best suited for different specific purposes. Fat is the body's long-term energy source and serves as a protection against famine and as fuel for long-duration, low-intensity exercise.

During periods of starvation, fat stores kept cavepeople alive. Those who were able to preserve fat stores had a much better chance of surviving (and, therefore, reproducing) than those who readily burned fat. During most of our bodies' evolution, our species survival has depended on fat. How times have changed. In the big picture, the agricultural revolution is a fairly recent achievement, and our bodies have not kept up. Before the agricultural revolution, if you reduced calorie consumption, it was because food was not available, not because you wanted six-pack abs for the beach or to run a 10K personal record. Now that we have grocery store shelves constantly lined with food, and we die from storing too much fat instead of from running out of fuel, our genetic tendencies may work against us.

Fat is the most difficult fuel to burn for a number of reasons. First of all, very little fat is stored in the muscle. Other fuels, especially carbohydrate, are stored directly in the muscle, so they may be accessed immediately for use. Fat is primarily stored in the fat cells under the skin. Before significant fat burning can occur, the muscle must send a signal to fat cells. Then fat must be mobilized into the bloodstream, circulate through the body and to the working muscles, be taken out of the bloodstream by the muscles, and finally burned. For most people, it takes 20–30 minutes for significant fat burning to begin. (This time shortens with increased fitness.)

Burning fat also requires more oxygen than burning carbohydrate. At low intensity, when the body is able to deliver plenty of oxygen to the muscle (and after the initial 20–30 minutes), the body prefers to burn fat as fuel. If intensity increases, the body may not deliver proportionally more oxygen to the muscle, so in order to meet the energy demand of the exercise, the muscle must shift to burning more carbohydrate and less fat. Increasing fitness will increase fat-burning intensity, but even for extremely fit athletes, fat burning occurs optimally at very low intensities and ceases completely at high intensity.

Correct exercise also increases a person's ability to burn fat. Adaptations in the heart, blood vessels, and muscles increase oxygen delivery and fat utilization. The mechanisms responsible for releasing fat into the bloodstream, transporting it into the muscle cells, and then burning it, work faster. Hormonal changes that prevent fat burning become less sensitive and those that increase fat burning trigger earlier in an exercise session.

More importantly, people who exercise correctly burn fat more effectively while at rest. All the changes that enable greater fat burning during exercise don't just vaporize when you take your running shoes off. Those who have trained their bodies to burn more fat through correct exercise burn more fat 24 hours a day than those who have not.

Exercise and Appetite

Exercise has a profound affect on hunger and satiety responses. Many of the factors that trigger overeating are negated by exercise.

Core body temperature is a major hunger trigger. Humans get hungry when they get cold. Exercise almost always increases acute core body temperature significantly, which reduces appetite. One exception is swimming, during which the water usually draws more heat away from the body than the exercise produces. The idea that swimming is not the best exercise for reducing body fat is not a myth.

Research consistently shows that people tend to eat more after swimming than after other types of exercise or when they do not exercise. One solution to this problem is a short trip to the sauna or hot tub, if they are available, after swimming. Raising core body temperature back to normal, or slightly above, reduces the tendency to overeat caused by cooler body temperature.

People who exercise regularly also tend to have a slightly higher basal core body temperature even at rest. This provides a constant built-in appetite suppressant.

Blood sugar is another key trigger for hunger and satiety. While incorrect exercise may cause low blood sugar and increased appetite, an optimal exercise program stabilizes blood sugar and provides chronic protection against blood sugar crashes.

Blood acidity affects hunger as well. Even low-intensity exercise generally increases the level of lactic acid in the bloodstream, which causes the blood pH to decrease. Lower blood pH causes feelings of fullness and decreases appetite.

Higher levels of free fatty acids in the bloodstream trigger satiety. Many types of exercise trigger the release of free fatty acids into the bloodstream, but sustained, low-intensity aerobic exercise is most effective at this.

Acute Responses of Resting Metabolic Rate

The body continues to burn calories at a higher than normal rate for a long time after exercise ceases. The duration and magnitude of these changes depends on the volume and intensity of the exercise. This phenomenon, often called the afterburn, may account for as much as 15 percent of the energy expenditure of the workout and may last up to 24 hours.

Increased Carbohydrate Storage

Exercise increases the body's ability to store carbohydrate. Athletes have bigger gas tanks than sedentary people. This provides a "safety net" for excessive carbohydrate intake. A person who is capable of storing a large amount of carbohydrate is less likely to store carbohydrate calories as fat. A large carbohydrate storage capacity also makes longer workouts possible, increasing the potential for both fat burning and conditioning.

Heat and Cold Sensitivity

People who exercise tend to be more sensitive to both heat stress and cold stress. These responses stimulate acute increases in resting metabolic rate and release of human growth hormone, both of which result in increased fat burning.

Energy Cost

Exercise burns calories, which is good. This is one relatively small, but still significant, benefit of exercise for weight loss. As you should understand after reading the preceding sections, the energy cost of exercise is not the primary benefit, but it does play a role.

Increasing Benefit

One factor that causes many people to underestimate the benefit of exercise in long-term weight management is that the benefits of exercise accelerate over time, while the apparent benefits of calorie restriction show themselves immediately.

As Figure 7.4 shows, exercise becomes an increasingly important part of body fat reduction over time. The long-term benefits are much greater than the short-term benefits. Dietary adjustments, especially

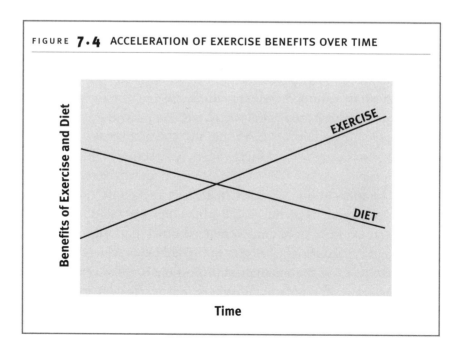

FIGURE **7.4** ACCELERATION OF EXERCISE BENEFITS OVER TIME

calorie reduction, play a greater role in short-term results than long-term results. Changes in resting metabolic rate and body chemistry take time. The cumulative effects of exercise, over a long period of time, will produce enormous changes in body shape and body composition. The results of exercise show themselves gradually, especially when weight is used as a measure of success.

When sedentary people begin an exercise program, their poor fitness limits how much work they can accomplish. Their bodies are not able to burn fat effectively and only moderate-duration, low-intensity exercise is possible. Initially, the acute benefits of exercise for weight loss are low.

Chronic benefits of exercise are more important than acute benefits, but they do take time. If an aggressive exercise program increases a person's resting metabolic rate by 150 calories per day, it will make enormous changes in that person's body composition over the course of a year, but the acute benefit is not great. Burning 150 additional calories today is not a big deal compared to the 54,750 additional calories (15.6 pounds of fat) burned in a year. Exercise provides very gradual weight loss, which accelerates consistently as increased fitness enables longer and more intense workouts and elevated resting metabolic rate has time to take effect.

In the short term, however, it is easier to eat fewer calories per day than to exercise. For the first several weeks of calorie restriction, the result will be the same. Eating less does produce short-term results. Over a relatively short period of time (approximately 14 days), the body will adjust resting metabolic rate, almost calorie for calorie, to match the decreased intake. Calorie restriction provides quick initial weight loss followed by a plateau and often weight regain.

Clearly exercise plays a critical role in long-term weight management—not because of the calories burned during exercise, but because of the chronic changes in resting metabolic rate and in how the body selectively burns and stores fuel. We will discuss how to target an exercise program to change body composition later.

Although the calories in/calories out paradigm is widely accepted in our culture, even among medical professionals, there is ample evidence derived from both laboratory research and real-life experience that indicates that it does not work for long-term weight management. This model requires many leaps of faith that are not borne out.

It ignores myriad complex interactions between nutrition, exercise, and how the body burns, stores, and alters fuel. These reactions, and the systems that control them, are extremely complicated.

Research that refutes the calories in/calories out paradigm includes the following:

- Metabolic rate responds directly to our behaviors. When you eat less without more complicated changes in your nutrition habits, your metabolic rate will match your calorie reduction—almost calorie for calorie. You can fool your body for only a short time. Win a battle, lose the war.
- Overweight people's bodies store and burn fuel differently than lean people's bodies, but this is in response to lifestyle and is largely within our control.
- Overweight people do not eat more than normal-weight people.
- Metabolic rate is driven and controlled by the endocrine system, which responds directly to many lifestyle factors including nutrition habits and exercise.
- Enzymes, which catalyze reactions, increase or decrease dramatically in direct response to nutrition (including dieting) and exercise.

Research is definitely important when assessing the effectiveness of a weight-loss method, but real-world results are even more important. Sometimes, the greatest value of research is explaining why a certain method already developed does or does not work.

Each year, millions of Americans spend billions of dollars on a weight-loss industry that consistently succeeds in making its clients fatter. Most people who use commercial weight-loss programs lose weight only to gain back more than they lost—ultimately becoming fatter for the experience. The average weight regain following a commercial weight-loss program, in the first year, is almost 120 percent of what was lost. Overweight people do generally try hard and basically comply with their programs. While they are easy to blame, programs fail people much more than people fail programs. If *most* people gain the weight back, it is not the individuals who are to blame, but the program.

When overweight people regain the weight lost using strategies derived from the calories in/calories out paradigm, they blame themselves, remembering that hot fudge sundae they ate in March, the trip to McDonalds in April, and the one slice of birthday cake they ate at their son's party in June. Look around. Don't you see lean people eating cake at birthday parties? In most cases, dieters who regain weight were set up for failure. They lost weight, drastically lowered their metabolic rates, and gained it back. They don't understand that reducing their metabolic rate holds tremendous long-term consequences. They blame themselves, instead of the program. They blame themselves because their willpower didn't work. You can't take a nut off a bolt with a hammer. Don't blame yourself for not being successful when you've chosen the wrong tool. You cannot use psychological tools to fight physiological problems.

If genetics is the key, then explain why some people lose weight and successfully maintain their ideal weight, while others continue to yo-yo. The answer is that they do it differently. They may have stumbled on to the appropriate techniques that we teach in this book by accident. They may have figured out how their own bodies work through trial and error. I promise you, however, that eating less food was not the only factor in their long-term weight management success.

ALL CALORIES ARE NOT THE SAME

Our bodies process the three primary sources of calories—fat, carbohydrate, and protein—very differently. Learning how each affects our energy level, digestive system, endocrine system, metabolic rate, feelings of hunger or satiety, and mood enables us to regain control of our bodies.

Calories consumed in the form of fat will be kept in the blood until they are burned or stored as fat. Most fat calories consumed will end up in fat storage. Increasing fat consumption has very little effect on metabolic rate. Basically, eating too much fat makes you fat and has other health-destroying consequences.

A recent fad, the low-carbohydrate diet, has been not only destructive to weight-loss efforts but is also extremely dangerous. Interestingly, this fad swept the country in the 1950s and didn't work, resurfaced in the 1970s and didn't work, and hit again in the

1990s. Guess what, it still doesn't work! The human body just doesn't evolve that quickly.

Calories consumed in the form of carbohydrates may be kept in the blood where they can be used as a fuel source, be stored in the muscles as glycogen, or be stored as fat. Two of three results of eating carbohydrate are good. Which of these results occurs is largely under our control. How our bodies use carbohydrates is affected by when we consume them, which types of carbohydrates we choose, as well as what other foods are eaten together with the carbohydrates. Carbohydrates are necessary for burning fat. Avoiding carbohydrates is absolutely not the answer to anyone's weight management problems. Incorporating them into a nutrition plan in such a way that they are used as fuel instead of stored as fat is the answer. Eat carbohydrate to feed your muscle cells, not your fat cells.

Calories consumed in the form of protein may be used to repair tissues (especially muscle), be used as fuel, or be stored as fat. Significant protein will be stored as fat only in extreme cases of overconsumption. This is very unlikely. Athletes trying to decrease body fat should eat a lot of protein. I recommend about 0.6 grams of protein per pound of bodyweight each day.

Underconsumption of protein, on the other hand, may lead to muscle atrophy, which results in decreased metabolic rate, which results in fat storage. Eating enough protein, spread throughout the day, maintains muscle mass and keeps metabolic rate high. This is one key to long-term weight management.

Fat Loss Versus Calorie Loss

Clearly, strategies derived from the calories in/calories out paradigm are shortsighted and do not work. A more accurate paradigm of body fat reduction would be:

FAT LOSS = FAT CALORIES REMOVED FROM STORAGE –
FAT CALORIES STORED

After all, isn't fat loss the real goal, not calorie loss? Therefore, doesn't it make sense to look specifically at fat and how calories are stored and used to see ultimately what causes them to end up as fat in storage or not—and to look at expenditure the same way?

Many factors that affect this formula aren't apparent in the calories in/calories out formula. There are also significant factors that affect the calories in/calories out paradigm that do not cause either fat burning or fat storage. The following list contains just a couple of the differences between the formulas. There are many more.

- If you have 40 minutes to exercise, according to the calories in/calories out formula, you should exercise as hard as possible to burn the greatest number of calories. However, hard exercise burns almost entirely carbohydrate and not fat, causing almost no fat to be removed from storage. Carbohydrate depletion does not lead to body fat reduction.

- According to the calories in/calories out formula, a plain bagel, having fewer calories, is a better breakfast choice than a bagel-with-egg white sandwich. However, the calories from the plain bagel are very likely to be stored as fat, while the calories from the bagel sandwich are likely to remain in the bloodstream until they are combined with fat and burned and where they will trigger sustained feelings of satiety. In reality, the addition of the egg whites reduces the amount of stored fat.

- The calories in/calories out formula suggests that the day before a party at which you will probably overeat, you should eat very little to "save up" calories for the splurge. This strategy is likely to increase overeating (because you get hungry), but even if you don't overeat, this strategy activates the fat-storing enzymes and causes greater fat storage from the same food. Eating normally through the day will reduce the amount of fat stored from the food eaten at the party.

- Reducing protein intake reduces caloric consumption. According to the calories in/calories out formula, this should produce weight loss. However, reducing protein intake will reduce metabolic rate directly (acute response); may cause muscle atrophy, which also reduces metabolic rate (chronic response); causes more carbohydrate calories to be stored as fat; and triggers feelings of hunger.

One powerful attraction of the calories in/calories out paradigm is its apparent simplicity. Unfortunately, the human body *isn't* so simple.

Learning how your body works and redesigning your lifestyle appropriately can be hard work initially. Inertia is a powerful foe to be overcome. Each of us is used to eating and exercising a certain way, and making changes can be difficult. However, once you have put in the work of learning how you are fighting your body and adjusting your habits accordingly, inertia becomes a powerful ally. It is not much more difficult to eat and exercise optimally for weight management than to do these things the wrong way. Using the principles outlined here is the only way to work with your body to become leaner—and working with your body is the only way to achieve and maintain the level of leanness you desire.

APPETITE CONTROL: HOW TO AVOID FIGHTING YOUR BODY

Hunger is not the enemy! Hunger is a good thing. Contrary to most people's beliefs and the popular interpretations of the calories in/calories out formula, hunger is not evil! Hunger is an important signal from your body and is something to be heeded and managed, not feared.

Hunger is a sign from your body that it needs nutrients, like an automobile's low-fuel light. Remember this: Hunger is a sign from your body of impeding damage. The consequences of ignoring it are metabolic changes that will make you fat! *If you fight hunger, you will get fat.*

Certainly physiological hunger is not the only cause of overeating. We may overeat the wrong foods out of habit and due to social and emotional factors. If these are indeed problems, we must develop better habits and modify our behavioral responses to social and emotional factors. However, hunger must be managed if we are to have a realistic opportunity to make these changes. The strategy of altering mental and emotional processes while fighting physiological responses is not realistic. Whether you face emotional issues with food or not, you cannot fight your body and win.

Deactivating the Fat-Storing Enzymes

One important aspect of becoming lean is avoiding triggers for fat storage. The strategies for accomplishing this go hand in hand with the strategies that will enable you to control hunger. Once calories are stored as fat, the body is extremely reluctant to give them up.

FIGHTING BIOLOGY WITH PSYCHOLOGY?

Many unsuccessful dieters get down on themselves because they do not have the willpower to eat the way they would like to. While I am not in any way negating the role psychology plays in weight management, I believe that using willpower to overcome physiological hunger is not a winning strategy. If you are hungry, you should eat, because you are going to eat anyway, and if you listen to the hunger you stand a good chance to control what and how much you eat. The longer you fight hunger, the more likely that it will overpower you and cause binge eating. Attempting to starve yourself when you need a 200-calorie snack may cost 1,000 calories later.

Removing fat from storage so that it can be burned is, at best, a slow and difficult process. Minimizing the number of calories that are stored as fat is one critical aspect of reducing body fat.

What your body does with the calories you eat depends on a number of factors, not just on how many calories you consume. Everyone has fat-storing enzymes, which take fat out of the bloodstream and store it in the fat cells. Over a long period of time, it is possible to reduce the number of these enzymes in your body. This will make reaching and maintaining low body fat levels possible. Your habits also determine how active these enzymes will be at any given time. Fortunately, the strategies we use to get rid of these enzymes in the long term and the strategies we use to reduce their activity in the short term are the same.

Most people, especially those who have repeatedly tried to lose weight, have trained their bodies to store fat very efficiently. Altering these destructive habits will reverse this tendency.

When you allow yourself to get hungry, it is a sign that your body is ready to store fat. You have, through mistakes in how you have eaten, created a bad situation. When you get really hungry, you are likely to overeat, but that is only part of the problem. The other part is that you have primed your endocrine systems to trigger maximal fat storage.

The answer is never to allow hunger to develop. This is the antithesis of the calories in/calories out mentality, which stresses willpower to help you not eat. Remember that the strategies derived from that formula do not work. You cannot fight biology with psychology.

I remember a commercial I heard on the radio years ago that went something like this: Did you ever try to stare down a chocolate chip cookie? I tried the other night. It took a large cheesecake, two candy bars, and half of an apple pie, but I didn't eat that cookie—until later!

The most destructive aspect of these attempts to fight biology with willpower is the psychological damage created in the form of negative self-image and negative thinking patterns. You are smart, not weak, because you eat when you are hungry. People who do not eat when they are hungry are not smart—they usually are fat.

There are a number of physiological variables that trigger hunger and satiety. Each of these provides one or more effective strategies for preventing hunger.

Avoid Evening Consumption

The fat-storing enzymes are generally most active in the evenings. Unfortunately, this is when most people consume most of the day's calories. Consume more calories earlier in the day and fewer at night unless you eat right after a workout.

Increase Eating Frequency

The human body has several gas tanks. We store different types of fuel in different places for different purposes. The beauty of the human body is that the capacities of each of our fuel storage sites respond directly to our own lifestyle. We teach our bodies. Teach your body that it needs to be able to store a lot of a certain fuel in a certain place, and it will learn—responding directly to the stimulation you provide with your eating and exercise habits.

Carbohydrate is a short-term fuel, designed to be stored in small quantities primarily right in the muscles where it can be immediately accessed for fuel. The typical person stores only 1,000 to 2,000 calories as carbohydrate. Consuming excess carbohydrate calories, beyond the body's limited ability to store them as carbohydrate, will result in storage of fat.

Fat is our long-term fuel. The human body is capable of storing hundreds of thousands of calories of fat, many times more than can be stored as carbohydrate. Very little fat is stored in the muscle, where it is readily accessible for immediate fuel needs. Instead, fat is stored under the skin where it can be used only for long-duration activity. Fat is our body's fuel for long-lasting activities.

Our bodies naturally want to store fat and give it up reluctantly. How would we trigger our bodies to want to store fat even more and give it up even more reluctantly? Simply make it go long periods of time without consuming fuel, and you trigger the need for greater storage of the fuel designed for that purpose.

Conversely, feeding the body frequently sends the signal that storing a large amount of fuel isn't necessary. Eat breakfast immediately upon waking and eat approximately every four hours throughout the day. Again, this strategy is not only designed to prevent overeating, but to decrease the activity of the fat-storing enzymes, reducing the number of calories stored as fat, whether you overeat or not. *Going long periods of time without eating makes you fatter even if you do not overeat afterward.*

What to Do When You Get Very Hungry

We have established that in a perfect world we would never go for long periods without eating, but sometimes that is not possible. A one-hour staff meeting goes three hours or you have to leave work to pick your child up from the school infirmary, so you miss lunch. While we should make contingency plans to prevent such problems, sometimes extended periods of time without eating are inevitable.

When you are forced to go a long time without eating and you find yourself very hungry, the key is to listen to your hunger, but minimize the damage. Eat a small snack, about 150 to 300 calories (depending on your size and activity level) that contains a small amount of carbohydrate and significant protein (aim for a 2:1 carbohydrate-to-protein ratio). Then, wait at least 20 to 30 minutes before having a meal. The goals are taking the edge off the hunger and deactivating the fat-burning enzymes before consuming a full meal. You will find that, when following this strategy, you will eat fewer total calories and fewer of the calories you do eat will be stored as fat.

Choose Low-Caloric Density Foods

Research consistently shows that people eat a fairly consistent amount of food each day, both in terms of volume and weight. Eating foods with a low caloric density, meaning relatively few calories for the volume and weight consumed, helps keep hunger at bay without overconsumption, even at reasonable levels of calorie intake. Obviously, feeling slightly full at each meal and appropriate snacking helps prevent overeating. Just how much broccoli would you have to eat at every meal to get fat from it?

The weight of food in the stomach plays a key role in triggering feelings of satiety. Our bodies are able to sense the pull of gravity on the stomach and trigger endocrine changes that keep us from being hungry. Foods that are heavy for their number of calories generally contain a lot of water. Compared to almost every food, water is extremely dense. Choosing high-water foods makes it easy to eat enough to prevent feelings of hunger without consuming too many calories.

The volume of food in the stomach also plays a key role in triggering satiety. The human stomach is very small, about the size of a fist. The walls of the stomach are able to expand dramatically in response to the food we eat. This stretching of the stomach walls also triggers feelings of satiety and eliminates hunger. Eating reasonably large portions of foods that have low caloric density is an effective strategy for managing hunger. Foods that have a high volume for their calorie content are usually high in fiber. Fiber is the part of the plant cell that the human digestive system cannot break down. Fiber contains calories, but since we cannot digest it, those calories simply pass through our digestive systems instead of being absorbed. No amount of fiber can contribute even a little bit to you getting fat, but it can and will help prevent overeating. Consuming foods that have a lot of water and fiber will help keep hunger under control without providing enough calories to cause fat storage.

How Heat and Cold Stress Affect Appetite and Metabolism

Few people realize the impact that heat and cold stress can have on weight management. For our bodies to function well, our core body temperature must be closely regulated. The body getting either too hot or too cold poses a serious threat to our safety. Changes in core body temperature in either direction cause immediate and intense reactions from the endocrine system in order to regain thermal regulation.

The eating triggered by decreased core body temperature prevents the body from being cold. First, digesting food releases heat and warms the body. Therefore, eating provides an immediate solution to the problem of being cold. Secondly, eating may provide an extra layer of body fat, which provides insulation against cold. Eating provides both an acute, short-term solution and a chronic, long-term solution to the problem of being cold.

This particular reaction poses a dilemma to people trying to lose weight. One symptom of low metabolic rate is a tendency to be cold all the time or to get cold easily. When the metabolic rate is reduced, the body tries to conserve energy and "waste" as little energy as possible as heat. The body actually becomes more efficient, which is the opposite of our goal. We want to be inefficient at rest so that we burn more fat.

Heat stress, on the other hand, tends to trigger feelings of satiety. Think about it, when are you usually hungriest? In August when it is 100 degrees outside or in December when it is 30 degrees? Almost everyone eats more in the winter.

Fortunately, we can choose to control our core body temperature if we are smart. Staying warm in the cold winter months may be a challenge, but making a special effort to dress especially warmly will make overeating much less likely. We can develop a number of strategies from this fact.

First, in general, try to stay warm all the time. Overdress when it is cold outside, even if you are just going to the car right in the driveway. Wear warm clothing while exercising outside. Even if you are comfortable running in shorts during the winter, and even though you sweat profusely, you may be lowering your core body temperature and increasing your appetite. Certainly you are losing one potential benefit of the workout—raising your core body temperature.

For those who have trouble with overeating at the evening meal and at night, a bowl of hot soup or a cup of hot tea will help take the edge off the hunger. Taken about 20 minutes before the evening meal, either of these will increase core body temperature as well as adding volume and weight to the stomach.

If you do get cold, take steps to warm back up immediately—before you eat. Drink hot beverages, keep your coat on for a few minutes after you come inside, or wrap up in a blanket.

Keep your home a little warmer in the winter. Your heating bill may go up slightly, but your body fat will decrease, which is well worth the trade-off for most people.

Many people come home from work stressed out and starving. I find that many of these people benefit tremendously from taking a very hot shower or bath and listening to relaxing music or reading a book before they head to the kitchen. The hot water raises core body temperature and encourages relaxation. By the time they make it to the kitchen for a snack, their hunger is moderated and it is easier to make healthy choices.

DEVELOPING A WORKOUT PLAN TO REDUCE BODY FAT

Developing a workout plan that conditions you to reach your triathlon goals *and* helps reduce body fat is possible. In fact, the strategy of training at low intensity or high intensity and avoiding medium-hard workouts is most effective for both purposes.

Frequency

Athletes trying to reduce body fat should exercise almost every day, but as triathletes, most of us already do that. I recommend weight training, during the appropriate times of year, two to three times per week. Building strength in the Base period will not only make you a faster swimmer, cyclist, and runner, but will also help you get leaner.

Intensity

Low-intensity exercise burns fat. High-intensity workouts trigger growth hormone release and increase metabolic rate. The same balance of training that develops your swimming, cycling, and running fits well with body fat reduction goals.

One suggestion is that you be conservative on basic endurance workouts. Most athletes burn fat most effectively in Zone 1 and the lower half of Zone 2. Go *very* easy on your basic endurance workouts.

Duration

Longer workouts are better. Especially for basic endurance workouts, increase duration more aggressively than intensity. One very long workout per week helps burn more fat and helps increase the ability to burn fat. Keep this workout at a very easy pace.

Exercise Mode

Obviously, if you will be swimming, cycling, and running for triathlon, these will be your primary exercise modes. Cycling, because very long duration workouts are practical, is very effective for your low-intensity fat-burning workouts. Running, because higher intensities are possible, is most effective for the high-intensity workouts. Don't forget serious weight training during the Base period.

Human Growth Hormone

Human growth hormone (HGH) helps release free fatty acids from the adipose tissue (fat storage) into the bloodstream where they may be burned. It also helps transport amino acids into the muscle and connective tissue cells where they may assist with workout recovery and with growth.

HGH is secreted by the anterior pituitary in response to the stress of starvation, heat, or intense exercise. HGH is likely to be released as a result of heavy strength training (more than 85 percent of the maximum weight you could lift for a single repetition) or high-intensity cardiovascular exercise (more than 75 percent of VO_2max).

Caffeine

Caffeine releases free fatty acids from the adipose tissues so they may be burned for fuel and increases resting metabolic rate. A strong cup of coffee or two about 45 minutes before a workout helps increase fat burning during the workout. Check with your doctor before using caffeine.

Summary

Stop thinking according to the calories in/calories out paradigm. Learn a little more about how your body works. Develop habits that work with your body instead of fighting it. Be patient. Follow these four guidelines and you are sure to race closer to your ideal race weight this season.

WEIGHT MANAGEMENT FACTS AND RESULTING STRATEGIES

Facts:

1. Over time, the body's metabolic rate adjusts upward with increased consumption of protein and carbohydrate, but not fat.
2. When protein and carbohydrate are stored as fat, the conversion process uses a significant percentage of the calories. Fewer calories are stored from 100 calories of protein or carbohydrate than from 100 calories of fat.
3. Even highly motivated individuals have great difficulty complying with extremely low-fat diets. Compliance is dramatically higher on moderately low-fat diets.

Strategy: Reduce fat consumption to moderately low level.

Facts:

4. Over time, the body's metabolic rate adjusts downward, almost calorie-for-calorie, to match decreased calorie consumption.
5. Metabolic rate adjusts downward relatively quickly in response to low-calorie diets and returns to normal levels very slowly, if at all, after calorie intake returns to normal.
6. Muscle is burned during periods of low-calorie intake, resulting in huge decreases in metabolic rate.

Strategy: Avoid extended periods of significant calorie reduction.

Facts:

7. Low-intensity exercise burns fat, while high-intensity exercise burns carbohydrate.
8. Fat-burning aerobic exercise at the appropriate intensity increases the percentage of fat burned at rest.
9. High-intensity aerobic exercise stimulates the metabolic rate.

Strategy: Balance low-intensity and high-intensity exercise optimally through each week to increase total metabolic rate and the percentage of fat burned. Avoid medium-hard workouts. Either go slowly and be very aerobic, or really push yourself hard.

Facts:

10. Heat stress increases metabolic rate dramatically and reduces appetite.
11. Carbohydrate calories consumed immediately following intense exercise are more likely to be stored as glycogen in the muscles than as fat.
12. Exercise reduces appetite because it results in increased core body temperature, more free fatty acids in blood, and decreased blood pH.
13. Overconsumption at the evening meal contributes greatly to most weight problems.

Strategy: Use exercise and heat stress before the evening meal to stimulate metabolism and trigger feelings of satiety (decrease appetite).

Facts:

14. Muscle is the only tissue in the body that burns fat; it accounts for a majority of total calories expended.

Strategy: Use resistance exercise to increase muscle mass and increase metabolic rate.

Facts:

15. People generally consume a very consistent weight and volume of food each day.
16. Fiber and water add significantly to the weight and volume of foods, without adding any calories.

Strategy: Reduce the caloric density of your diet by emphasizing foods high in both fiber and water.

Facts:

17. Eating increases metabolic rate significantly for several hours after a meal.
18. Small meals increase metabolic rate almost as much as large meals.

19. Extended periods without eating (four hours or more) activate lipogenetic enzymes, which store calories in fat cells.
20. After a few hours without food, the body reduces metabolic rate and may burn muscle.

Strategy: Eat more frequent, but smaller, meals spaced relatively evenly throughout the day.

Facts:
21. For approximately the first 20 minutes of exercise (even at the optimal fat-burning intensity), the primary source of energy is carbohydrate.
22. Approximately one hour into exercise at fat-burning intensity, the body secretes greater levels of cortisol. This increases fat burning dramatically.

Strategy: Make sure that fat-burning exercise sessions last well beyond 20 minutes. Shorter workouts can be beneficial, but should be higher intensity. Increase endurance to enable increased exercise duration. Consider eventually extending one workout per week well beyond an hour.

Facts:
23. When carbohydrates are consumed without protein or fat, an insulin response stores fat, increases hunger, and decreases energy level.

Strategy: Combine protein, fat, and carbohydrate in each meal to prevent the insulin response and maintain blood sugar level. Choose carbohydrate sources that are lower on the glycemic index.

Facts:
24. Exercise increases the body's ability to store calories as carbohydrate in the muscles and liver.
25. Repeated periods without food (four or more hours) increase the body's tendency to store calories as soon as they are consumed.

26. Frequent bingeing increases the body's ability to store calories as fat.

Strategy: Develop a "safety net" against occasional splurges by increasing your carbohydrate storage through exercise. Long workouts at low intensity accomplish this best. Decrease the body's tendency to store calories at all with frequent meals and by avoiding bingeing. Don't "train" the body to store fat efficiently.

You now have a tremendous amount of information about how active people can best reduce body fat. Be patient with yourself. Changing habits is a process that takes time, and once your habits have been changed successfully, reducing body fat takes still more time. Remember that perfection is not the goal. Developing and implementing a program that gets you as lean as you would like to be by the day of the big race—and gives you a chance to stay lean because your metabolic rate has not decreased—is the goal. Think long term.

REFERENCES

Ailhaud, G., et al. "Growth and differentiation of regional adipose tissue: Molecular and hormonal mechanisms." *Int J Obesity* 2 (1991): 87.

Alford, B., et al. "The effects of variation in carbohydrates, protein and fat content of the diet upon weight loss, blood vessels, and nutrient intake of adult obese women." *J Am Diet Assoc* 90 (1991): 534.

Bailor, D., et al. "A meta-analysis of the factors affecting exercise-induced changes in body mass, fat mass, and fat-free mass in males and females." *Int J Obesity* 15 (1991): 717.

Bjorntorp, P. "Adipose tissue distribution and function." *Int J Obesity* 2 (1991): 67.

Brand-Miller, Jennie, Kaye Foster-Powell, Thomas Wolever, Stephen Colagiuri. *The New Glucose Revolution*. New York: Marlowe & Company, 1996.

Brown, J., et al. "Parity-related weight changes in women." *Int J Obesity* 16 (1992): 627.

Burgess, N., et al. "Effects of very low calorie diets on body composition and resting metabolic rates in obese men and women." *J Am Diet Assoc* 91 (1991): 430.

Campaigne, B. "Body fat distribution in females: Metabolic consequences and implications for weight loss." *Med Sci Sport Exer* 22 (1990): 291.

Coppack, S., et al. "Adipose tissue metabolism in obesity; lipase action in vivo before and after a mixed meal." *Journal of Metabolism, Clinical & Experimental* 41 (1992): 264.

Cramps, F., et al. "Lipolytic response of adicipocytes to epinephrine in sedentary and exercise-trained subjects: Sex related differences." *Eur Appl Physio* 59 (1989): 249.

DenBensten, C., et al. "Resting metabolic rate and diet induced thermogenisis in abdominal and gluteo-femoral obese women before and after weight reduction." *Am J Clin Nutr* 47 (1988): 840.

Despres, J., et al. "Loss of abdominal fat and metabolic response to exercise training in obese women." *Am J Clin Physio* 261 (1991): 159.

Doolittle, M., et al. "The response of lipoprotein lipase to feeding and fasting." *J Biol Chem* 15 (1990): 4570.

Drewnowski, A., et al. "Taste responses and food preferences in women: Effects of weight cycling." *Int J Obesity* 16 (1992): 639.

Eckel, R., et al. "Weight reduction increases adipose tissue lipoprotein lipase responsiveness in older women." *J Clin Invest* 80 (1987): 992.

Freedman, D., et al. "Body fat distribution and male/female differences in lipids and lipoproteins." *Circulation* 81 (1990): 1498.

Fried, S., et al. "Nutrition-induced variations in responsiveness to insulin effects on lipoprotein lipase activity in isolated fat cells." *J Clin Nutr* 120 (1990): 1087.

Garrow, J. "Is body fat distribution changed by dieting?" *Acta Med Scand* 723 (1988): 199.

Geissler, C., et al. "The daily metabolic rate of the post obese and the lean." *Am J Clin Nutr* 45 (1987): 914.

Hattori, K., et al. "Sex differences in the distribution of subcutaneous and internal fat." *Hum Biol* 63 (1991): 53.

Hirsch, J., et al. "The fat cell." *Med Clin North Am* 73 (1989): 83.

Hodgetts, V., et al. "Factors controlling fat mobilization from human subcutaneous adipose during exercise." *J Appl Physiol* 71 (1991): 445.

Jensen, M., et al. "Influence of body fat distribution of free fatty acid metabolism in obesity." *J Clin Invest* 83 (1989): 1168.

Kay, S., et al. "Associations of body mass and fat distribution with sex hormone concentrations in post-menopausal women." *Int J Epidemiol* 20 (1991): 151.

Kern, P., et al. "The effects of weight loss on the activity and expression of adipose tissue lipoprotein lipase in very obese subjects." *N Engl J Med* 12 (1990): 1053.

Lanska, D. "A prospective study on body fat distribution and weight loss." *Int J Obesity* 9 (1985): 241.

Leibel, R. "Physiological basis for the control of body fat distribution in humans." *Ann Rev Nutr* 9 (1989): 241.

Markham, B. "Anatomy and physiology of adipose tissue." *Clin Plast Surg* 16 (1989): 235.

Miller, W., et al. "Diet composition, energy intake, and exercise in relation to body fat mass in men and women." *Am J Clin Nutr* 52 (1990): 426.

Rebuffe-Scrive, M., et al. "Effect of testosterone on abdominal adipose tissue in men." *Int J Obesity* 15 (1991): 791.

Rodin, J., et al. "Weight cycling and fat distribution." *Int J Obesity* 14 (1990): 303.

Rosbell, M. R., et al. "Effect of hormones on glucose metabolism and lipolysis." *J Biol Chem* 239 (1984): 375.

Ryan, T., et al. "Genesis of adipocytes." *Clin Dermatol* 7 (1989): 9.

Strokosch, G., et al. "Lipoprotein lipase." *N Engl J Med* 15 (1990): 477.

Tremblay, A., et al. "Impact of dietary fat content and fat oxidation on energy intake in humans." *Am Clin J Nutr* 49 (1989): 799.

Vague, J. "Sexual differentiation of the adipose tissue-muscle ratio: Its metabolic consequences." *Bull Acad Natl Med* 173 (1989): 309.

Weststrate, J., et al. "Resting energy expenditure in women: The impact of obesity and body fat distribution." *Metabolism* 39 (1990): 11.

Yost, T., et al. "Regional similarities in the metabolic regulation of adipose tissue lipoprotein lipase." *Journal of Metabolism, Clinical & Experimental* 41 (1992): 33.

C H A P T E R

8 Biking to Run Fast Afterward

Nobody runs as fast in a triathlon as in an open race of the same duration, so a 10-kilometer run off the bike will never be as fast as an open 10K. As race duration increases, this difference grows. Elite triathletes, however, have closed this gap considerably. Most triathletes, in their first race, don't run anywhere near as fast as they would in an open race, but as they improve, this gap decreases.

Closing the gap between triathlon running speed and open-race running speed is a multifaceted process. Optimizing running technique and performing brick workouts are key, but riding the bike in a way that balances bike speed with enabling effective running afterward also plays a great role. Details about turning in your best bike split are beyond the scope of this book. See Lynda Wallenfels's book *The Triathlete's Guide to Bike Training* (VeloPress, 2004) for more information about that. This chapter will cover what to do on the bike to enable optimal running afterward.

BIKE POSITION FOR RUNNING OFF THE BIKE

Optimizing position on the bike is a critical aspect of improving triathlon performance. While a full discussion of the biomechanics and aerodynamics of bike position for improving your bike split is beyond the scope of this book, your position on the bike will also affect running performance.

Saddle height is the most critical adjustment. Riding with a saddle that is too low reduces leverage. Riding with a saddle that is too high reduces efficiency and may lead to extreme saddle discomfort and injuries. A knee angle between 25 and 30 degrees optimizes pedaling efficiency and power. To the rider, this angle will seem like the leg is almost, but not quite, straight.

The next step in arriving at optimal position is determining fore-aft position (how far forward or backward the saddle is set). A more forward position allows a low torso position while maintaining a relatively open torso-femur angle. This allows greater power production in an aerodynamic position and shifts work away from the running muscles. Many riders cannot pedal efficiently with a relatively low torso position on a bike with a traditional 73-degree seat tube. These athletes should either purchase a bike with a more aggressive geometry (steeper seat tube angle) or use a forward seatpost.

The two primary power producers in cycling are the quadriceps muscles (front thigh) and the gluteus maximus muscles (butt). The quadriceps muscles extend the knee, and the glutes extend the thigh. These two muscle groups produce maximum power during different phases of the pedal stroke. The ideal triathalon position produces a horizontal torso with a maximal overlap between the power phases of the quads and glutes.

Terrain of the priority races also plays a role in determining the best saddle fore-aft position. An aggressive forward position may allow for efficient power production in an aerodynamic position and minimal use of the running muscles, but triathletes will not climb as well using this position. On a flat course, this position is a good trade-off for aerodynamics and for a faster run split. On a hillier course, a more powerful but less aerodynamic position might be preferable: A more aft position is generally preferred for hilly courses.

Determining optimal torso angle is the most critical step in aero positioning. Lowering torso position toward the horizontal decreases drag, but this may also reduce pedaling economy and decrease power production dramatically. Lower torso positions also use the running muscles more, which can possibly lead to greater fatigue when coming off the bike.

Flexibility plays an important role in getting to the best torso angle. Riders with tight hamstring and/or low back muscles will not produce power effectively in low positions. Riders with tight hip muscles will not be able to maintain a pedaling position that stays in the correct plane. Their legs will bow outward, which affects both power production and aerodynamics—and run speed afterward.

PEDAL STROKE TO PREVENT HAMSTRING FATIGUE

Learning to pedal effectively without overusing the running muscles is another important aspect of triathlon cycling and running. The hamstring muscle group is a secondary power producer during cycling, but it is one of the primary propulsion producers during running. Learning to pedal the bicycle powerfully and efficiently while minimizing use of the hamstring muscles will enable you to run much faster in triathlons. If you get off the bike with fatigued quadriceps, fast running is still possible. If the hamstrings are tight and fatigued, your best run is impossible. Figure 8.1 illustrates the most commonly used pedal stroke, as well as an alternate technique that is more effective and preferred.

If you suffer from hamstring fatigue while you ride, or when you run off the bike, make the following adjustments to your technique. You will find that you ride faster, farther, and without hamstring pain.

Most of a cyclist's power should come from the gluteus maximus and quadriceps muscles during the downstroke. These muscles combine to extend the upper leg at the hip and the lower leg at the knee. Other accessory muscles should be involved, but should not fatigue greatly and certainly should never be a limiting factor in cycling performance.

The way the hamstring muscles attach creates one difficulty for cyclists. Since the hamstring crosses both the hip and the knee joints, it has two major functions: hip extension and knee flexion. During all 360 degrees of the pedal stroke, a cyclist undergoes either hip extension or knee flexion. The hamstring muscles potentially contract throughout the entire pedal stroke without a moment to recover. No wonder they fatigue for so many riders.

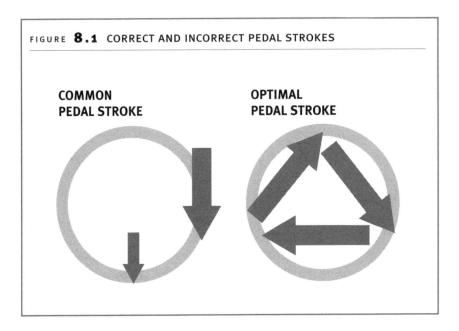

FIGURE **8.1** CORRECT AND INCORRECT PEDAL STROKES

**COMMON
PEDAL STROKE**

**OPTIMAL
PEDAL STROKE**

Each muscle involved in the pedal stroke must have periods of relaxation during which it recovers from the powerful contractions it has just been required to produce. The key is learning when in the pedal stroke the hamstrings are required to produce power in an efficient stroke and when they should be relaxed—and then learning to pedal that way all the time.

Remember these keys, as illustrated in Figure 8.1:

1. Try to feel that all your power is created in the top half of your pedal stroke.
2. Begin the downstroke early, pushing down diagonally from twelve o'clock toward four o'clock.
3. When the pedal reaches the three o'clock position, begin the backstroke. Try to pull your heel directly backward through the bottom bracket. This will not actually happen, but attempting to do this will develop the optimal stroke.
4. When the pedal reaches the seven o'clock position, pull upward and forward with the knee. Concentrate on using the hip flexor muscles, located in the front hip and upper thigh area, and relax the hamstrings.

A cyclist's pedal stroke can be broken down into three phases: the downstroke, the backstroke, and the upstroke. The hamstring muscles should contract powerfully through two phases and relax during the third.

Downstroke

Most of a cyclist's power is released during the downstroke. This phase of the pedal stroke, when performed properly, overlaps power output from hip extension (gluteus maximus and hamstrings) and knee extension (quadriceps). Misunderstanding how power should be applied during the downstroke causes many riders to lose this crucial overlap and overuse the hamstrings.

Many cyclists begin the downstroke late, at about two o'clock, and direct the power produced directly downward. This separates the optimal torque ranges of hip extension and knee extension and calls the hamstrings into play excessively. Since the quadriceps muscles are not activated properly, almost all the power must be produced by hip extension. To accomplish this, the hamstrings must create a very forceful contraction.

In an ideal downstroke, the power application begins early, at twelve o'clock, and is directed downward diagonally toward four o'clock. This activates the quadriceps optimally and lengthens the overlap between the peak torque-production of knee extension and hip extension. The quadriceps and gluteus maximus are the primary power producers, and the hamstrings contract moderately.

Backstroke

The backstroke is the one area of the pedal stroke in which the hamstring muscles should be very active, because only knee flexion provides power in this range. Hamstring relaxation during other ranges of the pedal stroke (during upstroke) prevents fatigue and enables powerful backstroke contractions without overusing the hamstrings.

Creating power effectively during the backstroke is key to climbing efficiency. When the pedals are in the twelve o'clock and six o'clock positions, neither leg is engaged in a downstroke. During this period, creating just a little bit of power allows a rider to conserve momentum and get through to the next downstroke with minimal speed loss. On the flats, due to the higher speeds and greater momentum from rider and bike weight, a rider can more effectively coast through dead spots in the pedal stroke.

A primary weakness of many riders is extending the downstroke too long and starting the backstroke late. This prevents the rider from unloading before bottom-dead-center and causes wasted energy pushing downward when the crankarm is moving directly backward.

Upstroke

Most cyclists create negative power during the upstroke by actually pushing down on the pedal and negating some of the power of the opposite leg's downstroke. During steady-state riding, efficient riders lift the weight of their foot, leg, and shoe off the pedal during the upstroke. This allows 100 percent of the power generated by the opposite leg's downstroke to be propulsive. We call this "unloading." This aspect of pedaling is critical. Unloading on the upstroke is one significant difference between elite and intermediate riders. Without correct unloading, the right and left legs actually fight each other.

The movements of the upstroke are hip flexion (lifting the knee) and knee flexion (lifting the foot). Since the hip flexors are active only in this range of the pedal stroke, and the hamstrings are active during each of the other phases, the hip flexor should be the primary muscle contracting during this phase. Efficient riders, especially since they have to get off their bikes and run efficiently, relax the hamstrings during this phase.

Attempting to pull up on the pedal through this phase places too much concentration on knee flexion and prevents hamstring relaxation. Lift the weight off the pedal and avoid creating negative power, but do not attempt to create power by actually pulling up on the pedal.

The hip flexors, once trained, are extremely fatigue resistant and are only active for about 25 percent of the pedal stroke. Obviously they can contract fairly powerfully with a 1:3 work-to-rest ratio.

There are two keys to taking advantage of the fresh hip flexor muscles and resting tired hamstring muscles. The first is keeping your concentration on lifting the knee and not the heel or the foot. If cyclists lift their knees powerfully, their feet and pedals will follow without contractions to bend the knee. The second key is thinking of the upstroke as a diagonally upward and slightly forward movement—instead of an upward and backward movement. Again, this places the emphasis on the hip flexor muscles, which should be contracting, instead of the hamstrings, which should be relaxing. When your pedal reaches the seven o'clock position, drive your knee diagonally upward, directly toward the handlebar.

Learn to use the hamstrings during the pedal-stroke phases in which they effectively deliver power and to relax them during the others. You will definitely run faster off the bike.

CADENCE

When you pedal a bicycle, your muscular system produces power to propel it, and your cardiovascular system delivers oxygen to the body, fuels your muscles, and removes waste products such as lactic acid from your body. Selecting your optimal cadence is a matter of keeping these two systems in balance. The optimal balance is different for each person.

Spinning (pedaling) at higher cadences reduces your watts-per-pedal stroke, a measure of the force required to produce a given wattage. This makes the workload more tolerable for the muscles. Most experts believe this is because fewer fast-twitch muscle fibers must be recruited to create the high torque levels required at low cadence. Pedaling with a too-low cadence increases reliance on fast-twitch fibers, which causes premature lactic acid accumulation and makes your legs burn.

Pedaling with high cadence, however, does waste some energy. Imagine setting your bike up on an indoor trainer and cutting off the chain. If you spun at 100 rpm, the workload would be zero watts, yet your heart rate would elevate significantly above resting. Just moving your legs fast does use energy. Research has consistently demonstrated that cycling at 40 to 60 rpm generates the lowest oxygen consumption for a given wattage. Pedaling at too high a cadence overloads the cardiovascular system's ability to deliver oxygen to the muscles. The most obvious symptom of this is ventilatory distress.

High-cadence pedaling works your cardiovascular system more, but it reduces the relative intensity of work for the leg muscles. The key, then, is pedaling with enough cadence to keep your watts-per-pedal stroke at a level your muscles can handle, but at a cadence that will not overload your cardiovascular system. The optimal balance is different for every rider.

Lance Armstrong has an extraordinary cardiovascular capacity. His heart and lungs can deliver enormous quantities of oxygen to his muscles. Yet Armstrong does not possess huge, muscular thighs. His muscles are much more likely to be overloaded by high watts-per-pedal stroke than his cardiovascular system is by the oxygen demand of the workload. Therefore, high-cadence pedaling, even at a slightly higher energy cost, is most effective for him. Jan Ullrich, on the other hand, is not gifted with the cardiovascular capacity of Armstrong, but he has much greater muscle mass in the hips and thighs. His legs are able to withstand high watts-per-pedal stroke, so he correctly minimizes the "wasted" energy to prevent cardiovascular limitation. Both Armstrong and Ullrich pedal using the cadence that is most effective for their unique physiologies.

Each cyclist brings a unique set of genetics and training to the sport. The basic rules are, if your legs hurt more than your lungs, increase cadence. If your lungs hurt more than your legs, use a lower cadence.

If you decide that higher-cadence pedaling might be more effective for you, now is the time to accustom your body to its different demands. Until you have learned the skills to pedal at very high cadence for long periods of time, you will be less efficient. Begin to develop leg speed now, and your new cadence will be smooth and natural by next year's race season.

Each athlete must experiment to find the cadence that works best. As you experiment, keep the following factors in mind:

> **Plan to train at different cadences:** Riding at a certain wattage at 100 rpm and the same wattage at 75 rpm produces different benefits. Specific, targeted training at higher and lower than your race cadence will pay big dividends. Even high-cadence cyclists need to do some low-cadence training to develop torque.

> **Train like you race:** While this may sound contradictory to the last statement, it isn't. Specifically targeting a particular system with overcadence or overtorque workouts is an excellent approach, but much of your riding should still be performed at close to race cadence. Athletes training efficiently perform 70 to 90 percent of their training significantly below the wattages they will be required to produce in competition.

Many get lazy on their long, slow rides and pedal at a lower cadence. The reduced cadence may, in fact, be more efficient at the greatly reduced wattage. Remember, though, that the purpose of these workouts is not to be efficient during the workout, but to make you more efficient at race intensity. Disciplining yourself to maintain race cadence even when riding slowly is critical.

Give high cadence time: If you decide that a higher race cadence might work for you, understand that it may take months for your legs to develop the skills to create wattage efficiently at the new cadence. Cardiovascular conditioning also takes time to develop, so start well before the season and be patient.

Try weight training: If you find you lack the super cardiovascular power to ride efficiently at high cadence, weight training can help you develop tolerance to lower-cadence, higher watts-per-pedal stroke riding. In fact, weight training has been shown to increase cycling efficiency for almost every rider at every cadence. More information on weight training is available in Chapter 11.

Most likely beneficiaries of high cadence: Those most likely to benefit from increasing cadence are those whose cardiovascular capacity exceeds their muscle power, such as women, small or thin riders, former runners, and masters riders. These athletes should work to develop a higher cadence style, but they should still incorporate specific high-force workouts to increase their ability to create torque. Analyze whether force and burning legs or ventilatory distress is most likely to limit you when riding hard for extended durations. If your legs limit performance, higher cadence may improve your results once you have adapted. Decide for yourself what style is likely to work, plan a program that will prepare you before your important races, and get started.

Most triathletes, even if they can ride faster with moderately low cadence, will run significantly faster off the bike after racing with high cadence. Developing the neuromuscular efficiency to pedal effectively at high cadence may take time, so be patient with it.

Make the effort to refine your bike position and pedal stroke, and work to develop the cadence that will give you the best opportunity to run to your potential after the bike on race day. Halfway through the run, you'll be glad you did.

R E F E R E N C E S

Gottschall, Jinger S. and Bradley M. Palmer. "The acute effects of prior cycling cadence on running performance and kinematics." *Med Sci Sport Exer* 54 (2002): 1518-22.

C H A P T E R

9 Event-Specific Issues

aces of different durations require different preparation. The key to adapting your training schedule to different race distances throughout the year is determining what your specific limiters will be for each A race and prioritizing accordingly. The timing of races is critical as well. As you plan your season, be sure to space out your races to be sure you have time to work on increasing speed for shorter-distance races or building endurance for longer races. Interspersing races randomly makes specific training for any event difficult. If everything is a priority, nothing is a priority.

SPRINT DISTANCE

Sprint-distance racing puts a premium on speed. The special challenge of sprint-distance training is that it demands that the athlete blend workouts from a number of different intensities.

A sprint-distance race is still an endurance event. The slow-twitch muscle fibers produce most of the energy for an event of this duration, and endurance training maximizes the power and speed these fibers can produce. Even though the duration is much shorter and the speed much higher than other distances, the duration of a sprint race is great enough that energy production is still over 95 percent aerobic. Sprint-distance triathletes still need to emphasize endurance training.

Lactate threshold training is key for events lasting from 30 minutes to five hours. Sprint-distance races obviously fall in that range for everyone. The FOG muscle fibers produce a significant amount of energy during a sprint-distance race and need to be trained to produce maximal power and to endure for the full duration of the event without fatigue.

Aerobic capacity training increases the aerobic capabilities of the fast-twitch muscle fibers. At sprint-distance speeds, every muscle fiber type contributes significantly and must be prepared. Aerobic capacity training, which increases the endurance of the sprint fibers, should be emphasized more heavily at sprint distance than for any other race.

Since most serious athletes will race at intensities that exceed lactate threshold, lactate tolerance (the muscles' ability to produce power and speed effectively despite acid accumulation) becomes a critical aspect of training. As described in previous chapters, waiting to train lactate tolerance until the last four to six weeks before a priority sprint-distance race is critical (it is a capacity quickly developed and quickly lost).

Proper pacing in a sprint race means pushing for the entire race duration. Experienced athletes will race at a level significantly over lactate threshold at an intensity at which lactic acid accumulates, but accumulates slowly so that it does not cause fatigue until the finish line. Even as you push the pace, concentrate on being smooth and efficient. Keep cadence on the bike and turnover on the run very high.

Race-pace workouts should have given you a clear idea of how hard you can push. Even though these workouts never approached race duration, almost every athlete can push longer in race conditions (although not necessarily faster).

Be sure to fuel and hydrate yourself. At the high intensity of sprint races, this can be a challenge. It seems less important to most athletes in short races, but you will not race your best if you neglect these details.

INTERNATIONAL DISTANCE

International distance is the most popular triathlon format. This distance puts the premium on speed endurance. Like sprint-distance racers, international-distance racers benefit heavily from endurance training.

Intermediate triathletes will compete at very close to lactate threshold intensity. Advanced and elite triathletes will sustain effort levels at slightly above lactate threshold, so this distance places a premium on lactate threshold training. For every athlete, increasing speed at lactate threshold in all three race segments is the primary goal of training. International-distance athletes will spend a higher percentage of training time in Zone 4 than those of any other race distance.

Aerobic capacity training will be an important component of race preparation for this distance—once an athlete is no longer endurance limited. For intermediates, LT workouts should be prioritized, but aerobic capacity workouts will have an important place in the Build period. For advanced and elite competitors, these are key workouts of primary importance during the Build.

Whether lactate tolerance becomes a priority at this distance varies dramatically depending on the level of the athlete. Beginner and intermediate triathletes will not race much of a race of this duration above lactate threshold, so lactate tolerance training will have a far greater recovery cost than it is worth. Performing lactate tolerance workouts costs enormously in terms of recovery time before future workouts. High-level amateurs and professionals will spend almost the entire race at intensity exceeding lactate threshold, so this type of training will become a primary priority during the Peak phase of training, while other aspects are put on maintenance.

Pacing

Pacing during an international-distance race varies for athletes of different levels. Most athletes will settle in at or slightly below lactate threshold for the duration. Advanced and elite athletes will slightly exceed lactate threshold, with pacing similar to a sprint race.

Ease into your bike pace gradually. Give your body a few minutes to redistribute blood to the legs after the swim. After about five minutes, settle into your pace and hold it for the duration. Some athletes back off just slightly for the final several minutes of the ride. Whether you back off or not, avoid the temptation to speed up because you sense the finish line. The transition area is not the finish line; you still have to run.

HALF-IRONMAN DISTANCE

The half-ironman triathlon presents unique challenges. This distance is short enough that a well-conditioned athlete pushes the pace throughout the race, but long enough to demand disciplined pacing and effective nutrition strategies. Preparing for a half-ironman requires balancing long workouts designed to improve endurance with higher-intensity workouts designed to increase the pace which can be maintained for the race duration. Half-ironman racing also requires plans for effective fueling, hydrating, and pacing.

Workouts

The two key workouts for a half-ironman triathlon are both brick workouts (bike followed by run). The first is a long brick workout at an easy pace. The second is a race-pace brick workout.

A half-ironman is a relatively long race. The endurance to hold up for race duration is always the triathlete's most important ability. A brick workout at a basic endurance pace, gradually increasing in duration, is key for building that endurance.

Begin with a one- to two-hour ride followed by a 30-minute to one-hour run. Experienced athletes who have already developed a solid endurance base can start at the high end of the range. Gradually build the duration of these workouts until a three- to four-hour ride followed by a one- to two-hour run is comfortable. These workouts should be completed at a basic endurance pace, Zone 2. Both the ride and the run should take place on flat to gently rolling terrain so that intensity can be kept under control. This workout is the priority during the Base period.

After establishing a solid endurance base, a race-pace brick becomes the priority workout. This workout increases cycling and should be performed at speeds that can be maintained for the half-ironman distances. During your Build phase, perform one of these workouts each week.

Workout intensity is based on each athlete's ability. Beginner and intermediate triathletes should be more concerned about developing the endurance to finish a half-ironman than about speed. Advanced and elite triathletes are not worried about being able to finish, but they are concerned with the pace they can maintain for the duration.

Begin with a ride of about one hour at endurance pace. After the hour is up, increase speed and attempt to maintain an intensity that can be sustained for the duration of the half-ironman race. For beginning athletes, this will be at endurance pace or just slightly faster. For intermediates, this will be somewhat faster than endurance pace and will probably fall in the upper half of heart rate Zone 3. Advanced athletes will maintain a subthreshold pace, approximately five to eight heartbeats per minute below lactate threshold, in the lower half of heart rate Zone 4. Increase this workout conservatively, and monitor recovery closely. This workout can bring quick improvements, but it can also lead quickly to overtraining.

Do this workout on terrain similar to that of the race course. Keep intensity steady and maintain relatively high cadence. Eat and drink exactly according to your race plan. Maintain the intensity that you could realistically hold for race duration. Harder is not better.

Begin running as soon after the ride as possible. For the first segment of the run, hold the pace that feels sustainable for race distance. Continue to eat and drink as you will during the race. After completing the race-pace segment, finish the workout with at least 20 minutes of easy running.

Begin using 30- to 45-minute race-pace segments on the bike and 20- to 30-minute race-pace segments on the run. Increase duration of the race-pace segments consistently, but gradually. These workouts develop efficiency at race intensity and allow you to practice the skills of pacing, hydrating, and fueling.

Race-pace workouts should never approach race duration. Even advanced athletes should build up to no more than 50 percent of race duration at race pace. Full efforts should be saved for race day. The time required for recovery from huge efforts, such as 75 percent of half-ironman distance at race pace, is not worth the benefit. Save those full efforts for race day and concentrate on consistent and efficient training until then.

Pacing

Very few athletes finish a half-ironman thinking that they didn't go hard enough early in the race. Consistent pacing is necessary to perform to your potential. Pace conservatively, especially during the first half of the bike and the first half of the run. A half-ironman is not nearly as intimidating as an ironman, but it is still a long race. A triathlete who rides two minutes too slowly during the first half of the bike has ample opportunity to gain back most of that time. A triathlete who rides two minutes too fast will lose much more than two minutes on the run because of the overly aggressive early pace.

Race-pace workouts will teach you the intensity that can be sustained on race day. Even though workouts don't approach race duration, the addition of a full taper, plus the excitement of the race atmosphere, usually allows a pace to be sustained longer. The effort that enabled effective running after the bike during workouts should do the same in the race.

Intensity should be steady throughout the race, but perceived exertion will gradually increase. The correct pace will feel easy early in the race. The same speed feels quite different at mile 10 of the bike than it does at mile 50. Performing to your potential is never easy, even on the best days.

IRONMAN DISTANCE

The ironman distance, for athletes of all levels, is a true test of endurance. Nobody races an ironman fast. The paces sustained by the winners of ironman races are, for those athletes, very slow. Ironman racing, even at the highest levels, is about training the body to keep going without falling apart. This is true to a much greater degree than even the most serious athlete usually realizes.

Most triathletes watch Ryan Bolton run his ironman races at mind-boggling paces and think he has trained his body so hard that he can push hard for the entire duration of the race without fatiguing. In fact, Bolton races significantly below his aerobic threshold. Even for Bolton, ironman racing is about the endurance to not fall apart, not about pushing. The paces he sustains in an ironman, even though they sound very fast to most of us, are slow and steady for him.

So, the first priority in ironman training is developing the endurance to continue sustaining a pace slightly slower than aerobic threshold for race duration. Second priority is increasing your speed at aerobic threshold.

Almost every ironman-distance triathlete performs almost all training faster than race pace. This is an enormous mistake. Higher-intensity training does have a place in ironman training, but the great majority of workout hours should be steady swimming, cycling, and running at or even below race intensity. The higher-intensity workouts demand recovery time that ironman distance athletes should spend very conservatively.

Training for ironman-distance racing, even more so than for shorter distances, is about prioritizing breakthrough workouts. Two or three key workouts per week really prepare an ironman athlete to go the distance. Other workouts either build these breakthrough workouts up or tear them down. Make sure that yours build them up.

Prioritize bike training for ironman racing. Becoming stronger and more efficient on the bike is the key to effective ironman racing. First, the bike is the longest segment of an ironman. Getting 2 percent faster here will cut more off your race time than getting 2 percent faster at the swim or run. Getting stronger on the bike will also improve your run split. Running is a costly and high-risk training mode; cycling is not. Increasing running volume beyond a certain point dramatically increases the risk of overtraining and injury. That is not true to the same degree with bike training. While a full discussion of ironman bike training is beyond the scope of this book, see *The Triathlete's Guide to Bike Training* by Lynda Wallenfels (VeloPress, 2004) for more information.

Fat: An Ironman's Friend

An athlete's body constantly burns some combination of fat, carbohydrate, and protein for fuel. At any intensity, protein is a relatively insignificant source, generally accounting for between 1 and 4 percent of energy expenditure. The percentages of fat and carbohydrate burned vary dramatically based on a number of factors. Training the body to use fat as a significant fuel source is an important goal for any athlete who competes in events lasting 30 minutes or more, but it is vital for ironman racing.

An athlete's body generally stores about 1,500 to 2,000 calories of carbohydrate, enough for about two hours of hard running or cycling. During the race we will consume as much carbohydrate as our systems can digest and absorb, but this is generally about one third of our energy expenditure. An ironman athlete continually works at a carbohydrate deficit. We can never digest as much carbohydrate as we burn. We start with a cushion—our carbohydrate storage—and hopefully work at a small enough deficit that we cut into that cushion gradually without running out of carbohydrate before the finish.

One hundred twelve miles is a long way to bike, and 26.2 miles is a long way to run. When you get fast enough to do a two-hour ironman, you can race on carbohydrate. Until then, you need to train your body to burn as much fat as possible so that it burns less carbohydrate. Getting the intensity right is the key. Low-intensity exercise burns a relatively even mix of fat and carbohydrate. Since burning fat requires more oxygen than burning carbohydrate, fat burning decreases and carbohydrate burning increases as intensity rises. The optimal intensity for fat burning can be most precisely gauged using a metabolic analyzer—the machine used for VO_2max testing. Usually optimal fat-burning intensity is in the middle of Zone 2.

Most ironman athletes do much of their training at too high an intensity to maximize fat burning. Everyone intuitively understands how important pacing is in an ironman race, but pacing yourself in training is just as critical. Remember that correct intensity in workouts is not about making it through the workout, but about stimulating specific metabolic adaptations. Go too hard, even in high Zone 2, during long workouts, and you train your body to efficiently burn a lot of carbohydrate, which is not a good thing for an ironman athlete. Staying at a realistic ironman race pace for the bulk of your training hours trains the body to produce the necessary power by burning a lot of fat—which will not run out before the finish line—and a moderate amount of carbohydrate.

Pacing

Pacing is absolutely critical in an ironman race. The challenges are twofold: The price paid for going out too hard is enormous, and a too-fast pace still feels relatively easy. Running out of fuel is the main danger in an ironman. We can't feel when our bodies shift from burning fat and carbohydrate to burning mostly carbohydrate. Regardless of fitness, an athlete who has depleted carbohydrate will fall apart. A Porsche that has run out of gas isn't any faster than a school bus that has run out of gas.

Going hard in the swim is a huge mistake. Many triathletes push the swim hard since they won't use their shoulders hard on the bike or run, but their legs will pay the price too. Increasing workout intensity triggers hormonal changes that decrease fat burning and increase carbohydrate burning. Those hormones don't just vaporize instantly when you strap on your bike shoes and helmet. Hard swimming causes triathletes to burn more carbohydrate on the bike and run. This effect lasts hours. Swim steady and easy, just like you will bike and run.

On the bike, be very careful. The first hour is most critical. Keep intensity steady and light. Begin fueling and hydrating immediately. Be patient. I never once had an athlete finish the last 10K of the run strongly and say, "If only I had pushed harder on the first half of the bike." An ironman-distance triathlete will almost never regret being too conservative. Remember how easy ironman goal pace for running is. You never need to go fast. You need to avoid falling apart.

Once you begin the run, begin fueling within five minutes. Most ironman-distance triathletes should stop consuming protein on the run and concentrate on water and carbohydrate, with some salt. Remember that sports nutrition products are not magic. I've pulled athletes off gel and substituted jelly beans with great success.

Keep turnover high even at very slow paces. Walk through aid stations to ease hydrating and fueling. Keep walk breaks short, but include them early. Walk one twenty-sixth of your total walking every mile. Don't wait until you *have* to walk to start walking.

FUELING AND HYDRATING
Before the Race
Race-day fueling begins hours before the race, at breakfast. The goal is to provide the body with adequate fuel without overloading the digestive system. Practicing this before workouts is critical. We can provide guidelines, but every athlete is different, and finding the unique combination of foods that will work best for you is a trial-and-error process. Consume 400 to 800 calories about three hours before a half-ironman. Try to consume 1 gram of protein for every 3 to 4 grams of carbohydrate.

Consuming water and carbohydrate immediately before the race can benefit you as well. Obviously fueling and hydrating during the swim are impractical, but food and water consumed directly before the swim starts can be delivered to the working muscles during the swim. We recommend consuming 100 to 300 calories of carbohydrate and 8 to 12 ounces of water immediately before the start. Make sure to consume this last feeding as soon before the start as possible. This prevents an insulin response, which could leave your blood sugar low at the race start.

During the Race

Even at sprint and international distances, fueling and hydrating during the race are necessary to run to your potential off the bike. Race duration is long enough to produce significant dehydration. Drink 20 ounces of water per 150 pounds of bodyweight per hour on the bike and run. Even though complete bonking is unlikely, consuming carbohydrate is a requirement for running well. Consume one to two calories of carbohydrate per pound of bodyweight per hour on the bike and run.

Even though fueling is recommended, for sprint- and international-distance triathlons, most of the energy to be expended is already stored in the body at the start. While fueling and hydrating during those races can be important, they become even more important at the half-ironman distance, when much of the required fuel must be consumed during the race. Complete bonking is a very real possibility, and slowing on the run because of glycogen depletion is very likely.

On the course, hydration is a top priority. A half-ironman triathlete should consume 20 ounces of water per 150 pounds of bodyweight per hour. Take this very seriously. Follow a plan and do not rely on thirst. Drink water or sports drink approximately every 15 minutes. The excitement of the race atmosphere can work against you in this area. Some athletes find it effective to set a watch to beep every few minutes to remind them to fuel and hydrate. Do not listen to the advice "drink as much as you can." With the moderate intensity and duration of a half-ironman, overhydrating is a possibility.

During a half-ironman, a triathlete should consume as much carbohydrate as can be digested and absorbed. For most athletes who have practiced fueling strategies during training, this amounts to about two calories of carbohydrate per pound of bodyweight per hour (300 calories per hour for a 150-pound athlete). Each athlete is different, so experiment with this during workouts to find out how much your digestive system can handle. Find how much carbohydrate you can digest without it sitting in your stomach.

Fueling and hydrating during an ironman race is everything. While maintaining adequate muscle glycogen and blood sugar level during a half-ironman is necessary to allow you to run to your limit, a well-conditioned athlete will generally still be limited by lactic acid accumulating in the muscles. At the ironman distance, running out of fuel is generally the primary limiter on the run.

As at every race distance, consuming about two calories of carbohydrate per hour per pound of bodyweight is critical. Make sure to keep carbohydrates in your stomach throughout the race. You start the race with a cushion of carbohydrate stored in your muscles and liver, but you will burn it at a higher rate than your stomach could possibly digest and absorb. So you will be cutting into that cushion throughout the race. Make sure your digestive system is putting carbohydrate into your blood constantly so that you cut into that cushion as gradually as possible. Running out of carbohydrate is the primary limiter in an ironman-distance race.

After water and carbohydrate, consuming sodium is the next priority. An ironman-distance athlete should consume 1 gram of salt, or 600 mg sodium, per 150 pounds of bodyweight per hour. Remember to add up all sources of sodium—including sports drinks, bars, and any other food consumed in addition to supplemental sodium. Subtract the sodium you will eat and drink before calculating supplemental sodium requirements.

Ironman-distance athletes should consume protein during ironman races. The body burns a very small percentage of its energy from protein, but over eight to 17 hours it can add up. If an athlete does not consume adequate protein over the course of an ironman, the muscles will literally eat themselves. Relatively small amounts of protein need to be consumed. I generally recommend 1 gram of protein per 15 pounds of bodyweight per hour for the first 80 miles of the bike. On the last few miles of the bike, reduce protein intake. Because of the vertical movements of running, you won't want protein collected in your gut. Out on the run, most triathletes will consume carbohydrate without protein.

The most important factor in choosing sports nutrition products for ironman-distance triathletes is palatability. The most scientifically advanced sports drink never helps triathletes if it remains only in their water bottles. Only those products that get consumed work. Choose products that taste good to you. Also, you don't have to use sports nutrition products. An ironman triathlete needs water, carbohydrate, salt, and protein. Any combination of drinks, gels, peanut butter and jelly sandwiches, cookies, sports bars, potato chips, pretzels, or any other food that provides the right amount of these nutrients can work for you.

I remember years ago seeing an ad in a well-known triathlon magazine for a well-known sports nutrition company featuring a champion triathlete. The ad pictured her bike with the sports nutrition company's logo all over it, but on closer inspection, a pouch on the bike contained two candy bars. Certainly the sports nutrition products helped her win races, but the candy bars provided needed fuel and were more likely to be palatable during tough stretches of the race when she needed fuel but didn't feel like eating.

Post-Race Nutrition

Immediately after the race, providing the body with the nutrients required to refuel and rebuild damaged tissue is critical to minimize recovery time. Make sure to consume at least 400 calories of carbohydrate and 100 calories of protein soon after the race. Several excellent products designed to be used immediately post-workout are on the market, but a meal works just as well. Post-workout nutrition is critical, but it does not have to be rocket science. A profound quote from Sam Callan, exercise physiologist and science and education manager for U.S.A. Cycling, is: "Eat a meal."

10 Refining Mental Skills

Mental skills are the most neglected aspect of racing for serious cyclists at all levels.

—Joe Friel

Genetics plays a huge role in sports. The greatest thing an athlete needs to do to win an Olympic gold medal in triathlon is select the right parents. Unfortunately, that is one thing over which we have no control. Preparing to perform our best in a triathlon means maximizing every factor over which we do have control.

Renowned sports psychologist Bruce Gottleib opened a presentation he made to coaches recently by asking how they prepared their athletes to pack for an important race. The coaches mentioned how important it was to pack a variety of clothes for changing weather, as well as bringing nutrition, race number, bike helmet, wet suit, shoes, water bottles, lubricants, and a vast array of other equipment. Gottleib then asked, "Who has instructed their clients to pack mental skills?" Dead silence ensued.

While most coaches understand that performing to our potential is as much a mental task as a physical task, only the top coaches understand that preparing for the performance is as much mental preparation as physical.

We all know that psychology plays a role on race day, but few athletes realize how great a role psychology plays in the 365 days of preparation. Train at 95 percent for a few key workouts, and you will not race to your potential regardless of how tough you are mentally on race day.

I recently had a conversation with one of my clients about incorporating more mental training into his race preparation. This athlete has a VO_2max of just over 80 ml/kg/min and has placed in the top three as a professional in the World Championships. He agreed to go along with whatever I suggested, but I sensed reluctance from an athlete that usually robustly attacks every task in front of him. I asked, "Do we have you do hill repeats in training because your legs are weak? Of course not. You have some of the strongest legs in the sport, but we train them to be even stronger. In the same way, you have a strong mind, but we want to make it even stronger by training it."

Triathletes invest enormously in preparing for our events. So many triathletes would never go to a race without the latest sports nutrition products, the fastest race wheels that money can buy, the lightest training flats, and thousands upon thousands of miles in their legs, but so many overlook the benefits that could be derived from a relatively small investment in training their minds.

IMPROVING PERFORMANCE THROUGH EFFECTIVE SELF-TALK

An athlete's thought habits play an enormous role in every aspect of training and racing. Thought habits affect the discipline we bring to our workouts and our lifestyle, our level of motivation, our confidence for workouts and races, how we approach workouts and races, and how well we focus on the specific task at hand. In short, every aspect of mental skills is greatly affected by our thought habits.

Improving self-talk habits may go a long way toward developing effective thought habits, which will dramatically influence race preparation and results. This is a powerful tool, not just for athletes with a "problem" but for everyone. Just as each athlete has physical and technical limiters that we need to focus on, even the best have psychological limiters as well. In the same way that a physical limiter is not necessarily a weakness—Lance Armstrong's limiters for the Tour de France are sustained climbing and time trialing, at which he excels—

athletes may improve performance by improving self-talk skills, even if they don't present any symptoms of psychological weakness.

The basic idea of self-talk is that every thought that crosses our minds makes an imprint on our brains, somewhat analogous to a computer program. Our culture, and to a degree our sport, constantly bombards athletes with negative messages. Research clearly shows that any message perceived by the brain, whether believed or not, affects our beliefs and attitudes. Beliefs and attitudes, of course, affect behaviors—in this context, our training and racing.

Napoleon Hill, author of the classic *Think and Grow Rich* (1937) says, "The impulse of thought which is repeatedly passed on to the subconscious mind is, finally, accepted and acted upon by the subconscious mind, which proceeds to translate that impulse into its physical equivalent."

Athletes have no control over the negativity they are bombarded with from the outside. However, research estimates that about 95 percent of the thoughts that run through our minds are internally generated, and we have complete control over those. If Viktor Frankl could learn to control his thoughts despite the physical and emotional abuse he received in a Nazi death camp, certainly athletes can control their thoughts despite negativity in their environments. Control of these thoughts enables athletes to develop specific attitudes and beliefs that their minds will then turn into reality.

The great human freedom is control over our thoughts. Animals function by the laws of stimulus and response. Humans have the ability to exercise control over our reactions to any environmental condition, thus controlling our thoughts. In training and racing, as well as success in other areas of life, successful people tend to do a better job of exercising this potential control.

Learn to catch yourself making self-deprecating statements. Even if intended humorously or as analysis, these statements affect attitudes and beliefs, which in turn affect behaviors—including behaviors that directly affect race preparation. Learn to reword these statements and constantly remind yourself that you perform certain skills well and that you are working diligently to improve weak areas.

Listen to your thoughts and, when you find negativity, counterprogram with positive thoughts. This may seem silly, but research demonstrates that it is powerful and will affect performance. My experience agrees with the research. The following sidebar lists some examples of negative thoughts redirected in more positive ways.

Effectively managing your thoughts, attitudes, and beliefs is just as important to your racing as improving your muscular endurance. There are many ways to use self-talk to improve a weakness, train more consistently and with more discipline, get down to race weight, and react quickly and appropriately during workouts and races.

MANIPULATING PSYCHOLOGICAL MODE FOR OPTIMAL TRAINING AND RACING

The difference between a warrior and an ordinary person is that a warrior sees everything as a challenge while an ordinary man sees everything as either a blessing or a curse.

—Don Juan

Sometimes high-intensity workouts and races are a complete thrill; other times they become drudgery. Every athlete has had workouts and races during which producing and sustaining super-high speed and heart rate was so challenging and exciting that the pain and effort almost went unnoticed. We were aware that we were hurting badly, but somehow everything was OK. Other times, eight

---

POSITIVE AND NEGATIVE STATEMENTS

Negative: I can't climb.

Positive: I am an excellent rider, and my climbing gets better every week.

Negative: I ride fast, but my run sucks.

Positive: I am a strong and efficient cyclist, and I am working hard on my running efficiency.

Negative: I'm just not meant to be a runner.

Positive: My swimming and cycling are well developed, and my run is continually improving.

two-minute hill repeats seem like incredible drudgery. Producing the necessary output and elevating heart rate seems impossible, and the pain becomes unbearable. Often the difference between these two experiences is the psychological mode from which we begin the workout or race. Few athletes understand what a powerful force this can be in training and racing. Even fewer realize that psychological mode is something that can and should be manipulated or know how to use the tools they have to do so effectively.

Sports psychologists understand that each athlete has an optimal level of arousal for performance. If arousal is too low, the athlete is undermotivated and won't perform maximally. If arousal is too high, the athlete will suffer from some degree of anxiety, which impairs performance. While athletes can learn to moderate arousal, the very best performances come during states of high arousal. Shifting to the appropriate psychological mode can raise your natural optimal arousal level. Instead of toning down your arousal, approach the event from a mindset that produces your best during conditions of high arousal.

Based on M. J. Apter's reversal theory (published in the *Journal of Personality* in 1984), these techniques enable an athlete to perform optimally at high levels of arousal. Instead of gearing down psychologically so they won't be overaroused, athletes can activate a different part of their psyche, which thrives on higher arousal, and maximize their performance. Racing is inherently a high-arousal activity—physically, mentally, and emotionally. The passion that can be an athlete's undoing can just as easily be what makes her great.

The Psychological Modes

At any given moment, athletes tend to be in one of two basic psychological modes. Recognizing and controlling these modes is a critical aspect of performing to potential. Each athlete can learn to switch to the appropriate psychological mode before each workout and race.

The first psychological mode is the achievement mode. Racing and very hard workouts tend to naturally activate this mode, even though it is less productive at these times. While in the achievement mode, athletes want to succeed—to climb faster, to pass their rivals, to win the race, to set a new personal record, or some other specific accomplishment. Unfortunately, this is not the ideal mode for racing or for hard workouts. When in the achievement mode, athletes find that high arousal produces anxiety and low arousal produces feelings of peace. Of course, racing and hard workouts are extremely high-arousal situations, both physically and psychologically. Maintaining high physical and emotional intensity while in this mode triggers frustration and increased perceptions of both exertion and pain, even while the athlete is performing well.

As an exercise physiologist and coach, I realize the importance of structure in training, goal setting, and in using numbers to control an athlete's training. I also realize that these numbers can take on a larger-than-life role in the athlete's mind and become more detrimental than beneficial. I remember one road cyclist I coached who set a 45-second personal record in a 40-kilometer time trial, but was infuriated because he could not hold the heart rate he had hoped to. Annual training plans, heart rate zones, periodization, and all the structured, goal-oriented, number-oriented tools—which are useful for preparing an athlete for peak performance—are intrinsically related to the achievement mode. These things have their time and place, but on race day the preparation is done, and it is time to shift modes and race.

The second psychological mode is the hedonic (pleasure-seeking) mode. When in this mode, athletes find high arousal to be extremely challenging, exciting, and thrilling, while they find low arousal to be boring. This is the ideal state of mind for racing and high-intensity training, but it is not an attitude that comes naturally at these times. The pressure of performing well tends to shift serious athletes into the achievement mode at the times they most need the benefits of the pleasure-seeking mode. While we all enjoy racing and hard training, we also have goals. We train hard and race to make progress—to *achieve*. Success is not measured by pleasure, but by results. Learning to shift into the hedonic mode at appropriate times, even though it will not be natural at those times, is critical to producing your best performances when you need to.

The achievement mode is appropriate for workouts that demand discipline or must remain at low intensity. Longer rides with strictly controlled low intensity demand the discipline and patience provided by this mode. An athlete in the pleasure-seeking mode would find these workouts endlessly boring. Ever attacked a hill during a long Base-phase workout that was supposed to be kept aerobic? I think we all have. This is the hedonic mode kicking in. Specific work on pedal-stroke technique and other important workouts that demand concentration, but require minimal intensity, may also benefit from this mode. The low intensity is boring, not stimulating, to the athlete engaged in the hedonic mode.

An old Italian adage says, "Imparte l'arte, e mettila da parte," which means learn the art and then put it aside. This is key on race day. You have done the disciplined, hard work. Now put that aside and go have fun. You'll race faster.

Focus on Feelings, Not Numbers

While heart rate, wattage, and miles per hour can be critical in training—sometimes used almost exclusively to govern workout intensity—I prefer to have athletes rely more on perceived exertion during races. Heart rate, wattage, and speed can be useful gauges, but overemphasis on the numbers tends to shift athletes into a mode in which high arousal becomes a negative. I like to teach my athletes to become intimately acquainted with how their body feels at the intensity level that will be required in their racing and to seek to reproduce those feelings on race day. Using heart rate, wattage, and even laboratory test results does improve training. However, during this training athletes need to remain tuned in to perceived exertion, even as they train by numbers, to learn to accurately perceive intensity on race day. Prepare by the numbers. Race by feel. Use the science, then put it aside.

Enjoy the Moment

I once coached an athlete through training to qualify for the Navy SEALS. He was a serious athlete and a regional champion, but his life-long goal was always the SEALS. After years of training for this goal, we sat down for a strategy session right before he left to take his big test. As we were leaving, I said to him, "Have fun." He became furious at me. He had worked so hard to prepare for this test, and he thought my telling him to have fun meant I thought that he wasn't taking it seriously. Serious and fun are not opposites—in fact, they can and should go together in cycling. Did you ever watch Michael Jordan score 50 points in a basketball game and see the huge smile on his face? Was he smiling because he scored 50 points or did he score 50 points because he was smiling? Apter's research says the answer to this question is both. Great athletes in every sport are at their best under intense pressure. They fall into the hedonic mode instead of the achievement mode, and the high arousal brings out their best. Great athletic performances are expressions of the joy of the sport.

Don't "Psych Up"

I do not like the idea of my athletes getting "psyched up" for races. This method of increasing arousal shifts them into the achievement mode and generally does not produce great performances. Athletes who have trained hard and long for an event will naturally be aroused come race day. Artificially increasing this is neither necessary nor beneficial.

Race Day as "Payoff"

> *The feeling I get at the starting line is that it's over—all the hard work and training are over. The race is the fun part.*
> —Julie Moss, professional triathlete

I like to remind athletes that they invest an enormous amount in preparing for their races. They train hard and with discipline. They avoid late-night partying. They eat a healthy diet. I like to have our athletes see race day as the payoff, not as the final exam. This kind of attitude shifts athletes toward the hedonic mode, which brings out their best on race day. Many great performances have resulted from athletes thinking they have stored many hours of hard training in their legs, and on race day they just "let it out."

Understanding how, when, and why to shift to the appropriate psychological mode for different workouts and races enables an athlete to enjoy discipline and control when appropriate and to relish the challenge, effort, and pain associated with high-intensity workouts and races when that is required.

NURTURING CONFIDENCE

> *If you think you can, or think you can't, you're right.*
> —Henry Ford

Confidence is one critical aspect of performance that athletes and coaches should take more seriously. Confident athletes are more likely to perform to their potential. Below are some ways to increase confidence.

Don't base goals just on winning and losing. In every race there will be far more losers than winners, and overemphasis on winning can undermine confidence. Our culture places such importance on winning and losing that we can begin to think these are the only outcomes that matter. Set goals and analyze results based, at least partly, on objectives that you can control. "I didn't win today, but I had a negative split on the run, kept turnover at the desired level, and hydrated and fueled effectively." Stay tuned to your personal goals regardless of competition outcome.

> *All the significant battles are waged within the self.*
> —Sheldon Kopp

Focus on strengths. In the days leading up to a priority event, focus on what you do well. Even while training plans and workouts are centered on a weakness, don't let your attention settle there.

Include test workouts. Many athletes develop confidence by seeing objective improvements in performance through training. Make sure that the tests you use focus on limiters for the priority races. If you do not improve, analyze what you might need to change in your training plan. When you do improve, let it sink in. Enjoy it.

Learn from failures. Everyone has terrible days in training and in races. Analyze every aspect of what went into the bad day and try to learn from it. Whatever you did to cause the bad day, you don't have to do again.

Keep a training log or journal. Record positive thoughts about preparation in your training log. This provides a daily reinforcement that you are doing what is necessary to achieve your goals.

Find your happy place. Most athletes can remember one day when everything clicked. Preparations went well, they stayed healthy, race nutrition clicked, they paced evenly, and they gave 100-percent effort. This could have been in a race or just one of those one-in-a-million days where you could push hard, and you knew you could keep going. When things get tough in a workout or race—or when a challenge intimidates you—remember that perfect-day feeling. You did it then, you can do it again.

Confidence is one of the most powerful weapons in athletics, affecting not only race day, but the 365 days of preparation as well. Make sure that you do everything in your power to develop your confidence

> *Confidence comes from committing yourself to do the preparation or quality work, talking to yourself in positive ways about what you have done and what you can do, drawing lessons from your experiences and acting on them, and remaining positive with yourself through the many challenges and struggles along the way. Confidence grows when you discover what focus works best for you and regularly call on the focus.*
>
> —Terry Orlick

MOTIVATION

> *All it takes is one totally obsessed guy and you'll be second every time.*
>
> —Scott Molina

Preparing to race to your potential in triathlon requires enormous sacrifice. Getting your body and mind ready to go as fast as possible in each triathlon discipline requires tremendous investments of time, money, sweat, and suffering. Triathletes of any level who continue to improve revolve their lives around training to a significant degree. In addition to swim, bike, and run workouts, we have weight-training workouts to squeeze in, additional meals to prepare, several extra showers per day, additional sleep requirements, massage and chiropractic care to schedule, a bike to maintain, training plans to write, and books about triathlon running to read. Serious triathletes, from beginner to professional, dedicate themselves enormously to their sport. Preparing to race your best in a triathlon is a 365-day-per-year commitment. Regardless of how much we love the sport, how do we maintain motivation and positive attitudes about something so demanding?

We have all known athletes with great ability but no consistent motivation. These athletes may have flashes of brilliance and produce some incredible performances, but they will always have huge ups and downs and will never develop to the level possible. I think sometimes that "consistent motivation" is redundant, because truly motivated athletes sustain their passion for their sport through tough times.

> *Effort only fully releases its reward after a person*
> *refuses to quit.*
> —William Arthur Ward

We have also known athletes with moderate ability who are driven to be their best. These athletes prepare with passion, balance, and consistency and never seem to have a bad race.

Are these just individual differences, like genetic talent, or is there something we can learn from the driven and disciplined athletes who always seem to make the most of their talent level? I believe the latter is true.

One thing that sets driven athletes apart is that their sport is woven into their lives. I remember when I started training for triathlon during college; my family asked, "Will you be able to have any social life?" I told them I would have just as active a social life, but I would be sitting on a bike instead of a bar stool. Driven triathletes subscribe to magazines such as *Inside Triathlon* and buy books like *The Triathlete's Guide to Run Training*.

Driven athletes also usually possess a well-refined work ethic. Most are relatively successful in their careers and with family, have an active social life, and frequently are active in church or other volunteer work.

The greatest key to the consistent and intrinsic motivation of the most driven athletes is their *process orientation* instead of *product orientation*. No matter how exciting winning the Hawaii Ironman® is, it is not worth the effort required unless the athlete enjoys the training. This doesn't mean you'll wake up smiling and feeling lucky when the alarm clock goes off at 4:30 A.M. before every early swim workout. Training becomes a grind for every athlete at some point, but the process as a whole is still a positive, enjoyable one, regardless of the outcome of races. Winning races will not make you happy; enjoying daily workouts in three sports that you love (four if you love weight training!) just might.

Highly motivated athletes seem to have an inherent understanding that any process will have ups and downs, and they don't let the problems that are sure to arise affect their motivation or passion. Remind yourself that you do triathlon because you love swimming, cycling, running, and the spirit of competition—not just because you love going faster than before, collecting trophies, and winning races.

I have made a habit of reading several autobiographies of the world's most successful people every year. Each time, I read about failures and struggles more than about dazzling successes. Thomas Edison, when asked how he could keep trying after failing so many times to find a material that would keep a lightbulb burning, said, "I don't see it as a failure. I have successfully identified over 10,000 materials that won't work and each attempt brings me closer to the one that will."

Motivation is the urge to succeed. Athletes are driven by both extrinsic motivators and intrinsic motivators. Extrinsic motivators originate from outside your own psyche. Athletes love getting a trophy at an awards ceremony, hearing praise from others, and seeing their name printed in the race results. Intrinsic motivation is derived from the pleasure that springs from a personal sense of achievement.

INSPIRATIONAL QUOTES

Read through these quotations from other successful people. If one particularly catches your attention, write it down somewhere you will see it frequently and incorporate it into your self-talk to provide motivation and inspiration.

> *We are what we repeatedly do. Excellence, then, is not*
> *an act but a habit.*
> —Aristotle

> *Every time I suffer, I'm a better man because of it.*
> —Lance Armstrong

> *The world breaks everyone and, afterward, many are*
> *strong at the broken places.*
> —Ernest Hemingway

Success is how high you bounce after hitting the bottom
—General George Patton

If you're willing to accept failure and learn from it, if you're willing to consider failure a blessing in disguise and bounce back, you've got the potential of harnessing one of the most powerful success forces.
—Joseph Sugarman

Courage is the first of human qualities because it is the quality which guarantees the others.
—Winston Churchill

When someone tells me there is only one way to do things, it always lights a fire under my butt. My instant reaction is "I'm going to prove you wrong."
—Picabo Street

Do not let what you cannot do interfere with what you can do.
—John Wooden

No one is ever defeated until defeat has been accepted as a reality.
—Napoleon Hill

Far better is it to dare mighty things, even though checkered by failure, than to take rank with those who neither enjoy much or suffer much because they live in the gray twilight that knows not victory or defeat.
—Theodore Roosevelt

Those things that hurt, instruct.
—Benjamin Franklin

What lies behind us and what lies before us are small matters compared to what lies within us.
—Oliver Wendell Holmes

The opposite of mediocrity is not winning. Recognizing a challenge, taking it head-on, and refusing to consider an easier, less gratifying path—that to me is escaping mediocrity.
—Ashley Powell

A successful person is one who can lay a firm foundation with the bricks that others throw at him or her.
—David Brinkley

We don't stop playing because we grow old, we grow old because we stop playing.
—C. Wyatt Runyan

All glory comes from daring to begin.
—William Shakespeare

Boldness has genius, power, and magic in it. Begin it now.
—Goethe

Behold the turtle. He makes progress only when he sticks his neck out.
—James Byrant Conant

Do not wait; the time will never be "just right." Start where you stand, and work with whatever tools you may have at your command, and better tools will be found as you go along.
—Napoleon Hill

Always bear in mind that your own resolution to succeed is more important than any other thing.
—Abraham Lincoln

You gain strength, courage, and confidence by every experience in which you really stop to look fear in the face. You must do the thing you think you cannot do.
—Eleanor Roosevelt

For to win one hundred victories in one hundred
battles is not the acme of skill. To subdue the enemy
without fighting is the acme of skill.

—Sun Tzu

What does not kill us makes us stronger.

—Frederick Nietzsche

I know of no more encouraging fact than the
unquestionable ability of man to elevate his life by
conscious endeavor.

—Henry David Thoreau

Only those who risk going too far can know how
far one can go.

—T. S. Eliot

SUGGESTED READING

Apter, M. J. "Reversal theory and personality: A review." *J Res Pers* 18 (1984): 265-88.

Csikszentmihalyi, Mihaly. *Flow: The Psychology of Optimal Experience.* New York: Harper and Row, 1990.

Frankl, Viktor. *Man's Search for Meaning.* New York: Washington Square Press, 1959.

Helmstetter, Shad. *What to Say When You Talk to Yourself.* New York: Simon & Schuster, 1982.

Hill, Napoleon. *Think and Grow Rich.* New York: Fawcett Columbine, 1937.

Jackson, Susan A. and Mihaly Csikszentmihalyi. *Flow in Sports.* Champaign, IL: Human Kinetics, 1999.

Orlick, Terry. *In Pursuit of Excellence.* Champaign, IL: Human Kinetics, 2000.

CHAPTER 11

Strength Training

TO BUILD A BIGGER ENGINE

While the fastest triathlon runners certainly will never win a bodybuilding contest, a well-thought-out strength-training program will absolutely improve triathlon running performance. Given the duration of triathlon races, performance will be limited by the muscles of the extremities, not the cardiovascular system. A fit triathlete has an extraordinarily strong cardiovascular system, but the winner is the athlete whose muscles hold up to the demands of racing.

Interestingly, the greatest benefit of strength training for triathlon running is improved economy. Strong runners can run fast using less energy than weaker runners. So it isn't that strength training enables you to sustain a higher workload, but that strength training enables you to run fast with a reduced workload.

Injuries are an ever-present risk with run training. Running is an extremely high-impact activity, and all runners will be injured at some point in their career. Peak performances almost always come after long periods of consistent, uninterrupted training. Beyond correcting technique and developing training schedules that balance volume, intensity, and recovery, strength training is a triathlete's best defense against injury. Strength training increases the strength of the connective tissues as well as the muscles.

Triathletes who perform serious strength training in the off-season also recover faster from workouts, especially runs. A strong runner will suffer less microtrauma—tiny tears in the muscles that cause soreness. Anything that speeds recovery and allows more training volume and intensity without overtraining will improve performance.

STRENGTH TRAINING FOR TRIATHLON

Remember that a triathlete is in the weight room to build strength. Triathletes are not interested in getting bulky muscles—that would only slow them down. Triathletes are also not going to build endurance in the weight room. A very long weight-training set is two minutes in duration, not even as long as a half-mile on the track. On a two-hour bike ride at 90 rpm, a triathlete's legs perform 10,800 repetitions. Which is going to increase endurance better, that or a two-minute weight-training set? Stronger muscles will have better endurance, but it is the strength developed in the weight room that increases performance, not endurance that would come from high-repetition sets.

PRIORITIZE INTENSITY OVER VOLUME

A triathlete's strength-training workouts should be short duration and high intensity, use a minimum number of sets, and have a slow speed of movement and relatively heavy weights. The athletes I coach, including world-ranked professionals, spend no more than 30 to 40 minutes in the weight room two to three times per week. I recommend a single very hard set for each muscle group. Increasing strength is accomplished with high-intensity workouts. Increasing volume beyond a single maximal-effort set delays recovery significantly without much additional return. Triathletes—who need to swim, bike, run, and lift weights—should get in the weight room, work their tails off for a short time and go home. I have found that this method develops strength very effectively and leaves time and energy for other workouts. Strength training is a very important supplement for a triathlete, but it should always remain a supplement and not dramatically interfere with the primary workouts.

Use Relatively Heavy Weights

To build strength, triathletes need to use relatively heavy weights. Increasing strength requires stimulating muscle fibers that are not used in your normal workouts. Weight training with light to moderate resistance is not effective. Beginning a strength-training program using light weights and building to moderate weights is important initially, but once the tissues have adapted to the demands of strength training, use relatively heavy weights.

A weight-training set should end because the muscle will no longer, even with 100-percent effort by the athlete, create the force necessary to lift the weight. This should occur before lactic acid builds up in the muscles and causes incredible pain. Weight-training workouts do require great effort and will cause some pain, but it should be the effort of lifting heavy weights, not the burning of pumping out reps, that causes momentary failure and ends the set.

Keep Movements Slow

I believe that weight-training movements should be kept extremely slow. Slow movements minimize momentum and require a more sustained contraction. This is much more effective than accelerating the weight initially, which builds up momentum that allows the muscle to relax. Slow, steady contractions increase strength much more effectively than the contract-relax-contract-relax rhythm of faster movements, which features built-in moments of relaxation due to momentum.

I recommend a style of strength training that uses repetitions with an eight-second lifting phase and a four-second lowering phase, with no pauses at any time during the set. This is an extreme style that requires tremendous discipline and concentration, but I have found it to be extremely safe, time efficient, and effective. Great care should be taken to accelerate the weight very deliberately at the beginning of each repetition and to avoid setting the weight down between repetitions. Anything that would cause the working muscle to relax, even for a split second, should be avoided. The idea of this style of weight training is to completely avoid buildup of momentum and maintain constant muscular contraction from the beginning of the set to the end.

Selecting the correct weight to be used is critical. Regardless of the style of lifting you prefer, each set should last between 40 and 80 seconds. With slow movements this will not produce a large number of repetitions, but duration of each contraction is key, not the number of repetitions. When you become strong enough that 80 seconds of continuous contraction is possible, you need to increase the weight by about 5 percent. This will reduce the set duration back toward 40 seconds, and you can gradually build back toward 80.

EXERCISES

I recommend using a single set of a single exercise for each major muscle group. Avoid doing too many sets or redundant exercises, as increasing the volume of the workout reduces the intensity, resulting in less-effective stimulation. Extra work will only delay recovery and unnecessarily interfere with swim, bike, and run workouts.

I recommend the following exercises using machines that can be found in most fitness centers:

1. **Leg Press:** Place feet at the very top of the platform, shoulder-width apart or narrower. Set seat so that knee angle is slightly less than 90 degrees and hip angle is significantly below 90 degrees. Press the platform out slowly until knees are almost straight. Lower slowly until knees are bent to a 90-degree angle and repeat. This exercise works the quadriceps muscles on the front of the thigh and the gluteus maximus muscles of the buttocks. Placing the feet too low on the platform puts most of the stress on the quadriceps and minimizes stress on the glutes.

2a. **Seated Leg Curl:** Sit on the machine with legs between the two roller pads. Slowly and deliberately pull the heels back toward the buttocks by bending the knees. Keep the toes pulled up toward the knees and avoid pointing the toes. This exercise works the hamstring muscles on the back of the thigh.

2b. **Lying Leg Curl:** Lie facedown on machine with knees lined up with machine's axis of rotation and heels hooked under the roller pads. Slowly bend your knees until your heels come up and touch your butt. Your hips may rise slightly off the machine; don't try to keep them all the way down. During the entire set, keep your toes pulled up toward your knees—don't point your toes or your calf muscles will assist and may fatigue before the target muscles have been effectively worked. This exercise works the hamstrings on the back of the thigh.

3. **Leg Extension:** Sit with your knees lined up with the machine's axis of rotation and your feet hooked under the roller pads. Slowly straighten your legs until they are completely straight. Make sure to achieve a full 180-degree angle—the last few degrees are very important. Lower the weight stack until your knees are bent to a 90-degree angle, without setting the weight down, and repeat.

4a. **Calf Raise:** Sit on a leg press machine with only the balls of your feet on the platform. Straighten your legs and lock out the knees (unless you feel pain or have a history of knee problems). Keeping the knees straight, lower the weight by dropping your heels. You should feel a deep stretch in the calves. Slowly point your toes, trying to shift your weight onto the big toe of each foot. Don't let your feet roll to the outside.

4b. **One-Legged Standing Calf Raise:** Stand on one foot on the edge of a stair with the ball of your foot on the stair and your arch and heel off the stair. Drop your heel to get a full stretch of the calf muscles, then slowly push up onto your toes and extend your ankle. As you push up, try to roll your weight onto the big toe as much as possible.

5a. **Seated Row:** Sit in front of a low pulley with your feet braced against the machine. Grip the handle with your palms facing each other. Keeping the elbows straight, slowly pull the shoulders back (squeeze your shoulder blades together and stick your chest out) without raising them toward your ears. Once your shoulders are pulled all the way back, slowly bend your elbows and pull back until the elbows are well behind the torso. Lower the weight until the arms and shoulders are fully extended and repeat.

5b. **Lat Pull:** Using a palms-away grip about six inches wider than shoulder width, slowly pull the bar down to the base of your neck where it meets the upper chest. Allow the bar to slowly rise back to the starting position and repeat for the designated number of repetitions.

6. **Bench Press:** Lie on your back with the bar lined up with your shoulders. Grip the bar at about six inches wider than your shoulders. Lower the bar to your chest and slowly press upward. Slowly lower and repeat.

7a. **Lateral Raise:** On a machine, place your elbows inside the pads, or stand with dumbbells hanging at your sides. Slowly raise your arms out from your sides. Make sure to rotate your arms from the shoulders, instead of "shrugging" the shoulders up toward the ears. This exercise works the outside of the shoulder.

7b. **Shoulder Press:** Grip a barbell using a palms-away grip about four inches wider than your shoulders. Slowly push the barbell upward until arms are fully extended overhead. Slowly lower the bar to your upper chest and repeat.

8a. **Low Back:** Sit in the machine with your hips pressed all the way back against the lower pad. Put both belts across your hips and legs and tighten as much as possible. Cross your arms on your chest and press back slowly against the upper pad with your upper back and shoulders until you feel a stopper. Lower the weight, rounding your back as you come forward. If you cannot hit the stopper, you are using too much weight. Make sure that the belts are tight enough that your hips cannot move forward or up during the movement.

8b. **Dead Lift:** Stand with a barbell on the floor directly in front of you. Bend over and grip the bar at shoulder width. Stand up, keeping your arms straight and lifting the bar to thigh level. Slowly lower the weight to the floor and repeat.

9a. **Leg Lifts:** Lie on your back on the floor with your arms at your sides. Very slowly raise your legs and bring your knees in to your chest, bending the knees as you lift. At the end of the movement, concentrate on rotating your pelvis upward as much as possible. During the entire movement, concentrate on squeezing the abdominal muscles, not just completing the repetition.

9b. **Crunches:** Lie on your back and cross your arms on your chest. Very slowly roll your shoulders forward and upward while keeping your lower back in contact with the floor. Pause at the top and return. As with the leg lifts, concentrate on squeezing the abdominal muscles, not just completing the movement.

9c. Sit-ups with a Twist: Lay on your back on the floor. Put your feet under the edge of a couch or have a friend hold them down. Lock your fingers behind your head. Bring your right elbow up to your left knee, go back down, and bring your left elbow up to your right knee. Repeat. Additional resistance can be created by holding a weight behind your head or using an incline board.

10a. Shoulder Internal Rotation: Attach a stretch cord to a doorknob or other stationary object at about waist height. Stand far enough away to create optimal resistance. Face 90 degrees away from the doorknob, so that it is directly to your right. Hold the stretch cord in your right hand with your elbow tucked firmly against your side and bent at 90 degrees—so that the forearm is horizontal and pointing toward the doorknob. Maintaining a 90-degree elbow angle, slowly rotate the upper arm, moving the hand away from the doorknob in an arc. Make sure to keep the elbow locked against your side and move only the forearm and hand. Repeat slowly for one minute. Resistance should be great enough that completing the final repetition is very difficult. Repeat with the left arm.

10b. Shoulder Internal Rotation: Grip a lat bar so that you have a 90-degree bend at both the elbow and shoulder. Begin with your upper arms horizontal and your lower arms vertical (pointing up). Rotate your hand and the bar forward until your lower arms are pointing down. Your elbows should remain in place, with the upper arm only rotating. This works small, weak muscles, so start very light.

11. Shoulder External Rotation: Attach a stretch cord to a doorknob or other stationary object at about waist height. Stand far enough away to create optimal resistance. Face 90 degrees away from the doorknob, so that it is directly to your left. Hold the stretch cord in your right hand with your elbow tucked firmly against your side and bent at 90 degrees so that the forearm is horizontal and pointing toward the doorknob.

Maintaining a 90-degree elbow angle, slowly rotate the upper arm, moving the hand away from the doorknob in an arc. Make sure to keep the elbow locked against your side and move only the forearm and hand. Repeat slowly for one minute. Resistance should be great enough that completing the final repetition is very difficult.

12. **Hip Flexors:** Use an ankle strap and a low pulley machine to work the hip flexors. Face away from the machine and lean forward on a chair or something similar for stability. Begin the exercise with the strap on your right ankle and the right leg fully extended behind you. Slowly drive the right knee forward, allowing the knee to bend. Ideally the range of motion at the hip will vary from about 45 degrees behind you to 45 degrees in front of you. Allow the leg to stretch out behind you again and repeat. Work this muscle particularly hard, as it is important in all three triathlon segments.

STRENGTH-TRANSFER TRAINING

While weight training with free weights and machines is one important aspect of strength training, a triathlete needs to be able to apply this new strength to swimming, cycling, and running. Transfer training provides additional resistance, but also trains the neuromuscular system to efficiently produce force in the specific movements that will be required on race day. This type of training bridges the gap between strength in the weight room and speed for the required duration on race day.

There are a number of different ways to accomplish transfer training. Triathletes often use hand paddles or webbed-fingered gloves during swim workouts in the appropriate training periods. We use hills or big-gear, low-cadence training on the bike. Both of these methods are very effective, but triathletes rarely plan or conduct effective strength-transfer training for running.

The run presents a different challenge in that we must create propulsion forcefully, but we must also hold our weight up. Running requires strength in muscles that act vertically and in muscles that produce horizontal propulsion. We need to do strength-transfer training for both groups of muscles.

Weighted Running

How do runners overload the muscles that act vertically in their stride? To overload the muscles that act horizontally, we run faster, but this does not significantly increase the stress on the muscles that act vertically. We run hills, which do include a vertical component of resistance, but the amount we can run on hills is limited. Few athletes, other than those living in Colorado, have a hill around that they could run up for an hour, and even then they would need to come back down.

Running while wearing a weight vest can be an effective way to increase overload on the quadriceps and calf muscles that act vertically. I have many of my athletes run with a weight vest at certain times of the year. This topic is discussed further in Chapter 1, which covers technique, and Chapter 13, which covers injury prevention.

I recommend that athletes with a force limiter use the weight vest heavily (pardon the pun) during the Preparation and Base periods, which focus on force and speed skills. As with any type of workout relating to running, start conservatively and build consistently and gradually.

Half-ironman and ironman-distance athletes may want to continue using the weight vest through the Build periods. Running with a weight vest simulates running with extremely fatigued cycling muscles. You train yourself to rely less on the quadriceps and run effectively with overloaded quadriceps without the risk of injury and overtraining that would come from actually experiencing repeated race fatigue. Running with an extra 10 pounds does feel very similar to running after 112 miles of cycling.

During the appropriate times of the season, include serious strength training and strength-transfer training in your routine. You will suffer fewer injuries and race faster as a result.

12

And on the Seventh Day He Rested

He who recovers fastest wins.

—Joe Friel

W hen we think of overtraining, we generally remember that time we squeezed in an extra track workout or decided that a 25-percent increase in our long run wouldn't really be a big problem. Few athletes realize that overtraining is really "under-resting" and that what happens outside of workout hours plays an enormous role.

Recovery is actually an active process; it is something we do, not something we don't do. Most athletes tend to think of recovery as not working out, but it is much, much more than that.

In 1995, I attended a one-week United States Cycling Federation camp at the Olympic Training Center in Colorado Springs. When I received the training schedule, I was startled, intimidated, and even frightened. We were scheduled for an enormous amount of work. We would wake up in the morning, do stretching and breathing exercises, have a light breakfast, and ride to the track. There we did set after set of lung-busting intervals, rode back to the center, had lunch, and took a short nap. After more stretching, I got a massage every day, and then we were back on the bikes for another brutally hard workout. We would shower, eat dinner, and have meetings until bedtime. The schedule included much, much more quality training than I had ever done in a week.

I was amazed at how my body held up to what seemed like a month's worth of hard training squeezed into a week, especially at a higher altitude. How was I faster at the end of such a brutal week than at the beginning of the week? The camp gave me many advantages for my recovery from the workouts. The nutritious meals provided to us, as well as the naps, snacks, massages, extra sleep, and the camp setting itself removed the physical and emotional stresses of everyday life. Instead of doing our laundry, we had professional massages. Instead of cooking our own breakfast, we slept an extra few minutes. That week really opened my eyes to how important it is for an athlete to incorporate habits into his life to maximize recovery.

Recovery is really the athlete's greatest resource. Athletes can train harder and longer, still absorbing and adapting optimally to the workouts, they will become faster. Therefore, athletes should take every reasonable step to accelerate recovery. Make this a priority and you will race faster.

> *Recovery is anything that promotes psychobiological well-being.*
>
> —Joe Friel

Recovery is more than just taking a day off from training; it is giving the body every resource it needs to adapt to the stimulation of previous workouts. Taking every step to maximize workout recovery is a critical part of training and needs to be planned.

OVERTRAINING

The point of taking steps to maximize workout recovery is to allow you to train at levels of volume and intensity that will maximize performance. Overtraining is a problem for almost every serious athlete at one point or another. Producing optimal performance is about constantly pushing right up to the line. We want to constantly provide the levels of volume and intensity that will keep you improving, but not enough to cause overtraining (see following table for a list of overtraining symptoms). Even for the most knowledgeable and experienced athletes and coaches, this involves guesswork. That is why we always write training schedules in pencil, monitor our bodies, and make adjustments along the way.

Overtraining occurs when the combined stresses in an athlete's life—including but not limited to training and racing stresses—exceed the body's ability to rebuild and recover between workouts. How does overtraining appear? The surest sign of overtraining is an unexpected decrease in performance, particularly in a breakthrough workout (see table for other indicators). Triathletes training correctly do go through cycles of fatigue. We do and should get tired during heavy training, hopefully cycling this fatigue so that we recover from the previous breakthrough workout before time for the next. Sometimes unknown and unexpected events adjust the balance of the stress-and-recovery system we have set up, and sometimes we just guess wrong. When performance significantly turns downward for two or three breakthrough workouts, you are probably overtrained. Every athlete will have a bad day in the process of training when perceived exertion is higher than usual, you aren't quite as fast as usual, and nothing feels sharp. A bad day is just a bad day. Several bad days in a row, especially in key workouts that were supposed to be good days, may be signs of overtraining. Whenever you have a bad workout, check the overtraining indicators table (page 220) and see if you have multiple symptoms. None of these symptoms is a sure sign of overtraining, but if you have several of them, you probably have some degree of overtraining.

Every time you get tired during heavy training is not overtraining. While most triathletes do not pay enough attention to overtraining, there are a few who let fear rule their workouts. While every triathlete should take serious steps to avoid overtraining, some take steps to avoid fatigue. Hard-training triathletes get fatigued. Every breakthrough workout should be fatiguing to some degree, and performance will temporarily decline as a result. Overtraining is persistent fatigue when it is time to train hard again and when you should be recovered.

If you do come down with a case of overtraining, the answer is pretty straightforward: reduced training load (especially intensity) and more and better rest. Obviously you should consider your workouts, but also look at your nutrition habits, stress, and sleep patterns, and make adjustments as necessary.

If there are no stresses other than workouts that may have caused the overtraining, first check your recovery weeks. Was volume significantly

TABLE **12.1** OVERTRAINING INDICATORS

BEHAVIORAL	PHYSICAL
Apathy	Reduced performance
Lethargy	Weight change
Depression	Resting heart rate change
Poor concentration	Muscle soreness
Sleep pattern changes	Swollen lymph glands
Irritability	Diarrhea
Decreased libido	Injury
Clumsiness	Infection
Increased thirst	Amenorrhea
Sluggishness	Lower exercise heart rate
Craving for sugar	Slow-healing cuts

Reprinted with permission from Joe Friel, *The Triathlete's Training Bible* 2nd ed. (VeloPress, 2004).

reduced and was intensity almost all endurance based? Remember that overtraining is a chronic process of under-recovering. It is not caused by a single very hard workout, but by an accumulation of stresses that outweigh recovery. Most overtrained athletes need lighter recovery weeks more than lighter heavy weeks. Always look at recovery first when you feel overtrained.

Most overtrained athletes who catch their condition early just need a recovery week and then can jump right back into training. Make adjustments to your schedule, your attitudes about the stress-recovery balance, and how you write your schedules.

If you work with a coach, and working with a qualified coach is the best way to keep the stress-recovery balance ideal, communicate with him or her frequently about recovery. Especially at the end of each training cycle, during your recovery week, let the coach know how the month's training went, how you recovered from the workouts, when you felt especially tired, and when you felt recovered. If you begin to feel tired, talk to your coach. It is impossible to be objective about your own recovery.

An athlete who is 10 percent undertrained will perform better than an athlete who is 1 percent overtrained, so monitor this carefully and make adjustments quickly. If overtraining is caught early, it remedies quickly and easily. If it is allowed to build up over time, it may drastically interfere with race preparations. Don't let that happen!

The keys to effective training are knowing where the line of overtraining is for you, so that you can "guess" effectively when designing training programs; monitoring your body and mind constantly for signs of overtraining, so you catch it early when you guess wrong; and pushing the edge only once per cycle—during the week that precedes the recovery week (usually week 3).

The following sections include a few methods that will maximize your body's recovery ability and let you train hard and long without pushing yourself into overtraining. Take this seriously; it is a big part of racing to your potential.

EARLY-SEASON PREPARATION

Athletes with a strong aerobic base will recover more quickly from workouts than those who lack in this area. For athletes competing in relatively short events, this is one of the primary benefits of Base training. High-volume training doesn't make an athlete faster in a two-hour race as much as it enables her to absorb more of the training that does increase speed. Take the Base period very seriously.

A solid base of strength training increases the ability to train hard and recover as well. After serious strength training, athletes suffer less microtrauma (tiny tears in the muscles and connective tissues) and will therefore be ready to train hard again sooner.

PRE-WORKOUT PREPARATION

Pre-workout preparation affects how an athlete recovers from training. Getting to group workouts early enough to allow adequate warm-up as well as making sure you are well hydrated and well fueled gives you the best chance of optimal recovery.

NUTRITION

Nutrition plays a huge role in workout recovery. Consuming adequate protein throughout the day (protein ingested in one large sitting is not absorbed well) provides a pool of amino acids to keep the muscles and connective tissues continually rebuilding from the previous workout.

A meal that combines protein and carbohydrate in about a 1:4 ratio immediately after (within 30 minutes of) each hard or long workout ensures optimal glycogen replacement and rebuilding of damaged tissues. Several drinks designed specifically for post-workout recovery are available now, and they work well.

Consuming enough protein is also critical, both post-workout and throughout the day. Overconsumption of protein does not become a major problem until you consume ridiculous quantities (300 grams or more). Base your diet on lean meat and you will recover from workouts better.

Hydrating immediately after a workout is important as well. Some athletes weigh themselves before and after hard or long workouts and consume 16 oz of water for every pound lost.

STRESS MANAGEMENT

Psychological stress has very real physiological manifestations and may impair workout recovery. While many of the sources of stress in an athlete's life may be beyond his or her control, steps can be taken to minimize some of them. One coach recommends that his athletes get their dental work taken care of early in the off-season to minimize the risk of interference with training. Athletes should analyze the stressors in their lives and take steps to minimize them whenever possible. Using a stress-relieving activity, such as meditation, can benefit recovery patterns.

ACTIVE RECOVERY

We all know that sometimes a light workout can promote recovery more than a day completely off. The goal is to exercise at an intensity that is great enough to stimulate circulation and some endocrine responses, but light enough to avoid demanding more recovery after the recovery workout.

Be very careful here. Even disciplined athletes will tend to go over-board. I believe that "recovery run" is an oxymoron for many athletes. I often have an athlete stay on an indoor trainer for active recovery workouts, and I have even recommended a brisk walk to a nationally ranked professional athlete. Be very conservative with active recovery workouts. It is basically impossible to make them too easy, and going just a little harder than necessary will reduce the effectiveness of tomorrow's workout.

REST

Even a day of complete rest needs to be planned out. It is more than just not working out. On rest and recover days, the athlete needs to avoid any activity that is even moderately stressful and take every possible step to promote recovery. I joke with one of my athletes that he has to rent a cart if he plays golf on rest and recover days because walking nine holes is too strenuous—but he knows I am only half joking. Eddie B used to say, "Never walk when you can stand or stand when you can sit." Every bit of energy that can be saved will make a difference.

The old principle of alternating one hard and one easy workout is not necessarily the best method. Alternating blocks of hard days and easy days is often more effective. This is an area that is difficult to offer specific advice on because each athlete seems to respond well to different patterns of work and recovery.

Afternoon naps can improve recovery to an amazing degree. I have found that 45 minutes is optimal. Longer naps don't seem to be more beneficial and may interfere with night sleep. For the same reason, avoid having athletes take evening naps. Taking regular naps may not be realistic for most of our athletes who work 40-, 50-, or 60-hour weeks, but I think most professional athletes should get in the habit of napping almost every day.

Just getting to bed a few minutes early really will have an impact. When my athletes head into a Build period, I generally suggest that they try to get an extra 20 to 30 minutes of sleep per night. Although this will not have a huge immediate impact, over time, the chronic benefit will be enormous.

MASSAGE

Massage may accelerate recovery dramatically. A professional massage after a heavy week of training or during an easy week can facilitate recovery. Self-massage is definitely not the same as a professional massage, but it can facilitate recovery, especially in the quadriceps. Glutes, hamstrings, and low back muscles can be self-massaged effectively using bodyweight and a tennis ball, rolling pin, or other object to focus pressure.

CHIROPRACTIC CARE

Chiropractic care can definitely accelerate workout recovery. My experience is that finding a chiropractor who is an endurance athlete and works primarily with endurance athletes is vital. I had several terrible experiences before I met my current chiropractor who is a triathlete and has improved my training dramatically.

HYPERBARIC CHAMBERS

For very serious athletes who wish to take advantage of every opportunity to optimize recovery, a hyperbaric chamber is a phenomenal tool. A hyperbaric chamber provides increased atmospheric pressure, which forces more oxygen into the blood and improves recovery dramatically. The model designed for home use is a seven-foot-long tube that zips shut and connects to a compressor. The athlete lies in the chamber, napping, while supersaturating her tissues with oxygen. Although it is an expensive investment, it provides amazing results.

SLEEP

Sleep is an enormously important part of successful athletic training. Poor recovery equals poor training, and sleep is a key to recovering well. According to the National Sleep Foundation, sleep deprivation is reaching epidemic proportions in the United States. Inadequate sleep accounts for accidents and lost productivity totaling more than $30 billion each year. Certainly if the mostly sedentary population suffers severely from inadequate sleep, this is an issue hard-training athletes should take seriously. Athletes need sleep to recover and repair tissues, and we tend to sleep less because training overfills already busy days.

Athletes and coaches study how to best combine exercise frequency, intensity, and mode to address our specific limiters and come to race day ready to perform to our potential. Unfortunately, to most coaches and athletes, rest is a passive process. I always try to help my athletes to understand that recovery is a process they need to attack proactively. A major part of that is getting enough sleep.

One of my top athletes made a point of getting 30 minutes per night additional sleep this year. He set a bedtime for himself and made every possible arrangement to improve the quality of his sleep. I believe this was one key component of his breakthrough season. When you divide his increased income by 30 minutes per night, he received a pretty good hourly wage for lying in bed.

The first step to improving quality of sleep is making sure to get enough hours of sleep. Individuals vary considerably in their sleep requirements, but I bet almost every athlete would benefit from a few additional minutes of sleep.

Many athletes are willing to train an additional hour per day, but they cannot find time for an additional 30 minutes of sleep per day. You do the math on that one. The following suggestions may help you on your quest for more or better-quality sleep.

Control caffeine. Caffeine can disrupt sleep. Caffeine's half-life in the bloodstream is between three and seven hours (depending on age and level of caffeine use—coffee junkies will metabolize caffeine faster), probably far longer than most people would estimate. I personally have moved my own 5:00 P.M. caffeine deadline back to 4:00 P.M., and my sleep has benefited tremendously. That said, caffeine's effect on sleep patterns is an individual response, and your friends who say coffee doesn't keep them from sleeping are probably right.

Keep consistent sleep patterns. Go to bed and rise at approximately the same hour every day. Sleep experts recommend waking within an hour of the same time each day. This is really a key. Set a bedtime and respect it as you would a workout. None of us would let a priority workout get squeezed out, but we do go to bed late the night before a priority workout and reduce its effectiveness.

Monitor bedroom temperature. Research shows that preferred temperature for sleeping is a significant factor that varies widely among individuals. Fortunately, it also shows that the temperature that produces optimal sleep patterns correlates very well with personal comfort. We sleep best at the temperature that feels most comfortable.

Avoid alcohol. While alcohol near bedtime may be relaxing and even help you get to sleep, it disrupts sleep patterns and negatively affects quality of sleep.

Time the evening meal. This presents quite a challenge for athletes, but sleep patterns are ideal if the evening meal is consumed at least three hours before bedtime. If this is not possible, one solution is dividing the evening meal and consuming half before the workout. The lighter dinner is likely to be less disruptive to sleep patterns.

Develop relaxing bedtime rituals. Developing patterns helps us fall asleep sooner after going to bed. Hot baths and reading seem to be most effective.

Use the bedroom just for sleeping. Avoid doing work or other activities in the bedroom as much as is practical. If the bedroom is for sleeping only, you are likely to fall asleep sooner after going to bed.

Keep the lights out. While there is considerable individual variability, most people sleep their best in a very dark sleep environment. Even a short, bright light may dramatically disrupt sleep patterns, so use a nightlight in the bathroom so you won't have to turn a bright light on during the night.

MONITORING RECOVERY

Even under ideal conditions, a hard-training athlete will feel tired and broken down at times. The key is that your recovery be basically complete by the next hard workout. Developing methods of monitoring recovery is important. Performance (speed) is the best indicator. If you are too tired to run at optimal speed during each workout, recovery is incomplete and adjustments are required. An aerobic time trial, which involves running at a predetermined heart rate and seeing how fast you run, may help you monitor the level of your recovery. How you feel subjectively is important, too. With heart rate monitors and now even GPS runner's speedometers available, this sometimes gets ignored. Make sure to perform a simple self-assessment every morning. This takes just a few seconds of squeezing and relaxing the muscles and making a mental note of how you feel.

Resting heart rate is a useful measure of recovery, as is the difference between sitting and standing heart rate. Just make sure that if you track these objective measures, you don't forget that subjective feelings are also important.

Appreciate the value of optimal workout recovery. Taking it seriously and following small steps to accelerate recovery will improve your training dramatically and ultimately help you to run faster on race day.

REFERENCES

Blomstrand E. and E. A. Newsholme. "Effect of branched-chain amino acid supplementation on the exercise-induced change in aromatic amino acid concentration in human muscle." *Acta Physiol Scand* 146 (1992): 293-98.

Dement, William C. *The Promise of Sleep*. New York: Dell Publishing, 1999.

Ivy, J. L., P. T. Res, R. C. Sprague, et al. "Effect of a carbohydrate-protein supplement on endurance performance during exercise of varying intensity." *Int J Sports Nutr Exerc Metab* 13 (2003): 388-401.

Miller S. L., C. M. Maresh, L. E. Armstrong, C. B. Ebbeling, S. Lennon, and N. R. Rodriguez. "Metabolic response to provision of mixed protein-carbohydrate supplementation during endurance exercise." *Int J Sport Nutr Exerc Metab* 12 (2002): 384-97.

Tarnopolsky, M. A., J. D. MacDougall, and S. A. Atkinson. "Influence of protein intake and training status on nitrogen balance and lean body mass." *J Appl Physiol* 64 (1988): 187-93.

Wolfe, R. R. "Effects of amino acid intake on anabolic processes." *Can J Appl Physiol* 26 Suppl (2001): S220-27.

CHAPTER

13 Off-Season Injury Prevention Program

T he frequency of injuries may be dramatically reduced by an off-season prevention program that develops strength, flexibility, and elasticity in tissues that are at high risk. Use this off-season to prepare your body fully for the high-volume, high-intensity training that will come later in the season.

Since the running action occurs primarily in a single plane, the tissues that act in that plane become disproportionately strong, while those that act laterally (side to side) atrophy. Programs developed only for performance enhancement usually neglect tissues that act laterally, thereby increasing the risk of injury. Most injuries do not occur in the tissues that develop propulsion, presumably because those tissues become so well trained. The off-season is the time to strengthen those "other" tissues to reduce the likelihood of injuries when hard-core training begins.

STRENGTH TRAINING

Strength training is a critical aspect of off-season preparation, as it affects the connective tissues as well as the muscles. Most strength-training programs are designed to improve performance but not to prevent injuries. Increasing strength in muscles that are not developed by our primary activities will maintain balance and reduce injuries.

Several muscles that are generally neglected in strength-training programs include those in the following list. When performing the suggested weight-training exercises, use relatively heavy weights and slow movements. Keep the duration of each set between 40 and 60 seconds.

Hip Abductors: The tissues along the outside of the hip and thigh are stressed every time a runner's foot lands. Weaknesses may cause serious injuries. Lay on your right side with legs straight and an ankle weight on the left leg. Keeping the knee straight, lift the leg upward (sideways) to about 30 degrees. Lower and repeat. This can also be replicated using a cable and low pulley on a weight machine.

Hip Adductors: The adductors pull the thighs together. Sit on a chair with a basketball between your knees. Squeeze the ball with your knees as hard as possible for 40 seconds. These muscles can also be worked effectively with a cable and low pulley on a weight machine, if available.

External Shoulder Rotators: The internal rotator muscles are strengthened by the catch and pull, but the external rotators are not. This strength imbalance stresses the connective tissues of the joint. Lay on your right side holding a dumbbell with your left hand. The left elbow should lay against the torso with the elbow just above the hip and bent to 90 degrees. Slowly rotate the upper arm to raise the dumbbell. The elbow should not move and the upper arm should only rotate.

Calves: Stand with the ball of one foot on the edge of a step and the rest of your foot hanging off the edge. Slowly push upward to full extension on your toes, then lower your body to the fully stretched position with the heel well below the edge of the step, and repeat.

Ankle Flexors: Strengthening the muscles that lift the foot will reduce a number of shin and foot injuries. Sit on the edge of a chair and hold a weight on your toes. Flex the foot upward, lower, and repeat.

FLEXIBILITY

While an effective stretching program may reduce injuries significantly, many athletes look to stretching as the cure-all answer to injuries. However, athletes do sometimes become injured because of overflexibility, and there are many other causes of injury. Be consistent with your stretching, but don't go to extremes and don't look to it as the way to prevent all injury.

The following stretches are recommended:

Hamstring: Sit on the floor with both legs out straight in front of you. Grab your ankles and gently pull your chest down toward your knees. Hold a moderate stretch for 45 seconds.

Gluteus Maximus: Lie on the floor on your back. Pull one knee into your chest, feeling the stretch in the glute muscle. Hold a moderate stretch for 45 seconds, switch sides, and repeat.

Quadriceps: Lie on the floor on your left side. Grab your right ankle and gently pull the foot backward, bending the knee and stretching the quadriceps muscle on the front of the thigh. Hold for a moderate 45-second stretch, switch sides, and repeat.

Calves: Stand with the ball of one foot on the edge of a step and the rest of your foot hanging off the edge. Lower your body to the fully stretched position with the heel well below the edge of the step, hold for 45 seconds, switch legs, and repeat.

Iliotibial Band (ITB): Sit on the floor with both legs straight along the floor in front of you. Bend the right knee and move the right foot across to the outside of the left leg. Move the right foot up toward the hip until it rests against the left leg, just above the left knee. Rotate your torso to the right and place your left arm on the outside of the right knee. Using the left arm, pull the right leg to the left. Feel the stretch along the right ITB, which runs across the outside of the hip and down the lateral aspect of the thigh. Hold for a 45-second stretch, then switch legs and repeat.

Posterior Shoulder: Hold your right arm so that it crosses the chest with the elbow straight. With your left hand, grab your elbow and pull it toward your left shoulder. Feel the stretch in the back of the right shoulder. Hold for a 45-second stretch, then switch arms and repeat.

Pectorals: Stand arm's length from a wall. Brace your right hand against the wall and rotate your torso to the left, stretching the chest and front-shoulder muscle. Hold for a moderate 45-second stretch, then switch arms and repeat.

Hip Flexors: From a standing position, extend your left foot forward of the other by three to four feet. Bend your left knee and pull your right hip forward and down, keeping the knee straight. Feel the stretch in the front of the hip and the upper front thigh. Hold for a moderate 45-second stretch then switch sides and repeat.

This is a very basic flexibility plan. Other specific stretches might benefit you as well. I recommend seeing a physical therapist, chiropractor, or other professional who can test you for strength and flexibility imbalances and provide you with a specific, customized stretching program.

PLYOMETRICS

Plyometrics are a type of training generally reserved for athletes in power sports, but they will increase tissue elasticity and improve neuromuscular interactions, which may improve injury resistance even for endurance athletes. Be careful when starting these exercises and build gradually. On each of these exercises, minimizing contact time between the feet and ground is critical.

Lateral Jumps: From a standing position, jump directly to your left, pushing off only with the right foot. Land on the left foot and immediately jump sideways back to the right. Land on the right and repeat without stopping for thirty seconds.

Lateral Hops: Standing with feet together, hop (with both feet) about six inches sideways to your left. Land on both feet and hop immediately back to your right. Repeat for 30 seconds without stopping.

Crossover Strides: Run directly sideways to your left, crossing your right foot over in front of your left. After about twelve steps, run back to the right using the same technique. Make sure not to rotate your hips in the direction you are running, but run sideways.

PROPRIOCEPTIVE TRAINING

Many forces are at play on the foot, ankle, and lower leg at foot-strike. Even on a relatively level surface, some irregularities cause each foot-strike to be slightly different from the last. Our bodies need to be able to perceive any irregularity in the surface and adjust immediately, contracting muscles to adapt to the surface. The body's ability to subconsciously make those adjustments happens through a system called proprioception. An athlete with well-developed proprioceptive abilities is less likely to suffer from injuries. Using a disk or a wobble board will train the tissues that control unintended movements and minimize the risk of running injuries.

WEIGHTED RUNNING

Proper use of a weight vest can significantly reduce running injuries. With any kind of strength training, tissues get thicker, stronger, and more elastic. This effect is specific to the movements involved. While strength training in the weight room is important and beneficial, it does not stimulate many tissues specific to running. Running with a weight vest will strengthen many tissues in the foot, calf, and lower leg more directly and more specifically than weight training does. Accomplishing this in the Preparation and Base periods, while volume and intensity are at their lowest, prevents injuries later when volume and intensity increase.

Use the weight vests conservatively and be sure to provide adequate recovery between sessions to optimize the benefits of this training while avoiding potential risks. Begin with only 2 pounds in the vest and add 2 more every several weeks until you can handle a maximum of 5 to 8 percent of your bodyweight. Use the vest for one or two easy runs per week. Do not perform long or intense runs with the vest. Weighted running can be a useful tool for building an injury-resistant body, but don't get carried away. A little bit goes a long way.

Your off-season should include weight training, stretching, plyometrics, and weighted running programs specifically designed to reduce injuries next year. Make sure to emphasize muscles that act laterally since training in swimming, cycling, and running does not develop these effectively. Also work to implement the techniques described in Chapter 1.

14 Special Preparation Factors

This chapter will discuss a number of aspects of training that will provide you with a small advantage over less-prepared competitors.

USING ALTITUDE IN TRAINING

Altitude can be a powerful tool for preparing to race to your potential. Our bodies adapt to altitude in ways that dramatically increase performance in endurance events. Air pressure decreases as altitude increases. Since our bodies rely on air pressure to push oxygen out of the air and into our blood, it is more difficult to deliver oxygen to the muscles at altitude. Our bodies adapt to this by improving. We make more red blood cells, among other things, and are able to deliver more oxygen to the muscles.

Spending time at altitude is a trade-off. Our bodies adapt to living at altitude, which can improve performance, but our workouts are less effective. If you train two hours a day at altitude, it is the other 22 hours that provide the benefit. The reduced oxygen makes us slower, so the two hours of training is actually slightly less effective.

Using altitude to improve performance can be tricky. Timing altitude exposure so that you benefit from the acclimation without interfering with workouts is a challenge.

Optimal time for altitude exposure is about four weeks, but that duration won't be practical for many athletes without the purchase of an altitude chamber for their home (an expensive, but very effective alternative). Stays at altitude of as little as one week may provide significant benefit, but we usually try to get the athlete to altitude for 10 to 14 days. This duration fits well with a family vacation and is practical for many athletes.

A red blood cell lives for about 80 days, so the benefit of altitude exposure lasts about that long. Performances are generally optimal three weeks after returning from altitude. This gives the body time to get used to the higher availability of oxygen to the muscles and the associated increase in training intensity.

The key with altitude training is to keep some speed while you get the benefits of high-altitude living. If you normally run 800-meter aerobic capacity repeats in 2:37, you will need to run them slower at altitude. With less pressure to oxygenate your blood, 2:37s will be too fast and will waste you for the rest of the week's workouts. I recommend slowing aerobic capacity pace by 2 to 3 percent at altitudes of 5,000 to 8,000 feet and 3 to 5 percent for altitudes above 8,000 feet.

Emphasize economy workouts heavily when training at altitude. If you will be at altitude one week, include two short economy workouts during that time. Since you have to run all aerobic workouts more slowly, the fast running will keep the neuromuscular interactions for high-speed running sharp, and economy workouts will not hamper recovery because of their short duration. Do not slow pace for economy workouts. Ideal pace for economy running is based on biomechanical factors—which do not depend on oxygen—not on metabolic factors.

When developing your annual plan, decide if a trip to altitude will be practical for you. The optimal time for altitude exposure has you returning home three weeks before your priority race.

TRAINING AND RACING IN THE HEAT

Training and racing in heat and cold present special challenges. Adjusting workouts properly and adapting the body to perform optimally despite these environmental stresses is critical. When training in the heat, the body will send more blood to the skin where it can lose heat and keep core body temperature down. This leaves less blood for the working muscles. Heart rate will be artificially elevated at lower temperatures.

Adjust running pace to the conditions. Heart rate (HR) may be slightly higher on your runs, but allow yourself to run slower and keep heart rate as close as you can to your normal training zones. I generally recommend keeping HR within five beats per minute (bpm) of what is optimal in normal temperatures. Conditions are not optimal, so slowing down is the best option. Holding pace will alter the workout and delay recovery.

High levels of heat and humidity mean less oxygen delivery to the muscles, so optimal training paces are slower. Do not ignore heart rate and force your normal running pace. While I understand that on a very hot day it may not be 100 percent possible to keep your heart rate all the way down to its usual levels, do the best you can. I generally want my athletes to keep heart rate within five bpm of their Zone 2 heart rate and make no adjustments for Zone 4 training. The conditions make your optimal pace slower today, so slow down. Better to have one suboptimal workout today than to fight the conditions, disrupt your recovery pattern, and make a bad week of training.

Unless you are specifically training for heat acclimation, have a large fan blowing right on your body and head during treadmill and indoor trainer workouts. You want your blood going to the working muscles to give them the best possible workout, not to the skin to cool you.

Heat is not as much of an issue on the bike, except for during climbing workouts. The wind the rider generates by riding relatively fast along a flat road cools the body considerably.

During the hottest months of the year, staying cool is critical to having effective workouts. Workouts early in the morning, late at night, or in shaded areas are most effective. Indoor workouts on a treadmill can be very effective as well. I frequently have athletes run a warm-up outdoors, then come inside and perform the high-intensity part of the run on a treadmill with a fan blowing on them. This improves the quality of the intense workout while still giving the athlete a run outdoors and shortening the treadmill workout.

Carrying water is critical during warm-weather runs. Most triathletes do a good job of hydrating during bike workouts, but a terrible job of hydrating for run workouts. It is always important to drink during runs of 45 minutes or longer, but especially when it is hot outside.

Early-season or late-season races in climates different from home can pose special challenges—even in moderately warm conditions—because your body has not acclimated to performing in the heat. I raced in Perth, Australia in mid-November one year. Mid-November is summer in Australia and winter in Washington, D.C., where I am from. Ninety degrees felt like 110 degrees. A lot of East Coasters in the United States head to Florida for the St. Anthony Triathlon and are surprised at how hot 85 degrees feels in April.

When producing your annual plan, determine what the likely weather conditions will be on race day. When training for the Hawaii Ironman®, expect it to be hot. If heat is expected, plan several workouts during Peak phase to prepare you specifically for the thermal regulation demands of the race. If you live where the temperature doesn't exceed 70 degrees and you'll be racing in the heat, wear a sweatshirt for one weekly hard run. I have instructed clients to perform indoor trainer workouts on the pool deck to simulate the heat and humidity they will face on race day. Be creative with this; there are many effective ways to accomplish heat acclimation. If thermal regulation is likely to be an issue on race day, make yourself hot during one hard workout each week for four to five weeks before the priority race.

Stimulating thermal regulation adaptations must be done during a workout. Sitting in a sauna, even though the extremely high temperatures will drive core body temperature way up, won't train your body to exercise effectively in the heat.

When racing in the heat, consuming enough water and sodium become even greater factors. In extreme conditions, I like my athletes to carry water. This can be used to drink or to pour over your head.

Find shade on the run. Make sure you stay on course and within the rules, but running a few extra yards to cross the street for shade can be a good trade-off. Wear sunscreen and a ventilated hat to keep the sun off your head. Keeping the hat wet can make a big difference.

TRAINING IN THE COLD

Training in the cold poses a different set of challenges. Comfort, not performance, becomes the primary issue. In fact, we are likely to perform very well even when uncomfortably cold.

For athletes working out in the cold, sustaining core body temperature is really not the issue. The real challenge is keeping our skin warm, especially at the extremities. Make sure to wear a windproof shell on the outside and dress in layers. A hat, gloves, and insulated socks will also make the cold more tolerable.

Another strategy you may find useful is warming up inside before going outdoors to finish the workout. Just 5 to 10 minutes of light aerobic activity will elevate core body temperature and increase circulation, both of which will prepare you to face the cold more comfortably.

ERGOGENIC AIDS

All triathletes would love to find a nutrition supplement that would help them race faster without any negative side effects. There are three very effective nutritional supplements: water, carbohydrate, and salt. Unfortunately, all your competitors will be consuming those, too, so you can't gain a great advantage there.

The key benefit of nutrition supplement—in fact the key benefit of good nutrition in particular—is that it allows us to train a little bit more effectively and recover a little bit faster during the 365 days of preparation for a big race. While that is the greatest contribution nutrition can make, and triathletes should focus their attention more heavily there, some ergogenic aids may benefit race-day performance. The following sections discuss two substances that may be of benefit. However, whenever you hear about a new wonder supplement, be skeptical. For every ergogenic aid that is effective, there are dozens produced and sold for great profit and no benefit to performance.

Sodium Phosphate

Sodium phosphate is the closest thing to an endurance athlete's wonder drug. Taking sodium phosphate enables your blood to carry a little bit more oxygen. This produces 1 to 2 percent greater output at any triathlon intensity. This is a very significant increase in output. Sodium phosphate is truly a nutrition supplement, not a drug as many so-called supplements are. We eat sodium phosphate every day in meat products, just not enough to maximally benefit our racing. The key to using sodium phosphate, often referred to as phosphate loading, is that you cannot benefit from this supplement frequently. In fact, phosphate loading before more than two events per season (or three if they are perfectly separated by four months) reduces the benefit to almost nothing. The general prescription for phosphate loading is taking 1 gram of sodium phosphate with food four times per day for four days before the race and once on race morning.

Caffeine

Caffeine can improve performance through both physiological and psychological benefits. Caffeine helps transport fatty acids out of fat cells and into the bloodstream where they can be used for fuel. This reduces reliance on carbohydrate for fuel early in a workout or race, which extends endurance. After consuming caffeine, perceived exertion at any intensity is lower. Check with your doctor before beginning or increasing caffeine consumption.

PLYOMETRIC WORKOUTS

Plyometric exercises improve the legs' ability to produce running power efficiently. This type of exercise increases the elasticity of the muscles and connective tissues and trains the neuromuscular system to create forceful contractions more quickly and with greater efficiency.

Begin with the 2-Legged Hop drill (see Chapter 1) for several sets of 30 seconds with 30-second recoveries between reps. This exercise is the most basic plyometrics exercise for running. More aggressive exercises are available, but this exercise is a good starting point, as well as a good reminder for experienced runners whose legs have started to feel sluggish. Gradually increase volume and intensity, remembering that any single-legged drill is much more intense than double-legged drills. Variations to this and other plyometrics exercises are described in Appendix A.

As with all high-intensity running, conservatism and consistency are keys. Plyometrics are high-intensity exercises even if they are not at all fatiguing. The intensity of the impact provides opportunities for injury. A few minutes of plyometrics exercises before each run will help you run faster and more efficiently, but remember that a little bit of plyometrics goes a long way. Be careful and increase volume and intensity very gradually.

PART FOUR

Racing

CHAPTER

The Art of the Taper

Y ou have trained long and hard, and the big A-priority race is quickly approaching. Now it is time to rest. Most athletes and coaches are aware of the need for a taper, but few understand the nuances of planning a taper appropriately. Learning to get the taper just right is a critical aspect of performing to your potential on race day.

The basic idea of the taper is to get fully rested and fresh, but athletes rarely perform at their best immediately after rest. The taper is a two-part process beginning with rest and then including enough high-intensity work to sharpen skills and fine-tune fitness without causing fatigue.

Rest diminishes symptoms of fatigue, which enables you to perform more strongly. Unfortunately, rest can also diminish certain factors that are critical to optimal performance. In particular, blood volume and movement economy may be dramatically reduced even with just a few days of reduced intensity.

The key to tapering, then, is providing enough rest to remove any residual fatigue while inserting enough volume and intensity to maintain fitness and sharp, efficient neuromuscular interactions. Timing is the important part of the equation.

DURATION OF TAPER

A number of factors affect the ideal duration of a taper. Higher-level athletes (high-level amateurs and professionals) need longer tapers, not shorter ones. Although these athletes do have the physical resources to recover more quickly from hard training, they also are able to use greater resources in training on a chronic basis and "dig a deeper hole." In addition, after years of hard training, their bodies will be more resistant to detraining, and fitness will be lost more gradually with reductions in training.

The greater an athlete's level of conditioning, the longer the taper should be. An athlete who has struggled with consistency in training and has not yet come into form may do better to spend an extra week catching up and use a shorter taper.

The greater the race duration, the longer the taper should be. High-volume training demands more rest time than high-intensity training. Many aspects of high-end fitness, including lactate threshold, aerobic capacity, lactate tolerance, and high-speed economy detrain faster than long-distance aerobic fitness. Lactate tolerance, in particular, detrains very quickly. The more critical that is as a limiter, the shorter the taper must be. I generally recommend the following taper lengths for athletes, based on event duration.

- Three- to four-week taper for ironman-distance races
- Two- to three-week taper for international-distance and half-ironman triathlons
- Ten-day to two-week taper for sprint-distance triathlons
- One-week taper for B- and C-priority races

TRAINING VOLUME

Decreasing volume is the most critical factor in a taper. How this is structured will depend on the athlete, the normal training schedule, and the event being trained for. For a four-week taper, volume will be approximately 80 percent, 70 percent, 60 percent, and 40 percent of normal weekly volume. For a two-week taper it might be 75 percent and 50 percent.

Maintain frequency. The goal is to reduce the workload and get rested, not take lots of rest days. Maintaining frequency is critical for maintaining economy and for psychological reasons. Doing some workout—even a 20-minute Zone 1 spin on the bike—will help you optimize performance.

Perform a short set at race intensity, nowhere near race duration, every 72 to 96 hours during the taper. These workouts improve race-pace economy, but they allow full recovery between workouts. The volume of this training should be moderately light at the beginning of the taper period and reduce throughout. These workouts are not to make you stronger, but to sharpen your movements at race pace and maintain efficiency. Even though these workouts include some speed, they should be *very* light.

Light economy workouts can also be very effective. A warm-up, six 200s with 400-meter jog recoveries, and a cool down keep your stride sharp without fatiguing you.

THIRD-DAY-BACK SYNDROME

Athletes tend to be sluggish for their first two workouts after a block of rest. We want to make sure that the priority race isn't one of those. If a full rest and recover day is included in the final week before an A race, place it three or four days out. Do not take either of the last two days before the race off. Sandler and Lobstein discuss this pattern, which I call the "third-day-back syndrome," in their book *Consistent Winning* (Rodale, 1992). They studied records of endurance athletes in the 1970s and 1980s and found that many athletes rested fully the week of a race (with no quality workouts) and then performed at their best Monday or Tuesday after the race. Their research indicates that *reasonably* heavy workloads on the two days before races may produce peak performance if the athlete is fully rested early in the week.

THE FINAL DAYS

Use some light quality training in the several days before the event to increase blood volume, sharpen the neuromuscular interactions that enable economical movements, and develop confidence that the taper has worked. This should *not* be a heavy workout, but it should be challenging enough to "wake up" the muscles. The amount of quality training should be very low and should be specific to the event.

Make sure to ask yourself how these workouts went before race day and reinforce how strong you are feeling to bolster confidence.

Keep bricks extremely light during the taper, because even light bricks are relatively demanding.

Do very short race-pace reps running and swimming two days out and cycling and swimming the day before the race. Even light race-pace running workouts are more demanding than swimming and cycling, so allow an extra day before the race.

XTERRA triathletes need to climb on the bike in the days before the race. I often have them perform 3 x 40-second to one-minute climbs, all with full recovery between reps. I also have them do some specific work on handling skills during the final days before the race.

Any athlete can benefit from some very light economy running in the days leading up to an A race. Keep these reps shorter than normal (about 30 seconds), emphasize full recovery between reps, and allow one day between this workout and the race.

NUTRITION

The few weeks before a priority race are not the time to experiment with diet. High-volume athletes may need to reduce the volume of food they eat during a taper, but I recommend that my athletes eat the same foods that comprise their normal diet.

SLEEP

The taper enables busy athletes to get extra sleep, and this is an important factor. Athletes who nap regularly should continue to do so, but do not add naps if they are not already routine, as they may interfere with sleeping at night. I try to give my athletes fewer morning workouts, enabling them to sleep a little later, and shorter, less-intense evening workouts may make getting to sleep earlier realistic.

REST

I write "Rest & Recover" on my athlete's schedules rather than "Off." I think this reinforces that resting is more than just not working out. Several years ago I had an athlete go dancing until 2:00 A.M. three times during the week before the world championships. Obviously, she did not race well. Tapering athletes should stay off their feet as much as possible. Little things matter.

REPLACEMENT ACTIVITY

Plan something restful with the extra time you have during a taper. Go to the movies or a concert, or read a new book. I remember driving past the home of a client who lived near me on the day before his A race and seeing him digging postholes. Athletes who are used to training three-plus hours a day won't just sit around—unless they plan a stimulating sitting-around activity.

INDIVIDUAL DIFFERENCES

How hard training should be the day before the A race may be a very individual thing. I coached one athlete who thrived on relatively hard workouts the day before races. I rested him heavily early in the week and worked him fairly hard Friday or Saturday before Sunday races.

Review your training logs from previous years and find the five to eight days (workouts or races) you performed the best. Analysis of patterns in the days leading up to these performances may yield useful insight. The athlete I described in the previous paragraph performed his best in Sunday races after long, hard Saturday workouts. This is not the norm, and I am not suggesting that this is the optimal taper, but each athlete is slightly different. Also, do not underestimate the effect of the psychological factors of the taper period on race performance. Just as each athlete's body responds somewhat differently, each psyche will do the same. If you are an exercise addict, find a way to feed your addiction while getting fresh and rested for important races.

GENERAL POINTERS

Triathletes need to keep swimming during their tapers. Swim economy is lost most quickly with time off, and the swimming muscles are less likely to need heavy rest than the legs. Keep high-cadence work on the bike and keep the frequency up. Do just a little torque work (light, low-cadence economy sets) if climbing will be important during the race. I like to get triathletes' running muscles rested early and then get frequency back up in the second half of the week. Keep these workouts light, though. My preferred taper has a light swim and short ride two days before the race, and a similar swim and run the day before the race, with just a little work at race pace. Emphasize long, slow strokes when swimming, high cadence in easy gears when cycling, and high turnover and short strides when running.

Athletes will have more time available during the taper, and since they aren't training their bodies as hard, they can spend a few extra minutes a day training their minds. This is the perfect time to add visualization. Spend five to 10 minutes a day in a quiet place imagining yourself going through the race. Use as many of your senses as you can to feel what race day will be like. Be realistic. If you aren't a good climber, don't imagine yourself flying by everyone on the climbs with ease. Imagine yourself struggling, hurting, and suffering on the climbs, but maintaining smooth and efficient form and keeping a positive attitude.

Many athletes have a hard time following a correct taper because they feel they are losing valuable training time and think if they could just squeeze one more killer workout in they would be stronger on race day. This tendency is not just for beginners and intermediates. A pro mountain biker, ranked in the top three in the United States, had a breakthrough race. I had coached her for three years, but afterward she told me she had finally gained enough trust in me to follow the taper exactly as written. The first time she really followed the taper, she had her best race ever.

Remember all the sacrifices you have made to prepare for an optimal performance on race day, and sacrifice that one last workout you are dying to get in. My staple statement is, "The work is done now. It is too late to do anything now to increase your fitness, but it is not too late to do something to decrease your fitness." It is never too late to make yourself tired for a race.

Even though B- and C-priority races are not usually important enough to warrant a full taper (because you don't want to miss that much training for a lower-priority race), it can be a good idea to do a "practice taper" before a B or C race.

PHOSPHATE LOADING

Discussed in more detail elsewhere in this book (see Chapter 13), sodium phosphate is a powerful and effective ergogenic aid. The general prescription for phosphate loading is taking 1 gram of sodium phosphate with food four times per day for four days before the race and once on race morning. This is the most effective nutrition supplement I have ever used. Be sure you check with your doctor before taking any supplement.

FINAL PREPARATIONS

Two Days Before

Two days before the priority race is the time to get all the logistical issues settled. Decide what you will eat race morning. Put the cassette you plan to race onto your race wheel and your race wheels on the bike. Get your race-day nutrition, clothes, paperwork for registration, maps to the race start, and all your equipment together.

Have a good workout today and make sure to follow the post-workout nutrition strategy that provides the best recovery for you.

The Day Before

The final day before the race, increase carbohydrate consumption to about 4.5 to 5 grams per pound of bodyweight. It is critical to have the gas tanks full at the start line. Some athletes find that decreasing fiber intake the day before the race and decreasing protein intake in the evening helps prevent bloated feelings on race morning.

Have everything prepared for race morning as early as possible. Have your race wheels on the bike. Have breakfast as prepared as possible. Have your race clothes laid out and your race-day bag packed.

Race Morning

Make sure the alarm clock goes off early enough on race morning that you won't be rushed. The stress of hurrying won't help you race well, even if you do get everything taken care of. Develop a routine for race mornings. On the days of important races, it will be less stressful to simply fall into a familiar routine.

I think it is generally a mistake to wake up early to get a feeding at the exact physiologically optimal time. The sleep is more valuable.

Warming Up

Allow yourself plenty of time to warm up on the bike, the run, and then the swim. Keep the warm-up relatively light, with a few accelerations to race pace. Fuel and hydrate after the bike and run warm-up, and then prepare for the swim. Keep your swim warm-up as close to the race start as possible. Even when you cannot swim anymore, keep your arms moving and make sure your muscles do not cool down. Even treading water instead of standing on the bottom will help keep you warmed up.

The Start

Again, make sure to give yourself enough time. Nothing should be rushed on race morning. When the gun goes off, get into a rhythm with long, slow strokes. Do not overkick. Save your legs for the bike and run.

Planning every small detail of race preparation will help you enter the race fully confident that you are as ready as you possibly could be. Make sure to take advantage of anything that might help you perform your very best on that day.

REFERENCES

Sandler, Ronald and Dennis Lobstein. *Consistent Winning*. New York: Rodale Press, 1992.

16 Race-Day Running

Ideal performance on the run begins before you even pull your running shoes onto your feet. Biking quickly but efficiently plays an enormous role in your run split. A full discussion of cycling preparation is beyond the scope of this book, so we will only cover the ways cycling affects your running.

Dehydrated and glycogen-depleted triathletes do not run fast. Maintaining hydration and refueling on the bike are critical. Consume about two calories of carbohydrate per hour per pound of bodyweight. Drink about 2 ounces of water per hour per 15 pounds of bodyweight. For half-ironman and ironman-distance races, consume 4 milligrams sodium per hour per pound of bodyweight. Be consistent. You should eat and drink every 15 to 20 minutes throughout the bike.

Triathletes consistently run faster after maintaining high cadence on the bike. Higher-cadence riding reduces the force the muscles are required to produce to maintain any speed and requires less use of the sprint muscle fibers. Even strong cyclists who are able to push a big gear and sustain the effort for the duration of the bike segment will lose more time on the run by doing so. Riding a minute faster in a big gear is not a good idea if it costs you two minutes on the run. Train yourself to maintain a cadence of 92 to 100 rpm even on very easy rides. Your run splits will improve.

Ease up slightly for the last half-mile of the bike, increasing cadence further and using an even easier gear. The transition from bike to run is the most difficult part of the race for most triathletes. Reducing the lactic acid levels in the legs and getting breathing fully under control will enable a smoother transition. Giving up just a couple of seconds here will improve your run split by more than it costs your bike split.

IN TRANSITION

Watch a professional triathlete in transition. Nothing looks rushed or hurried, just smooth—but they are out in just a few seconds. Good transitions are smooth. Concentrate on smoothly moving through your plan without excessive hurrying. Overexcitement in transition will hurt your running.

Plan your transitions. Know the order in which you will put on your helmet, sunglasses, race number, and so on. Do these the same way every race. Several practice transitions the day before the race will help.

Most triathletes should not eat or drink in transition. During transition and for several minutes after, the body is rerouting blood from the cycling muscles to the running muscles. This is not the time to add water and calories to the stomach, drawing more blood there. Wait just two or three minutes and the water and fuel will be absorbed better and with reduced risk of stomach irritation.

OUT ON THE RUN

Heading out of the transition area is likely to be one of the most difficult parts of the run. Don't assume that your legs will only feel worse as time goes by. Your legs are accustomed to riding, and it usually takes a few minutes for the body to adjust to running.

Right from the very start of the run, get your turnover up. This will probably require very short strides at first. As your legs adjust to running, stride length will return naturally. Don't force it. Keep the turnover high and let your stride lengthen out as your cycling legs loosen up and become running legs.

About one-half mile into the run is a good time to think about fueling and hydrating. By this time, the bounce should have returned to your stride and breathing should be controlled. Once the body has adjusted from cycling to running, begin to give it water and sugar.

Fall into race pace and concentrate on monitoring intensity through heart rate, perceived exertion, and mile splits. Understand that the first part of the run may be the worst. Don't assume that the fatigue of transferring from bike to run will last.

PACING

After the first half-mile of the run, the legs should loosen up. The first half-mile may be the slowest section of the run, but be patient with yourself while you transition from cyclist to runner.

Once your running legs return, settle into running at goal pace. Use perceived exertion, heart rate, and mile splits to pace yourself. You should have run many miles in the past several months at this exact pace, so it should feel natural even though your levels of fatigue and pain will be higher than in training. If you find yourself below race pace, adjust gradually. An international-distance triathlete hitting the first mile marker 20 seconds slower than goal pace needs to run less than four seconds per mile faster than goal pace to make up the difference. Avoid overcorrecting, a major cause of pace fluctuations, which drives fatigue to a higher level.

Expect heart rate to be higher than normal. Fatigue from the bike and excitement from the race atmosphere may push your heart rate well beyond normal race-pace levels. Analyze exertion based on heart rate, ventilation, burn in legs, and responsiveness of legs, along with splits and heart rate.

As we become more fatigued, we tend to think that we can only feel worse as the race continues on. In every race, even on our very best days, how we feel will fluctuate. There will be peaks and valleys. If you start feeling bad, fuel and hydrate, moderate pace slightly, check that you are using economical techniques (especially high turnover), and you will probably feel better in a few minutes. When things start to get back under control, consider pushing just a little bit more. Racing to your potential is supposed to hurt. If you find that you cannot hold pace, make subtle adjustments and review again in a couple of minutes.

Avoid asking yourself if you are going to quit—and by quit I mean stop racing, not necessarily dropping out of the race. If you ask yourself that question often enough, you'll give in. Even if you tell yourself to keep going 99 percent of the time, the race will be a failure because of that 1 percent. Decide that, barring the likelihood of injury, you will give 100 percent today—regardless of how well you perform. Quitting racing is not an option. The pain of pushing is temporary; the pain of quitting lasts.

Ryan Bolton once told me, "If your attitude starts to turn down, eat some sugar." Very frequently a feeding brings a mental lift as well as a physical lift. Blood sugar level affects our brain as well as our muscles, and I have found that to be excellent advice.

Remember to follow your strategy for fueling and hydrating. We tend to lose track of these things in the excitement of the race when we feel good. Farther down the road we won't feel so good if we don't stick to our plan.

WHEN FATIGUE SETS IN

A triathlete's legs are going to fatigue in every race. Pushing 100 percent hurts, it exhausts fuel reserves, it dehydrates, and it causes acid accumulation in the muscles and in the blood. How does a triathlete continue running fast and efficiently as the legs fatigue?

When we want to run faster, we generally think about increasing the force and the speed of our push-off. This increases both turnover and stride length. When our legs are fresh this works well and our speed increases quickly and easily, but it does require more forceful contractions from the muscles that create propulsion. Toward the end of the race, the muscles can't do this. This approach is analogous to a fatigued cyclist who can't keep cadence up deciding to shift to a harder gear, thereby asking the fatigued muscles to create even greater force while increasing cadence.

I recommend that triathletes, when they feel their legs fatiguing toward the end of the race, concentrate on driving the knee forward more powerfully during leg recovery. The propulsive muscles are tired from driving your bodyweight forward at a sustained speed for a long time. The muscles that drive leg recovery, the hip flexors, have only been driving the weight of your leg forward, not your entire bodyweight. No matter how fatigued a triathlete gets from sustained hard running, the hip flexors should be able to drive the knee forward quickly. This increases turnover, enabling the athlete to run faster without greater force production from the propulsive muscles (they fire more frequently, but not more forcefully).

Plan every aspect of your run ahead of time. Think through your pacing goals, nutrition, and mental strategies. Practice these strategies in C-priority races, race-pace workouts, and bricks, and you give yourself the best opportunity to run fast on race day.

R E F E R E N C E S

Gottschall, J. S. and Bradley Palmer. "The acute effects of prior cycling cadence on running performance and kinematics." *Med Sci Sports Exer* 54 (2002): 1516–21.

Epilogue

This book was a greater challenge for me than expected. After six years studying exercise physiology, nutrition, biology, and psychology at Virginia Polytechnic University and nine years of coaching, I did not realize just how complicated preparing a triathlete to run well can be until I sat down to put it in writing. So many factors go into training a multisport athlete. Volumes have been written about the physiology of training, which is but one important factor in preparing for triathlon. Biomechanics, nutrition, psychology, lifestyle-management, and a host of other areas of expertise play into developing and implementing effective training methods and making use of all the preparation on race day.

Although comprehensive coverage of the topic was beyond the scope of this book, we did touch on running economy. I encourage every reader to take that section of the book seriously, because that is where the greatest gains are to be made. Do the same with your swimming and cycling.

The information contained in this book reflects the latest in scientific research and experience that I know of today. Certainly, training methods will continue to move forward and improve. In the next few years I am sure we will see new and better methods developed.

In the preface I stated that the goals of this book were to help you to run a little bit faster in your next race and to enjoy the sport of triathlon a little bit more. I hope this has happened and that reading *The Triathlete's Guide to Run Training* will make your triathlon career a little bit more successful.

APPENDIX A
Run Workout Menu

ENDURANCE WORKOUTS

Endurance workouts are most prominent during the Preparation and Base periods of training, but most of your training should be endurance work throughout the year. Monitor intensity closely during endurance workouts. Doing these workouts too intensely will not make you faster, but it will deplete you for the workouts that are designed to make you faster.

Recovery. Do these workouts preferably on flat, soft terrain such as a packed dirt or gravel trail, and run in Zone 1. Keep all movements extremely quick and light. Use a metronome to monitor turnover, staying at approximately 180 steps per minute, and keep stride length extremely short. These workouts may also be done on a treadmill.

Athletes vary considerably in their bodies' reactions to recovery running. Some athletes benefit from an additional weekly run, which improves economy and accelerates workout recovery. Others find that extra runs on non-breakthrough days lead to fatigue and injuries. Many athletes should swim, bike, or crosstrain for active recovery and avoid active recovery running.

Basic Endurance. The staple workout for all triathlon training is a basic endurance run. This workout is used for long runs and for moderate-duration midweek runs. Do this workout on flat to gently rolling terrain. After a few minutes of warm-up in Zone 1, maintain Zone 2 intensity throughout the run. Monitor turnover with a metronome, staying at approximately 180 steps per minute. Be sure to fuel and hydrate adequately.

FORCE WORKOUTS

Also see all hill workouts under muscular endurance, aerobic capacity, and anaerobic capacity workouts.

Weighted Running. Do a 20- to 90-minute run wearing a weight vest, keeping intensity in Zone 2. Use a metronome to monitor turnover, keeping it at about 180 steps per minute. Concentrate on keeping your foot-strike directly beneath your hips and notice the increased jarring and breaking when your foot strikes out in front. Begin this workout with 20 minutes and about 2.5 pounds in the vest, and increase your duration gradually to 40 to 90 minutes and weight to a maximum of 5 to 8 percent of bodyweight. Most triathletes benefit from these workouts in the Base period, and force-limited athletes benefit from maintenance workouts of this variety throughout the year.

Horizontal Resistance Running. Increasing the force requirements for horizontal propulsion will benefit force-limited runners. Since gravity works vertically, some artificial resistance is required. These workouts can be done with a partner and should be emphasized during the Base period. With a yoga belt tied around your hips, run while pulling your partner. Your partner should hold the end of the belt slightly higher than your hip level so you cannot overcome the resistance by extending the knee. Maintain a Zone 2 pace and have your partner provide enough resistance to increase intensity to Zone 3. Concentrate on feeling the falling-forward body position.

This workout is effective strength-transfer training to teach the muscles to contract forcefully. This is an especially good workout for athletes who have trouble developing the feel of using the hip muscles for propulsion instead of the thigh muscles.

Hill Fartlek. On a rolling course, run easily on flats and downhills, but run hard up every hill. The hard segments could be at lactate threshold (LT) or six-minute time trial (TT6) pace depending on the purpose and training period. Use a metronome to monitor turnover and keep it at 180 steps per minute or higher. Concentrate on driving the knee quickly uphill and pulling the foot back and down powerfully into the ground, instead of just allowing gravity to pull you down into contact with the ground.

MUSCULAR ENDURANCE WORKOUTS

Tempo. Run on a flat to gently rolling course. After a thorough warm-up in Zones 1 and 2, increase pace slightly to maintain Zone 3 intensity for a 20- to 40-minute segment. Finish the run in Zone 2. This workout should only be used during the Base period, as it may deplete the legs for high-intensity workouts in the Build or Peak periods.

Cruise Intervals. Cruise intervals are excellent as an introduction to lactate threshold training or anytime an LT workout is appropriate but extra-quick recovery is required for the next breakthrough workout. On a flat to gently rolling course or on a treadmill, complete four to six intervals of four to six minutes at Zone 4 intensity, with one- to two-minute recoveries between intervals at a Zone 2 pace. Use a metronome to monitor turnover and keep it at about 180 steps per minute.

Hill Cruise Intervals. This workout is the same as cruise intervals, except it is done on a long, steady grade of 2 to 4 percent. Run four to six minutes up the hill and jog back down. Use a metronome to monitor turnover and keep it at 180 steps per minute or higher. Concentrate on driving the knee quickly uphill and pulling the foot back and down powerfully into the ground, instead of just allowing gravity to pull you down into contact with the ground.

Crisscross Threshold. On a flat to gently rolling course, run for 15 to 30 minutes, alternating between Zone 4 and Zone 5a. Then for two to three minutes, run in Zone 4. Increase pace for two to three minutes to an intensity that will plateau you in Zone 5a. Continue to alternate between these intensities for the duration of the crisscross segment.

Lactate Threshold Tempo. On a flat to gently rolling course, run at a steady tempo in Zone 4. The LT segments should be 12 to 20 minutes each in high Zone 4 or 15 to 40 minutes in low Zone 4. Use a metronome to monitor turnover and keep it at about 180 steps per minute.

AEROBIC CAPACITY WORKOUTS

Hill Intervals. On a relatively steep hill with a 4- to 8-percent grade that takes one to three minutes to run up, do four to 12 repeats. Jog slowly back down the hill for recovery. Do not walk. Heart rate should reach Zone 5b by the end of the second and every successive interval. Use a metronome to monitor turnover and keep it at 180 steps per minute or higher. Concentrate on driving the knee quickly uphill and pulling the foot back and down powerfully into the ground, instead of just allowing gravity to pull you down into contact with the ground.

Hill Repeats. On a relatively steep hill with a 4- to 8-percent grade that takes two to four minutes to run up, do three to six repeats, walk downhill for one minute, and jog the remainder slowly for recovery. Intensity should climb to Zone 5b by the end of each repeat. Use a metronome to monitor turnover and keep it at 180 steps per minute or higher. Concentrate on driving the knee quickly uphill and pulling the foot back and down powerfully into the ground, instead of just allowing gravity to pull you down into contact with the ground. Monitor joints and connective tissue carefully during these workouts and stop the workout if injury seems likely. Allow adequate recovery between workouts.

Aerobic Capacity Intervals. Run four to six intervals that take two to four minutes to complete at TT6 pace. You should achieve Zone 5b heart rate by the end of the second and each succeeding interval. For recovery, jog half the distance of the interval. For example, run 5 x 800 meters with 400-meter recovery jogs. Experienced athletes may conduct these workouts on roads or trainers, using time instead of distance to measure repetitions. Recovery segments would also be measured by time and kept equal in duration to the interval.

I highly recommend doing these workouts on a track for the first cycle each season to allow yourself to relearn the perceived exertion and heart rate responses of running at TT6 pace. Remember that running faster than TT6 pace is detrimental to the goals of this workout.

Aerobic Capacity Repeats. These workouts should only be included in the schedules of advanced sprint- or international-distance athletes during Build 2 or Peak periods after they have successfully completed a phase of aerobic capacity intervals. This is a very stressful aerobic capacity and lactate tolerance workout.

Run three to five repeats of four to five minutes each at TT6 pace. Heart rate should reach Zone 5b by the end of each repeat. Walk for one minute and jog for four minutes or longer to allow almost complete recovery between reps (complete recovery will take several days).

For motivated athletes, these can be very effective workouts, providing physical and psychological benefits, but they are very costly. A little bit goes a long way and they require a lot of recovery time before the next breakthrough workout.

LT-AC Sets. This workout, similar to cruise intervals for lactate threshold training, provides an excellent benefit and allows quicker recovery than standard aerobic capacity (AC) workouts. This is an excellent introduction to AC training in the Build 1 period and is also very effective during Peak period. This workout counts as a lactate threshold (muscular endurance) workout and an aerobic capacity (anaerobic endurance) workout.

Run two to four reps of four to 10 minutes each in high Zone 4, followed immediately by two to four minutes at TT6 pace. Walk and jog for at least five minutes to allow almost complete recovery between reps.

LACTATE TOLERANCE WORKOUTS

See also aerobic capacity repeats, aerobic capacity hill repeats, and crisscross threshold workouts.

Lactate Tolerance Interval and Repeat Training. Any aerobic capacity workout can be modified to improve lactate tolerance. Follow the instructions for the workout, except accelerate from TT6 pace to economy pace for the last 30 seconds of each interval or the last minute of each repeat, keeping recovery period durations the same. Be sure to maintain a solid Zone 2 pace during interval recoveries. When adjusting aerobic capacity workouts this way, reduce the number of reps to one-half to two-thirds of the number originally recommended.

Races. Two-mile to 5K running races make excellent lactate tolerance workouts. Races are always the most demanding workouts, so make sure to allow adequate recovery in the following days.

ECONOMY WORKOUTS

Strides. Run for 20 to 40 seconds at economy pace with three or more minutes of recovery between. Use a metronome to monitor turnover and keep it at 180 steps per minute or higher. Get turnover as high as possible on these sets. I recommend conducting these workouts on a track from time to time to make sure you have a feel for optimal pace. Remember that these are not sprints and running them too fast may reduce economy. The goal is maximizing turnover, not running speed. Learn to run at economy pace with extremely high turnover while maintaining relaxation.

Running this workout barefoot on grass can be beneficial, but be sure the area is smooth and free of debris such as rocks.

Pickups. Within an endurance run, insert 3 to 12 20-second accelerations to economy pace at extremely high turnover. Allow full recovery between reps.

Hill Sprints. This can be an effective economy workout for athletes training for a race with a hilly run course. On a steep hill with a 6- to 8-percent grade, sprint up for 20 seconds three to six times. Concentrate on driving the knee quickly uphill and pulling the foot back and down powerfully into the ground, instead of allowing gravity to pull you down into contact with the ground. Keep turnover at 180 steps per minute or higher. Higher is better!

PLYOMETRIC WORKOUTS

The following are relatively gentle plyometrics workouts. Many more aggressive plyometrics exercises exist, but the injury risk and extended recovery time from the higher intensity is not worth any potential benefit for most triathletes.

Two-Legged Hop. Stand in the running posture with your arms at your sides and begin to "bounce," hopping just a couple of inches in the air. Make sure that the knee angle stays constant and that all vertical movement comes from the elastic recoil action in the feet and calves. Concentrate on relaxation, especially in the quadriceps. Begin with three to five sets of 30 seconds with a 30-second recovery in between.

The purpose of this drill is to develop the ability to create power from the elastic recoil of the feet and calves instead of the thighs. Mastering this drill develops the skills of storing and releasing energy quickly through elastic recoil, creating quick contractions in the quadriceps to prevent knee bend at foot-strike, and maintaining relaxation in the thighs when contractions are unnecessary. This drill also increases the strength, endurance, and elasticity of the muscles and connective tissues of the foot and calf.

Single-Leg Jumping. Perform the previous drill, but bend one knee to a 90-degree angle and jump on one leg. This effectively doubles the workload, so perform the two-legged hop consistently for at least a month before adding single-leg jumping.

Running in Place. From the two-legged hop, begin alternating support between the right and left legs. Lift one foot up directly toward the hips (just a few inches at first) while bouncing on the other. Establish a quick rhythm, but *be careful not to raise your body from the knees using the quadriceps. The knee angle of the support leg should remain constant, and the quadriceps should remain relaxed. All of the power for the movement should come from the "bouncing" of the feet and calves.*

As you lift the legs in this drill, move the knee forward and the heel backward equally. Lift the leg until the lower leg is parallel to the ground.

Notice that during this drill your feet always remain directly underneath your hips. Try this drill with a foot-strike 6 inches out in front of your hips. If you can do it at all, significant energy is wasted on balance and support—energy that should be directed to propulsion.

This drill furthers the goals of the previous drill, and forces runners to place their foot-strikes directly below the center of mass, landing on the balls of the feet and using elastic recoil.

Running in Place with High Knees. From the running in place drill, begin lifting your knees in front of your body up to hip height so that the upper leg is horizontal. Be careful not to lean backward while performing this drill. This variation emphasizes the importance of a powerful knee drive to initiate recovery and develops strength and endurance in the hip flexor muscles.

Running in Place with Heel-Flick. From the running in place drill, begin kicking your heels backward as if kicking yourself in the butt. This drill emphasizes the importance of a quick and relaxed heel-flick and develops strength and endurance in the hamstring muscles. This is the best drill for developing ideal body position.

TEST WORKOUTS

Test workouts help an athlete determine if training is progressing effectively and boost confidence in preparation for priority races, and they may also be motivating. Many athletes find that the frequent feedback from test workouts keeps their passion for training sharp. In a sense, these workouts serve as a smaller carrot dangling within closer reach, compared to the big carrot of a race that may be many months in the future. Athletes vary on this, so include test workouts during every training cycle if they work for you, but don't feel that they are necessary. Make sure that test workouts are specific to your race limiters and the training objectives of the period you are in at the time.

Aerobic Time Trial. Aerobic time trials are test workouts conducted at a specific intensity, instead of maximal speed, for the duration. They are best done on a track or relatively flat loop that can be used repeatedly for the same test. Run for a designated distance or duration at a specific heart rate. Measure and record time as well as average heart rate. Make sure to complete a thorough warm-up before starting the time trial.

Remember that conditions, including environment and level of recovery, will have an enormous effect on tests. When you plan test workouts, try to place them at times when you will be well recovered. When you record and analyze results, take conditions into account.

The following time trials may be useful depending on the training period and your race limiters:

- Zone 2: Run with heart rate at the top of Zone 2 for 20 to 60 minutes.
- LT: Run with heart rate at the top of Zone 4 for 12 to 30 minutes.

Race-Pace Time Trial. Run at race pace for a duration that is significantly less than race distance. Monitor and record average heart rate and perceived exertion. Also note the trend in heart rate; averaging 160 bpm with low 150s early in the climbing to mid-160s toward the end of the run is a different result than a steady 160 throughout. Sprint-distance triathletes should run 1 mile at race pace. International-distance triathletes should run 1 to 2 miles at race pace. Half-ironman-distance athletes should run 2 to 6 miles at race pace. Ironman- and ultra-distance athletes should run 6 to 12 miles at race pace.

LT Time Trial. Check average heart rate and time over a given loop, maintaining heart rate as close to LT as possible.

Time Trial Basics. Time trials are all-out efforts for a given distance or duration. These can be extremely costly, both physically and mentally, so don't include them more than once per cycle. You can use any course on which a time trial can be repeated. Common time trials include the following.

- TT6: This is used to determine the pace for aerobic capacity training. Repeat this every training cycle that includes aerobic capacity training.

- 30-Minute Time Trial: A 30-minute time trial will be improved by increasing lactate threshold, lactate tolerance, economy, pacing skills, and mental toughness. Do not use this too often!

APPENDIX B
Brick Workout Menu

ENDURANCE BRICK WORKOUTS

Endurance Brick. Complete a long ride on a flat to gently rolling course, staying Zone 2. Transition as quickly as possible, and do a long run on a mostly flat course, also staying Zone 2. Doing this workout on a soft surface is ideal. Total time for this workout will be between two and six hours. Generally, the bike will comprise about two-thirds of the duration and the run about one-third, but this can be adjusted in either direction to prioritize limiters. All triathletes could use this workout in the Base period. Ironman-distance triathletes and endurance-limited triathletes should also use this workout in the Build period.

Long Ride Brick. After a very long ride (two to six hours), transition as quickly as possible and do a 15-minute run in Zone 2. This workout develops the ability to run efficiently soon after getting off the bike and doesn't significantly extend recovery time from the long ride. Doing this workout Sunday after a Saturday long run works very well.

Reverse Brick. After a long run, transition as quickly as possible and go for a one- to two-hour Zone 2 ride. This allows you to extend the duration of the workout without the risk of injury and overtraining that extending the run would. This is especially effective early in the Base period or for run endurance–limited triathletes.

FORCE BRICK WORKOUTS

Weighted Running Off the Bike. Use a weight vest on a long ride brick. This workout should only be used by force-limited athletes who have used the vest through the Base phase and are in the Build phase. The weight vest can be very effective for 15 minutes after a long ride, but do not use the weight vest for endurance bricks with longer runs.

Hill Brick. Ride and run on a hilly course at intensities ranging from Zone 2 to Zone 4. On the bike, stay seated on climbs to build force. This is an effective workout for force-limited triathletes during the Base period and for triathletes training for a hilly race during the Base and Build periods.

MUSCULAR ENDURANCE BRICK WORKOUTS

Lactate Threshold Brick. Ride for one to two hours in Zone 1 and 2. Increase intensity to Zone 4 for a segment of 20 to 40 minutes. Then, transition as quickly as possible and run at Zone 4 intensity for 15 to 30 minutes. Cool down.

Bike Lactate Threshold Brick. This is an excellent workout for cycling-limited triathletes, especially those with strong running background who have trouble running to their capabilities off the bike. After a thorough warm-up, perform two to six sets of bike LT bricks. Ride for six to 12 minutes in high Zone 4, transition as quickly as possible, and run 1 to 2 miles at Zone 2 intensity. Concentrate on getting turnover up right away without forcing stride length, and allow your stride to open up gradually as the cycling legs become running legs. Transition back to cycling shoes and repeat for the desired number of repetitions.

Race-Pace Brick. After a thorough warm-up, ride at race intensity for one-third to one-half of race duration. Transition as quickly as possible and run at race intensity for one-third to one-half of race duration. In this workout, follow your race strategies for pacing, fueling, hydrating, and mental processes. Simulate race-day conditions as closely as possible, but do not exceed one-half of race duration.

Lactate Threshold Brick Intervals. After a thorough warm-up on both bike and run, perform 20 to 60 minutes of LT brick intervals. Ride for four to six minutes in high Zone 4, transition as quickly as possible, and run three to four minutes at high Zone 4 intensity. Transition back to cycling shoes as quickly as possible and repeat for an unbroken set of the predetermined duration. Use fueling and hydrating guidelines for international-distance races during this workout. This workout can be done anywhere, but bringing the trainer to the track gives you pace feedback during the run.

AEROBIC CAPACITY BRICK WORKOUTS

Aerobic Capacity Brick Repeats. Take your bike and trainer to a track. After a thorough warm-up on both bike and run, perform three to six sets of brick repeats. Ride three minutes on the bike at CP6 intensity (six-minute time trial effort), followed immediately by running 400 to 800 meters at TT6 pace. Jog 400 meters, transition back to cycling shoes, pedal easily for three to five minutes, and repeat for the desired number of sets.

Running Aerobic Capacity Brick Repeats. This is an especially effective workout for run-limited sprint- or international-distance triathletes. After a thorough warm-up on both bike and run, complete three to five sets of repeats. Ride at Zone 4 intensity for four to six minutes, transition as quickly as possible to the run, and run at TT6 pace for three to four minutes. Jog several minutes, transition back to cycling shoes, pedal easily for almost complete recovery, and repeat.

LACTATE TOLERANCE BRICK WORKOUTS

Lactate Tolerance Brick. Perform any of the aerobic capacity brick workouts, but add one minute of all-out effort to the end of each cycling segment and run each repetition above TT6 intensity. Allow greater recovery time between repetitions and limit repetitions to one-half the number recommended for aerobic capacity training.

APPENDIX C
Sample Training Schedules

NOTE: All distances are given in yards.

All time is given in hours and minutes, unless otherwise stated.

SPRINT DISTANCE: BEGINNER/INTERMEDIATE

	WEEK #1	WEEK #2	WEEK #3	WEEK #4
BASE PHASE				
MON.	Easy Swim	Easy Swim	Easy Swim	Rest & Recover
TUES.	Run :30 Z2	Run :35 Z2	Run :40 Z2	Run :30 Z2
	WEEK 1–4: Concentrate on maintaining very high turnover with very short stride length.			
	Weight Training	Weight Training	Weight Training	Weight Training
WED.	Easy Swim	Easy Swim	Easy Swim	Easy Swim
	Ride :45 Z1–2	Ride 1:00 Z1–2	Ride 1:15 Z1–2	Ride :45 Z1–2
	WEEK 1–3: Hold high cadence (95+ rpm)			
THUR.	Run :35 Z2, include 4 x 20 sec. strides	Run :40 Z2, include 4 x 20 sec. strides	Run :45 Z2, include 4 x 20 sec. strides	Run :30 Z2, include 4 strides
	Weight Training	Weight Training	Weight Training	Weight Training
FRI.	Easy Swim	Easy Swim	Easy Swim	Easy Swim
SAT.	Run :45 Z2, include 4 x 20 sec. strides	Run :55 Z2, include 4 x 20 sec. strides	Run 1:05 Z2, include 4 x 20 sec. strides	Run 1:00 Z2, include 4 strides
SUN.	Ride 1:00 Z1–2	Ride 1:15 Z1–2	Ride 1:30 Z1–2	Ride 1:00 Z1–2
BUILD PHASE				
MON.	Easy Swim	Easy Swim	Easy Swim	Rest & Recover
TUES.	Run @ Track: 6-min. Time Trial; 3 x 200 @ Econ Pace, jog 400	Run @ Track: 4 x 400 @ AC Pace, jog 200; 3 x 200 @ Econ Pace, jog 400	Run @ Track: 6 x 400 @ AC Pace, jog 200	Run :30 Z2
WED.	Swim w/ Race-Pace Work	Swim w/ Race-Pace Work	Swim w/ Race-Pace Work	Easy Swim
	Ride :45 w/ :10 low Z4	Ride :55 w/ :15 low Z4	Ride 1:05 w/ :20 low Z4	Ride :45 Z1–2
	WEEK 1–3: Hold high cadence (95+ rpm)			
THUR.	Run :40 Z2	Run :50 Z2	Run 1:00 Z2	Run :30 Z2
FRI.	Easy Swim	Easy Swim	Easy Swim	Easy Swim
SAT.	Run 1:00 Z2, include 4 x 20 sec. strides	Run 1:10 Z2, include 4 x 20 sec. strides	Run 1:20 Z2, include 4 x 20 sec. strides	Run 1:00 Z2, include 4 strides
SUN.	Ride 1:30 w/ 2 x :10 low Z4	Ride 1:30 w/ 2 x :12 low Z4	Ride 1:30 w/ 2 x :14 low Z4	Ride 1:00 Z1–2

SPRINT DISTANCE: ADVANCED/ELITE

	WEEK #1	WEEK #2	WEEK #3	WEEK #4
BASE PHASE				
MON.	Easy Swim	Easy Swim	Easy Swim	Easy Swim
TUES.	Run 1:00 w/ 3 x [:06 low Z4 /:02 rec]	Run 1:00 w/ 4 x [:06 low Z4 /:02 rec]	Run 1:00 w/ 5 x [:06 low Z4 /:02 rec]	Run 1:00 Z2
	WEEK 1–4: Concentrate on maintaining very high turnover with very short stride length.			
	Weight Training	Weight Training	Weight Training	Weight Training
WED.	Masters Swim	Masters Swim	Masters Swim	Masters Swim
	Ride 1:30 w/ 2 x :10 low Z4	Ride 1:45 w/ 2 x :12 low Z4	Ride 2:00 w/ 2 x :14 low Z4	Ride 1:30 Z1-2
	WEEK 1–3: Hold high cadence (95+ rpm)			
THUR.	Run 1:00 Z2, include 4 x 30 sec. strides	Run 1:10 Z2, include 4 x 30 sec. strides	Run 1:20 Z2, include 4 x 30 sec. strides	Run :30 Z2, include 4 strides
	Weight Training	Weight Training	Weight Training	Weight Training
FRI.	Masters Swim	Masters Swim	Masters Swim	Masters Swim
SAT.	Run 1:20 Z2, include 4 x 20 sec. strides	Run 1:30 Z2, include 4 x 20 sec. strides	Run 1:40 Z2, include 4 x 20 sec. strides	Run 1:00 Z2, include 4 strides
SUN.	Ride 2:00 Z1–2	Ride 2:30 Z1–2	Ride 3:00 Z1–2	Ride 2:00 Z1–2
BUILD PHASE				
MON.	Easy Swim	Easy Swim	Easy Swim	Rest & Recover
TUES.	Run @ Track: 6-min. Time Trial; 3 x 200 @ Econ Pace, jog 400	Run @ Track: 4 x 800 @ AC Pace, jog 200; 4 x 200 @ Econ Pace, jog 400	Run @ Track: 5 x 800 @ AC Pace, jog 200; 5 x 200 @ Econ Pace,	Run :30 Z2
WED.	Swim w/ Race-Pace Work	Swim w/ Race-Pace Work	Swim w/ Race-Pace Work	Easy Swim
	Ride 1:30 w/:15 high Z4	Ride 1:30 w/:20 high Z4	Ride 1:30 w/:20 high Z4	Ride 1:30
	WEEK 1–3: Hold high cadence (95+ rpm)			
THUR.	Run :40 Z2	Run :50 Z2	Run 1:00 Z2	Run :30 Z2
FRI.	Easy Swim	Easy Swim	Easy Swim	Easy Swim
SAT.	Run 1:00 w/ :20 low Z4, include 4 x 30 sec. strides	Run 1:10 w/ :25 low Z4, include 4 x 30 sec. strides	Run 1:20 w/ :30 low Z4, include 4 x 30 sec. strides	Run 1:00 Z2, include 4 strides
SUN.	Ride 1:30 w/ 2 x :10 low Z4	Ride 1:30 w/ 2 x :12 low Z4	Ride 1:30 w/ 2 x :14 low Z4	Ride 1:00 Z 1–2

INTERNATIONAL DISTANCE: BEGINNER/INTERMEDIATE

	WEEK #1	WEEK #2	WEEK #3	WEEK #4
BASE PHASE				
MON.	Easy Swim	Easy Swim	Easy Swim	Rest & Recover
TUES.	Run :40 Z2	Run :50 Z2	Run 1:00 Z2	Run :30 Z2
	WEEK 1–4: Concentrate on maintaining very high turnover with very short stride length.			
	Weight Training	Weight Training	Weight Training	Weight Training
WED.	Easy Swim	Easy Swim	Easy Swim	Easy Swim
	Ride :45 Z1–2	Ride 1:00 Z1–2	Ride 1:15 Z1–2	Ride :45 Z1–2
	WEEK 1–3: Hold high cadence (95+ rpm)			
THUR.	Run :40 Z2	Run :50 Z2	Run 1:00 Z2	Run :30 Z2
	Weight Training	Weight Training	Weight Training	Weight Training
FRI.	Easy Swim	Easy Swim	Easy Swim	Easy Swim
SAT.	Run 1:00 Z2	Run 1:10 Z2	Run 1:20 Z2	Run 1:00 Z2
SUN.	Ride 1:00 Z1–2	Ride 1:15 Z1–2	Ride 1:30 Z1–2	Ride 1:00 Z1–2
BUILD PHASE				
MON.	Easy Swim	Easy Swim	Easy Swim	Rest & Recover
TUES.	Run @ Track: 6-min. Time Trial; 3 x 200 @ Econ Pace, jog 400	Run @ Track: 4 x 400 @ AC Pace, jog 200; 3 x 200 @ Econ Pace, jog 400	Run @ Track: 5 x 400 @ AC Pace, jog 200; 3 x 200 @ EconPace	Run :30 Z2
WED.	Swim w/ Race-Pace Work	Swim w/ Race-Pace Work	Swim w/ Race-Pace Work	Easy Swim
	Ride :45 w/ :10 low Z4	Ride :55 w/ :15 low Z4	Ride 1:05 w/ :20 low Z4	Ride :45 Z1–2
	WEEK 1–3: Hold high cadence (95+ rpm)			
THUR.	Run :40 Z2	Run :50 Z2	Run 1:00 Z2	Run :30 Z2
FRI.	Easy Swim	Easy Swim	Easy Swim	Easy Swim
SAT.	Run 1:20 Z2	Run 1:30 Z2	Run 1:40 Z2	Run 1:00 Z2
SUN.	Ride 1:30 w/ 2 x :10 low Z4	Ride 1:30 w/ 2 x :12 low Z4	Ride 1:30 w/ 2 x :14 low Z4	Ride 1:00 Z1–2

INTERNATIONAL DISTANCE: ADVANCED/ELITE

	WEEK #1	WEEK #2	WEEK #3	WEEK #4
BASE PHASE				
MON.	Easy Swim	Easy Swim	Easy Swim	Easy Swim
TUES.	Run 1:00 w/ 3 x [:06 low Z4 / :02 rec]	Run 1:00 w/ 4 x [:06 low Z4 / :02 rec]	Run 1:00 w/ 5 x [:06 low Z4 / :02 rec]	Run 1:00 Z2
	WEEK 1–4: Concentrate on maintaining very high turnover with very short stride length.			
	Weight Training	Weight Training	Weight Training	Weight Training
WED.	Masters Swim	Masters Swim	Masters Swim	Masters Swim
	Ride 1:30 w/ 2 x :10 low Z4	Ride 1:45 w/ 2 x :12 low Z4	Ride 2:00 w/ 2 x :14 low Z4	Ride 1:30 Z 1-2
	WEEK 1–3: Hold high cadence (95+ rpm)			
THUR.	Run 1:00 Z2	Run 1:10 Z2	Run 1:20 Z2	Run :30 Z2
	Weight Training	Weight Training	Weight Training	Weight Training
FRI.	Masters Swim	Masters Swim	Masters Swim	Masters Swim
SAT.	Run 1:20 Z2	Run 1:30 Z2	Run 1:40 Z2	Run 1:00 Z2
SUN.	Ride 2:00 Z1–2	Ride 2:30 Z1–2	Ride 3:00 Z1–2	Ride 2:00 Z1–2
BUILD PHASE				
MON.	Easy Swim	Easy Swim	Easy Swim	Rest & Recover
TUES.	Run @ Track: 6-min. Time Trial	Run @ Track: 4 x 800 @ AC Pace, jog 200; 3 x 200 @ Econ Pace, jog 400	Run @ Track: 5 x 800 @ AC Pace, jog 200 3 x 200 @ Econ Pace, jog 400	Run :30 Z2 include 4 strides (30 sec. each)
WED.	Swim w/ Race-Pace Work	Swim w/ Race-Pace Work	Swim w/ Race-Pace Work	Easy Swim
	Ride 1:30 w/ :30 low Z4	Ride 1:30 w/ :30 low Z4	Ride 1:30 w/ :30 low Z4	Ride :45 Z1–2
	WEEK 1–3: Hold high cadence (95+ rpm)			
THUR.	Run :40 Z2	Run :50 Z2	Run 1:00 Z2	Run :30 Z2
FRI.	Easy Swim	Easy Swim	Easy Swim	Easy Swim
SAT.	3 Brick Intervals: Ride :06 @ Race Pace, Jog 400, Ride :05 recovery	4 Brick Intervals: Ride :06 @ Race Pace, Run 1200 @ Race Pace Jog 400, Ride :05 recovery	5 Brick Intervals: Ride :06 @ Race Pace, Run 1200 @ Race Pace Jog 400, Ride :05 recovery	Ride 2:00 Z2 Run 1:00 Z2
SUN.	Ride 2:30 Z1–2	Ride 3:00 Z1–2	Ride 3:30 Z1–2	Rest & Recover

HALF-IRONMAN DISTANCE: BEGINNER/INTERMEDIATE

	WEEK #1	WEEK #2	WEEK #3	WEEK #4
BASE PHASE				
MON.	Easy Swim	Easy Swim	Easy Swim	Rest & Recover
TUES.	Run 1:00 Z2	Run 1:10 Z2	Run 1:20 Z2	Run :30 Z2
	WEEK 1–4: Concentrate on maintaining very high turnover with very short stride length.			
	Weight Training	Weight Training	Weight Training	Weight Training
WED.	A.M. Easy Swim	A.M. Easy Swim	A.M. Easy Swim	A.M. Easy Swim
	Ride 1:00 Z1–2	Ride 1:20 Z1–2	Ride 1:40 Z1–2	Ride 1:00 Z1–2
	WEEK 1–3: Hold high cadence (95+ rpm)			
THUR.	Run 1:00 Z2	Run 1:10 Z2	Run 1:20 Z2	Run 1:00 Z2
	Weight Training	Weight Training	Weight Training	Weight Training
FRI.	Easy Swim	Easy Swim	Easy Swim	Easy Swim
SAT.	Run 1:10 Z2	Run 1:20 Z2	Run 1:30 Z2	Run 1:00 Z2
SUN.	Ride 1:30 Z1–2	Ride 2:00 Z1–2	Ride 2:30 Z1–2	Ride 2:00 Z1–2
BUILD PHASE				
MON.	Easy Swim	Easy Swim	Easy Swim	Rest & Recover
TUES.	Run 1:00 Z2	Run 1:10 Z2	Run 1:20 Z2	Run :30 Z2
WED.	Swim w/ Race-Pace Work	Swim w/ Race-Pace Work	Swim w/ Race-Pace Work	Easy Swim
	Ride :45 w/ :10 low Z4	Ride :55 w/ :15 low Z4	Ride 1:05 w/ :20 low Z4	Ride :45 Z1–2
	WEEK 1–3: Hold high cadence (95+ rpm)			
THUR.	Run :40 Z2	Run :50 Z2	Run 1:00 Z2	Run :30 Z2
FRI.	Easy Swim	Easy Swim	Easy Swim	Easy Swim
SAT.	Run 1:30 Z2	Run 1:40 Z2	Run 1:50 Z2	Run 1:00 Z2
SUN.	Ride 3:00 w/ 1st 2:30 Z1–2 :30 @ Race Pace	Ride 3:30 w/ 1st 2:45 Z1–2 :45 @ Race Pace	Ride 4:00 w/ 1st 3:00 Z1–2 1:00 @ Race Pace	Ride 2:00 Z 1–2
	Run :15 easy	Run :15 easy	Run :15 easy	

HALF-IRONMAN DISTANCE: ADVANCED/ELITE

	WEEK #1	WEEK #2	WEEK #3	WEEK #4
BASE PHASE				
MON.	Easy Swim	Easy Swim	Easy Swim	Easy Swim
TUES.	Run 1:15 w/ 3 x [:06 low Z4 / :02 rec]	Run 1:20 w/ 4 x [:06 low Z4 / :02 rec]	Run 1:00 w/ 5 x [:06 low Z4 / :02 rec]	Run :45 Z2
	Weight Training	Weight Training	Weight Training	Weight Training
WED.	Masters Swim	Masters Swim	Masters Swim	Masters Swim
	Ride 1:30 w/ 2 x :10 low Z4	Ride 1:45 w/ 2 x :12 low Z4	Ride 2:00 w/ 2 x :14 low Z4	Ride 2:00 Z1-2
	WEEK 1–3: Hold high cadence (95+ rpm)			
THUR.	Run 1:00 Z2	Run 1:10 Z2	Run 1:20 Z2	Run :30 Z2
	Weight Training	Weight Training	Weight Training	Weight Training
FRI.	Masters Swim	Masters Swim	Masters Swim	Masters Swim
SAT.	Run 1:40 Z2	Run 1:50 Z2	Run 2:00 Z2	Run 1:00 Z2
SUN.	Ride 2:00 Z1–2	Ride 2:30 Z1–2	Ride 3:00 Z1–2	Ride 2:00 Z1–2
BUILD PHASE				
MON.	Easy Swim	Easy Swim	Easy Swim	Rest & Recover
TUES.	Run 1:00 w/ :20 low Z4	Run 1:10 w/ :25 low Z4	Run 1:20 w/ :30 low Z4	Run :30 w/ 1:00 low Z4
WED.	Masters Swim	Masters Swim	Masters Swim	Masters Swim
	Ride 1:30 w/ :20 low Z4	Ride 1:30 w/ :25 low Z4	Ride 1:05 w/ :30 low Z4	Ride :45 Z1–2
	WEEK 1–3: Hold high cadence (95+ rpm)			
THUR.	Run 1:00 Z2	Run 1:20 Z2	Run 1:30 Z2	Run :30 Z2
FRI.	Easy Swim	Easy Swim	Easy Swim	Easy Swim
SAT.	Ride 2:00 Z2 w/ :30 @ Race Pace	Ride 2:30 Z2 w/ :45 @ Race Pace	Ride 3:00 Z2 w/ 1:00 @ Race Pace	Ride 2:00 Z 1–2
	Run :15 @ Race Pace, :45 easy	Run :25 @ Race Pace, :45 easy	Run :35 @ Race Pace, :45 easy	Run 1:00 Z2
SUN.	Ride 2:00 Z1–2	Ride 2:00 Z1–2	Ride 2:00 Z1–2	Rest & Recover

IRONMAN DISTANCE: INTERMEDIATE

	WEEK #1	WEEK #2	WEEK #3	WEEK #4
BASE PHASE				
MON.	Easy Swim	Easy Swim	Easy Swim	Rest & Recover
TUES.	Run 1:00 Z2	Run 1:10 Z2	Run 1:20 Z2	Run :30 Z2
	WEEK 1–4: Concentrate on maintaining very high turnover with very short stride length.			
	Weight Training	Weight Training	Weight Training	Weight Training
WED.	Easy Swim	Easy Swim	Easy Swim	Easy Swim
	Ride 1:30 Z1–2	Ride 1:30 Z1–2	Ride 1:30 Z1–2	Ride 1:30 Z1–2
	WEEK 1–3: Hold high cadence (95+ rpm)			
THUR.	Run 1:00 Z2	Run 1:10 Z2	Run 1:20 Z2	Run :30 Z2
	Weight Training	Weight Training	Weight Training	Weight Training
FRI.	Easy Swim	Easy Swim	Easy Swim	Easy Swim
SAT.	Run 1:20 Z2	Run 1:30 Z2	Run 1:40 Z2	Run 1:20 Z2
	Ride 1:00 Z1	Ride 1:00 Z1	Ride 1:00 Z1	
SUN.	Ride 2:00 Z1–2	Ride 2:30 Z1–2	Ride 3:00 Z1–2	Ride 1:00 Z1–2
BUILD PHASE				
MON.	Easy Swim	Easy Swim	Easy Swim	Rest & Recover
TUES.	Run @ Track: 3 x 400 @ AC Pace, jog 200; 3 x 200 @ Econ Pace, jog 400	Run @ Track: 4 x 400 @ AC Pace, jog 200; 3 x 200 @ Econ Pace, jog 400	Run @ Track: 5 x 400 @ AC Pace, jog 200; 3 x 200 @ Econ Pace, jog 400	Run :30 Z2
WED.	Long Easy Swim	Long Easy Swim	Long Easy Swim	Long Easy Swim
	Ride 1:20 w/ :20 low Z4	Ride 1:30 w/ :25 low Z4	Ride 1:40 w/ :20 low Z4	Ride :45 Z1–2
	WEEK 1–3: Hold high cadence (95+ rpm)			
THUR.	Run 1:30 Z2	Run 1:30 Z2	Run 1:30 Z2	Run 1:30 Z2
FRI.	Very Long Easy Swim	Very Long Easy Swim	Very Long Easy Swim	Long Easy Swim
SAT.	Run 1:50 Z2	Run 2:00 Z2	Run 2:10 Z2	Run 1:00 Z2
	Ride 1:00 Z2	Ride 1:00 Z2	Ride 1:00 Z2	
SUN.	Ride 3:00 Z1–2	Ride 3:30 Z1–2	Ride 4:00 Z1–2	Ride 3:00 Z1–2
	Run :15 @ IMRP	Run :15 @ IMRP	Run :15 @ IMRP	
IMRP = Ironman race pace				

IRONMAN DISTANCE: ADVANCED/ELITE (IRONMAN)

	WEEK #1	WEEK #2	WEEK #3	WEEK #4
BASE PHASE				
MON.	Easy Swim	Easy Swim	Easy Swim	Rest & Recover
TUES.	Run 1:30 Z2	Run 1:30 Z2	Run 1:30 Z2	Run 1:00 Z2
	Weight Training	Weight Training	Weight Training	Weight Training
WED.	Long Easy Swim	Long Easy Swim	Long Easy Swim	Long Easy Swim
	Ride 2:00 Z1–2	Ride 2:00 Z1–2	Ride 2:00 Z1–2	Ride 1:30 Z1–2
THUR.	Run 1:00 w/ :20 low Z4	Run 1:00 w/ :25 low Z4	Run 1:00 w/ :30 low Z4	Run 1:00 Z2
	Weight Training	Weight Training	Weight Training	Weight Training
FRI.	Long Easy Swim	Long Easy Swim	Long Easy Swim	Long Easy Swim
SAT.	Run 1:40 Z2	Run 1:50 Z2	Run 2:00 Z2	Run 1:30 Z2
	Ride 2:00 Z2	Ride 2:00 Z2	Ride 2:00 Z2	
SUN.	Ride 3:00 Z1–2	Ride 3:30 Z1–2	Ride 4:00 Z1–2	Ride 3:00 Z1–2
	Run :15 @ IMRP	Run :15 @ IMRP	Run :15 @ IMRP	
BUILD PHASE				
MON.	Easy Swim	Easy Swim	Easy Swim	Rest & Recover
TUES.	Ride 1:30 Z2	Ride 1:30 Z2	Ride 1:30 Z2	Run 1:30 Z2
	Run 1:30 Z2	Run 1:30 Z2	Run 1:30 Z2	
WED.	Long Easy Swim	Long Easy Swim	Long Easy Swim	Long Easy Swim
	Ride 2:00 w/ :30 low Z4	Ride 2:20 w/ :35 low Z4	Ride 2:40 w/ :40 low Z4	Ride :45 Z1–2
THUR.	Run 1:30 Z2	Run 1:30 Z2	Run 1:30 Z2	Run 1:00 Z2
FRI.	Very Long Easy Swim	Very Long Easy Swim	Very Long Easy Swim	Long Easy Swim
SAT.	Ride 3:30 Z2	Run 4:00 Z2	Run 4:30 Z2	Run 1:00 Z2
	Run 1:00 Z2	Run 1:15 Z2	Ride 1:30 Z2	Ride 2:00 Z2
SUN.	1:00 Easy Open-Water Swim	1:00 Easy Open-Water Swim	1:00 Easy Open-Water Swim	Rest & Recover
	Ride 2:00 Z1	Ride 2:00 Z1	Ride 2:00 Z1	

IMRP = Ironman race pace

APPENDIX D
Glycemic Index of Common Foods

NOTE: Glycemic index (GI) is a measure of how quickly carbohydrate from the food enters the bloodstream.

BEANS		CEREALS		CONVENIENCE FOODS		DESSERTS	
Baby Lima	0.32	All Bran	0.44	Hamburger & Bun		Angel Food Cake	
Baked	0.43	Bran Chex	0.58		0.61		0.67
Black	0.30	Cheerios	0.74	Chocolate Cake		Banana Bread	0.47
Brown	0.38	Corn Bran	0.75		0.38	Blueberry Muffin	
Butter	0.31	Corn Chex	0.83	Pizza, Cheese	0.60		0.59
Chickpeas	0.33	Cornflakes	0.83	Pop Tarts™	0.70	Bran Muffin	0.60
Kidney	0.27	Cream of Wheat		Popcorn	0.72	Danish	0.59
Lentil	0.30		0.66	**COOKIES**		Fruit Bread	0.47
Navy	0.38	Crispix	0.87	Graham Crackers		Pound Cake	0.54
Pinto	0.42	Frosted Flakes	0.55		0.74	Sponge Cake	0.46
Red Lentils	0.27	Grapenuts	0.67	Oatmeal	0.55	**FRUIT**	
Split Peas	0.32	Grapenuts Flakes		Shortbread	0.64	Apple	0.38
Soy	0.18		0.80	Vanilla Wafers	0.77	Apricot, Canned	
White Rice, High		Life	0.67	**CRACKERS**			0.64
Amylose	0.59	Muesli	0.60	Kavli Norwegian		Apricot, Dried	0.30
BREADS		NutriGrain	0.66		0.71	Apricot Jam	0.55
Bagel	0.72	Oatmeal	0.49	Rice Cakes	0.82	Banana	0.62
Croissant	0.67	Oatmeal, 1-minute		Rye	0.63	Banana, Unripe	
Kaiser Roll	0.73		0.66	Saltine	0.72		0.30
Pita	0.57	Puffed Wheat	0.74	Stoned Wheat		Cantaloupe	0.65
Pumpernickel	0.49	Puffed Rice	0.90	Thins	0.67	Cherries	0.22
Rye	0.64	Rice Bran	0.19	Water Crackers		Dates, Dried	1.03
Rye, Dark	0.76	Rice Chex	0.89		0.78	Fruit Cocktail	0.55
Rye, Whole	0.50	Rice Krispies	0.92			Grapefruit	0.25
White	0.72	Shredded Wheat				Grapes	0.43
Whole Wheat	0.72		0.69			Kiwi	0.52
Waffles	0.6	Special K	0.54			Mango	0.55
Pancakes	0.67	Swiss Muesli	0.60			Orange	0.43
		Team	0.82			Papaya	0.58
		Total	0.76			Peach	0.42
						Pear	0.36

GLYCEMIC INDEX OF COMMON FOODS (CONTINUED)

FRUIT CONT.	
Pineapple	0.66
Plum	0.24
Raisins	0.64
Strawberries	0.32
Strawberry Jam	0.51
Watermelon	0.72

SPORTS PRODUCTS	
AllSport™ (orange)	0.53
Clif Bar® (cookies & cream)	1.01
Cytomax™ (orange)	0.62
Ensure™ vanilla	0.48
Gatorade™ (orange)	0.89
METRx® (vanilla)	0.74
Poweraid® (orange)	0.65
Powerbar® (chocolate)	0.83
PR*Bar® (cookies & cream)	0.81
XLR8w	0.68

GRAINS	
Barley	0.22
Brown Rice	0.59
Buckwheat	0.54
Bulgur	0.47
Chickpeas	0.36
Couscous	0.65
Hominy	0.40
Millet	0.75
Rice, Instant	0.91
Rice, Parboiled	0.45
Rye	0.34
Sweet Corn	0.55
Wheat, Whole	0.41
White Rice	0.88

JUICES	
Agave Nectar	0.11
Apple	0.41
Grapefruit	0.48
Orange	0.55
Pineapple	0.46

MILK PRODUCTS	
Chocolate Milk	0.34
Ice Cream	0.50
Milk	0.34
Pudding	0.43
Soy Milk	0.1
Yogurt	0.38

PASTA	
Brown Rice Pasta	0.92
Gnocchi	0.68
Linguini, Durum	0.50
Macaroni	0.46
Macaroni & Cheese	0.64
Spaghetti	0.40
Spaghetti, Protein Enriched	0.28
Vermicelli	0.35
Vermicelli, Rice	0.58

SWEETS	
Honey	0.58
Jelly Beans	0.80
Life Savers	0.70
M&Ms Peanut	0.33
Skittles	0.70
Snickers	0.41

MEATS	
Beef	0.0
Chicken Nuggets	0.46
Lamb	0.0
Pork	0.0

APPENDIX E

Race Nutrition

SPRINT- AND INTERNATIONAL-DISTANCE RACE NUTRITION

Race-Day Breakfast

- Consume five to eight calories per pound of bodyweight two to three hours prior to the start of the races.
- Prioritize low-GI carbohydrates.
- Minimize fiber at this meal.
- Include about 1 gram of protein per 10 pounds of bodyweight.
- Choose foods that digest easily and do not cause gastric distress.

Pre-Race

- Eat regularly, but lightly: about 100 calories per hour between breakfast and the race start. Emphasize low-GI foods with very little protein. Stay with liquid or easily digestible foods.
- Drink a bottle of sports drink in the last hour before the race start.
- Drink a mixture that includes sodium between breakfast and the race. If you drink plain water, make sure to have a sodium source with it.

Bike

- Consume one to two calories per pound of bodyweight throughout the bike segment.
- Consume only carbohydrate calories.
- Carry all of the fuel you require; depend on aid stations only for water. It is fine to use fuel from the aid stations if it is available, but have enough with you that you don't require fuel from any other source.
- Do not use solid food throughout the race.
- Consume 1 ounce of water per 7 pounds of bodyweight per hour. Mixed drinks count as water.

Run

- Consume about 100 calories several times during an international-distance run and once during a sprint-distance run. All calories consumed should be carbohydrate.
- Drink only plain water, not a sports drink, when consuming gels.
- Consume as much water as you can, up to 1 ounce per hour per 7 pounds of bodyweight.

HALF-IRONMAN-DISTANCE RACE NUTRITION

Race-Day Breakfast

- Consume eight to ten calories per pound of bodyweight three to four hours prior to the start of the race.
- Prioritize low-GI carbohydrates.
- Minimize fiber at this meal.
- Include about 1 gram of protein per 10 pounds of bodyweight.
- Choose foods that digest easily and do not cause gastric distress.

Pre-Race

- Eat regularly, but lightly: about 100 to 200 calories per hour between breakfast and the race start. Emphasize low-GI foods with very little protein. Stay with liquid or easily digestible foods.
- Drink a bottle of sports drink in the last hour before the race start.
- Drink a mixture that includes sodium between breakfast and the race. If you drink plain water, make sure to have a sodium source with it.

Bike

- Consume two calories per pound of bodyweight per hour throughout the bike segment.
- Consume about one half gram of protein per 10 pounds bodyweight per hour in the early and middle parts of the bike segment. Discontinue protein consumption for the last hour of the bike.

- Carry all of the fuel you require; depend on aid stations only for water. It is fine to use fuel from the aid stations if it is available, but have enough with you that you don't require fuel from any other source.
- Do not use solid food throughout the race.
- Consume 1 ounce of water per hour per 7 pounds of bodyweight per hour. Mixed drinks count as water.
- Consume about 600 mg of sodium (1 gram of salt) per 150 pounds per hour on the bike and run. Getting too much salt is not a problem unless carried to excess. Remember to include the sodium from all sources.
- Some athletes report that their minds wander, causing them to miss feedings. Try setting a watch to beep every 15 minutes as a reminder.

Run

- Consume at least one calorie per pound of bodyweight per hour. All calories consumed should be carbohydrate.
- Drink only plain water, not a sports drink, when consuming gels.
- Consume as much water as you can, up to 1 ounce per 7 pounds of bodyweight.

IRONMAN-DISTANCE RACE NUTRITION

Race-Day Breakfast

- Consume ten to twelve calories per pound of bodyweight four to five hours prior to the start of the race.
- Prioritize low-GI carbohydrates.
- Minimize fiber at this meal.
- Include about 1 gram of protein per 10 pounds of bodyweight.
- Choose foods that digest easily and do not cause gastric distress.

Pre-Race

- Eat regularly, but lightly: 100 to 200 calories per hour between breakfast and the race start. Emphasize low-GI foods with very little protein. Stay with liquids or easily digestible foods.
- Drink a bottle of sports drink in the last hour before the race start.

- Drink a mixture that includes sodium between breakfast and the race. If you drink plain water, make sure to have a sodium source with it.

Bike

- Consume two calories per pound of bodyweight per hour throughout the bike segment.
- Carry all of the fuel you require; depend on aid stations only for water. It is fine to use fuel from the aid stations if it is available, but have enough with you that you don't require fuel from any other source.
- Use solid food as little as possible throughout the race, especially during the last hour of the bike and during the run.
- Consume 1 ounce of water per 7 pounds of bodyweight per hour. Mixed drinks count as water.
- Consume about 600 mg of sodium (1 gram of salt) per 150 pounds per hour on the bike and run. Getting too much salt is not a problem unless carried to excess. Remember to include the sodium from all sources.
- Some athletes report that their minds wander, causing them to miss feedings. Try setting a watch to beep every 15 minutes as a reminder.

Run

- Consume at least 1.5 calories per pound of bodyweight per hour. This should be almost entirely carbohydrate.
- Drink only plain water, not a sports drink, when consuming gels.
- Consume as much water as you can, up to 1 ounce per hour per 7 pounds of bodyweight.

Glossary

adaptation: The body's ability to adapt to stresses over time to reduce the stress of the stimulation. In short, our bodies get better at whatever we ask them to do.

aerobic: Metabolizing using oxygen.

aerobic capacity (AC): The maximal volume of oxygen that an athlete's muscles can use in one minute of maximal exertion. Aerobic capacity is also known as VO_2max.

anaerobic: Without oxygen; exercise that demands greater energy expenditure than the heart, lungs, and blood can supply oxygen for. Anaerobic metabolism can produce enormous amounts of energy in the short term, but it cannot sustain output very long.

anaerobic endurance: The ability of an athlete to dramatically exceed lactate threshold effort for an extended duration.

anaerobic threshold (AT): The highest intensity at which the body can recycle lactic acid as quickly as it is produced. At anaerobic threshold, lactic acid is not accumulating in the muscles, but a slight increase in intensity causes accumulation. This is also known as lactate threshold.

Base period: The training period during which the basic abilities of endurance, force, and speed skills are prioritized.

bonk: A condition of extreme fatigue caused by depletion of glycogen (carbohydrate) to fuel the muscles.

breakthrough workout: A key workout designed to stimulate changes that improve some specific aspect of the athlete's fitness.

brick: A workout that has the athlete switch from cycling to running with minimal time for recovery as will be required on race day.

Build period: The training period following Base during which muscular endurance, speed endurance, and power are prioritized. Endurance, force, and speed are maintained.

cadence: The number of revolutions per minute in a swim stroke, pedal stroke, or running stride.

carbohydrate: A form of fuel consumed in our diet, stored in our muscles and liver as glycogen, and converted to the sugar glucose to be burned by the muscles for energy. Carbohydrate is consumed primarily in starches, sugar, fruits, and vegetables.

cool down: The segment of low-intensity exercise at the conclusion of a workout that is designed to ease the transition from exercise to resting.

crosstraining: A workout mode that is different from the specific sport that will be required in competition.

duration: The length of time of a workout or some specific segment of a workout.

elastic recoil: The mechanism through which energy is stored in an athlete's muscles and connective tissues after they are stretched and then returned when the tissues return to original length in an elastic response.

endurance: The ability to continue exercise for an extended duration, to resist fatigue.

fast oxidative glycolytic (FOG) muscle fiber: A muscle fiber characterized by intermediate force and speed production, intermediate aerobic capabilities, and intermediate anaerobic capabilities; also called speed endurance fibers.

fast-twitch muscle fiber: A muscle fiber characterized by high-force, high-speed contractions. Fast-twitch fibers have very high anaerobic capabilities and very low aerobic capabilities, making them well suited for sprinting.

fat: A fuel consumed in the diet and produced in the body from other fuels. Fat is the most concentrated form of biological fuel and is a significant fuel for athletes during long, slow workouts.

force: The ability to overcome great resistance; the ability to exert strength.

frequency: The number of workouts per week.

glucose: The type of sugar that humans ultimately make from every carbohydrate and burn in the muscles for fuel.

glutes: The largest and strongest muscles in the body, located on the posterior hips (butt); these act in hip extension.

glycemic index (GI): A system of rating carbohydrates according to how quickly they are digested and absorbed into the bloodstream.

glycogen: The body's storage form of carbohydrate made from glucose and stored primarily in the muscles and in the liver.

goal pace: The speed the athlete hopes to be able to maintain in the highest-priority races of the year.

hamstring: The muscle located on the back of the thigh that is responsible for flexing the knee and that assists with extending the hip.

human growth hormone (HGH): A powerful hormone secreted by the pituitary gland that stimulates growth of tissues as well as fat burning.

intensity: A measure of the level of effort the athlete exerts during exercise.

interval training: A method of training characterized by relatively short periods of high-intensity training with periods of low-intensity training to allow recovery. Recovery periods during interval training are short enough to prevent complete recovery between high-intensity efforts.

lactate threshold (LT): The highest intensity at which the body can recycle lactic acid as quickly as it is produced. At anaerobic threshold, lactic acid is not accumulating in the muscles, but a slight increase in intensity causes accumulation; also known as anaerobic threshold.

lactate: Another term for lactic acid.

lactic acid: A by-product of anaerobic breakdown of glucose due to energy expenditure that exceeds the level that the heart, lungs, and blood can deliver adequate oxygen for. Lactic acid creates the burning feeling in the muscles that results from hard exercise.

muscular endurance: The ability of a muscle or group of muscles to continue to repeatedly contract against resistance for an extended period without fatigue.

overtraining: Extreme, chronic fatigue caused by exceeding the body's ability to recover from and adapt to stressful workouts.

Peak period: The period during which training volume is greatly reduced and intensity is maximized to bring the athlete to the highest level of fitness.

periodization: The process of structuring the year into distinct periods with specific purposes and priorities that differ between periods.

power: A combination of force and speed.

Preparation period: The conservative training period during which athletes prepare their bodies for the more aggressive training to follow.

progression: The theory that volume and intensity should gradually increase over time, with each training segment building on previous segments.

protein: A nutrient that serves, among other things, as the building block for muscles. Few athletes consume enough protein. Lean meats are the best source of protein in an athlete's diet, but it can also be found in dairy products, egg whites, and supplements.

quadriceps: The muscle located on the front thigh that is responsible for extending the knee.

Race period: The period during which the athlete has achieved the desired level of fitness and training is designed to maintain that fitness while resting for important races.

recovery: A period of training when rest is emphasized.

repeat training: A workout that alternates high-intensity segments with low-intensity recovery segments. Recovery segments are long enough to allow almost complete recovery from the high-intensity effort.

repetition: One of a series of workout tasks that are repeated a number of times.

set: A group of repetitions.

slow-twitch muscle fiber: A type of muscle fiber characterized by low-force, low-speed contractions, but great resistance to fatigue. Slow-twitch muscle fibers have very high aerobic capabilities and very low anaerobic capabilities.

speed: A measure of how fast an athlete is moving.

tapering: The act of reducing training volume and intensity just prior to an important race.

training: A term used to collectively refer to all of an athlete's preparations for competition.

training zone: A range of intensity determined to be effective for stimulating specific adaptations in athletes. The most common training zones are ranges of heart rate, but speed and wattage may be used effectively as well.

Transition period: The period during which volume, intensity, and structure of training are greatly reduced to allow maximal physical and psychological recovery from the pressures of training and racing in the previous season.

turnover: A measure of revolutions per minute of a runner, usually referred to as number of foot-strikes per minute or stride cycles per minute (foot-strikes divided by two).

ventilatory threshold: Intensity equal to anaerobic threshold or lactate threshold, measured by comparing an athlete's ventilation and oxygen consumption. This term can be used interchangeably with anaerobic threshold or lactate threshold.

VO$_2$max: The maximal volume of oxygen that an athlete's muscles can use in one minute of maximal exertion. VO$_2$max is also known as aerobic capacity.

volume: A quantitative measure of training, generally expressed in amount of time spent exercising.

warm-up: The period of low-intensity exercise at the beginning of a workout that is intended to ease the transition from resting state to exercising state.

work interval: The high-intensity effort separated by recovery segments during interval or repeat training.

workload: A measure of training stress that is the result of the combination of exercise frequency, intensity, and duration.

Index

running volume and, 185
oxygen use, 88, 147, 235, 237

pace, 255-56
  aerobic capacity, 94-97
  consistency, 183, 255
  economy, 98-99
  field testing, 94
  monitoring, 99
  by race distance, 180-87
  race intensity, 184-85
  time trial (TT6), 94, 96, 118, 262
  in training, 186
pacing skills, 127
pain, 195, 255
Peak period, 80, 111, 112
peaking, 76, 109
pedal stroke, 171-75
perceived exertion, 100-101, 184, 197,
  255
periodization, 70, 73-74
phosphate loading, 239-40, 251
physiological testing, 103
pickups, 266
plyometric workouts, 232-33, 234,
  240-41, 266-68
posture, 29
power, 48, 72
Preparation period, 75-76, 110, 111
priorities. See training priorities
process orientation, 201
proprioceptive training, 233
propulsion, 14, 21, 34-38
  for acceleration, 15
  drills, 39
  sources of, 16, 45, 52, 171-72, 173
protein, 132, 138-39, 153, 163, 222
  as energy source, 152
  during race, 189
psyching up, 198
psychological modes, 194-98
pull-through, 35-36, 38
purpose, x
push-off, 21, 23, 40
  force required for, 20, 30, 46, 50

quadriceps muscles, 1, 18, 45, 231
  cycling power production, 170, 171
  in hill running, 60
  overload training, 215
quitting, 255-56

race-pace workouts, 60, 80, 112, 248
  bricks, 125, 126-27, 182
  duration, 183
  as indicators, 180, 184
Race period, 81, 111, 112
race preparation, 179-90
races, 198, 253-57

duration, 124, 179
open, 169
pacing, 255-56
prioritizing, 67-68, 250
race day, 251-52
scheduling, 179
as workouts, 67, 68, 79, 266
race-simulation workouts, 81, 127
range of motion, 48
recoil. See elastic recoil
recovery, 75, 217-37. See also rest;
  tapering
  active, 86-87, 217, 222-23, 261
  from bricks, 127
  cost, 83, 88, 90, 96
  from economy workouts, 122
  from lactate tolerance training, 119,
    120
  leg. See leg recovery
  maximizing, 221
  monitoring, 226-27
  overtraining. See overtraining
  in Peak period, 80
  as process, 225
  reducing, 96, 99
  between repetitions, 122
  resources, 84, 190
  scheduling, 122, 219-20
  speed of, 208
  stress and, 219
  super-threshold training, 93
  weeks, 114, 115
  from weighted running, 46
  workouts, 86, 222-23, 261
repeat training, 95, 264-66
rest, 4, 74-75, 112, 223. See also
  recovery; tapering
  ratio to work, 96
  during taper, 248-49
rhythm, 31-32
running, 1, 4-5, 123. See also triathlons
  acclimating to, 125
  after cycling, 123-24
  barefoot, 11
  race-day, 253-57
running economy, 9-11, 69. See also
  economy training; efficiency
  as limiter, 111, 114
  models, 15-16
running in place, 33, 34, 268

saddle position and height, 170
Scott, Steve, 12
season, planning, 6, 65-81
  advanced ability training, 71-73
  annual, 65
  Base period, 76-78
  basic ability training, 70-71
  Build period, 78-80

About the Author

Ken Mierke has been a professional multisport and cycling coach, as well as owner of Fitness Concepts, for nine years. Fitness Concepts currently has a staff of ten professional coaches and well over 100 clients. Mierke has coached eleven national champions, both professional and amateur, and placed 28 multisport athletes on Team USA (top twelve in the country in their age group).

Mierke holds a B.S. in exercise physiology from Virginia Polytechnic Institute and State University with emphases in biology, psychology, and nutrition. He is currently pursuing an M.S. in sport psychology.

As Director of Training for Ultrafit, Mierke personally mentors associate coaches for their first year with Ultrafit and provides instructional articles to educate all the associate coaches. Mierke owns a metabolic analyzer and has personally performed over 6,000 VO_2max tests, aerobic threshold tests, and lactate threshold tests. This has provided him with an incredible education in cardiovascular dynamics, as well as enabling him to objectify efficient techniques in running.

Mierke has raced triathlon competitively for 14 years. He has competed at the I.T.U. World Championships four times, winning gold medals twice and silver medals twice in the physically challenged division (he has muscular dystrophy).

In 1996, Mierke was nominated by his athletes to carry the Olympic torch—an event that proved to be one of the highlights of his life.

Mierke's writing is published regularly in international publications such as *Inside Triathlon* and *VeloNews*, local sports magazines such as *Metro Sports Washington DC*, *Metro Sports New York*, *Spokes*, *Rocky Mountain Sports*, and online sources such as Joe Friel's E-Tips newsletter (www.Ultrafit.com) and the Active.com newsletter.

For more information on seminars and clinics or for personal coaching, Mierke can be contacted at CoachKen@erols.com or by fax at (703) 935-8378.